A Noble Pursuit

The Sesquicentennial History of the

New England Historic
Genealogical Society

1845-1995

A Noble Pursuit

The Sesquicentennial History of the

New England Historic Genealogical Society

1845-1995

JOHN A. SCHUTZ

1995

New England Historic Genealogical Society

BOSTON, MASSACHUSETTS

Dust jacket and frontispiece: 101 Newbury Street, Boston home of the New England Historic Genealogical Society since 1964, from the first-floor garden and from the air. Photographs (taken in August, 1994) by Warren Ford; color printing courtesy of the Lehigh Press, Inc., of Cherry Hill, New Jersey.

Contents

Preface

The sesquicentennial of any private, benevolent society is an unusual event that raises questions about its longevity and usefulness. For the New England Historic Genealogical Society, chartered in March 1845 by the Massachusetts General Court, there never has been any question of its usefulness, but for almost half of its life, members have wondered about its chief purpose. The men who founded the Society in Boston were drawn from the law, business, and antiquarian pursuits. They wanted a place to discuss New England history, American traditions, and their own family history. They gathered mostly as a group of amateurs infatuated by ancestry, antiquity, and heraldry. The catholicity of their interests helped them to be tolerant of each other and congenial toward a broadly-based male membership.

Time has a way of obscuring events and people of 150 years ago—even dramatic and exciting moments in the nation's history. When the Society was chartered, James K. Polk had just become President of the United States and faced crises that involved negotiations with Great Britain, hostilities with Mexico, and the acquisition of lands in the American West, including the Oregon territory, California, the southwest, and Texas. The unbelievable gold rush was still to come and the terrible struggle of the Civil War was already rising as a threat to the Union; the outbreak of war was anticipated by sensitive people when Charles Ewer, Lemuel Shattuck, John Wingate Thornton, Samuel G. Drake, and William H. Montague founded the Society. From its beginning the NEHGS has welcomed all men seriously interested in history and genealogy; from 1898 women were elected to membership and equally welcomed. Place of birth or race has never been a qualification for admission, but obviously most members are descended, in at least a few lines, from the founders of New England, passengers on the *Mayflower* or the *Mary and John*, or members of the Winthrop Fleet. Society interests have evolved in 150 years so that today members consult records of New England's black settlers and ancestors of its Irish, Italian, Greek, and German pioneers. Descendants of these people are also members of the Society.

For all its institutional life, the New England Historic Genealogical Society has been located in Boston, on Beacon Hill until 1964 and at 101 Newbury Street ever since. The Society has always associated itself with the leaders and officials of New England, with those in government, the law offices, and the courts, and with the business and professional communities in Boston and across the Charles River far beyond Cambridge—westward, in fact, to the Pacific Ocean. From the beginning, too, it has collected books, almost anything written, until it was forced to become selective. Today, it possesses probably the largest national collection of books and pamphlets on New England families. Its manuscripts include probably the largest collection of family documents in America.

The Society library is likewise a research institution, with copies of most reference works, published New England genealogies, and town and county histories; vast holdings of vital, probate, Bible, and town and church records; and a supplementary collection of microfiches and microfilms. It has access to the LDS Family Search Program on CD-ROM and extensive film records as well on the Maritime Provinces of Canada.

Since 1847 the Society has funded the *New England Historical and Genealogical Register*, the oldest continuously published antiquarian journal in the country. Many historians and genealogists have made their professional homes at the Society and published their research in the *Register*. Since the 1970s the Society has engaged a group of genealogists to work in the library as researchers, advisors to members, and editors of a publication program that has become increasingly more extensive with the years. These staff researchers have added an unusual prominence to the Society's contribution to the intellectual life of New England and the development of genealogy as a scholarly activity. In the past twenty years, Gary Boyd Roberts, David Curtis Dearborn, George F. Sanborn, Jr., Jerome E. Anderson, and Jane Fletcher Fiske have joined the staff. Other editors or directors include Julie Helen Otto and Robert Shaw of NEXUS, Marie E. Daly, Scott A. Bartley, Nathaniel Shipton, and Robert Charles Anderson, director of the Great Migration Study Project. Together with William M. Fowler, Jr., president of the Society, and Ralph J. Crandall, the executive director, and other officers, the fifteen Trustees have been able to define the current objectives of the Society and use its resources for their realization.

The Society has expanded its programs beyond 101 Newbury by providing a large lending library and expert research service, by sponsoring yearly tours to England, Scotland, and Wales, and by conducting a national series of regional seminars. These extended services bring Society staff into nearly every part of the United States. Thus its membership of approximately 16,000 is kept in personal touch with genealogical scholarship at Newbury Street. Since 1983, the Society has published the NEHGS NEXUS, a bimonthly newsletter which provides current information on the Society, its activities, and house publications. It is a magazine, too, of opinion and queries, and permits genealogists wherever they live to keep in touch with other researchers in family history. It regularly publishes genealogical materials, but defers to the quarterly *Register* for the placement of definitive articles.

In 1995, the Society celebrates a major anniversary of usefulness and service, an accomplishment probably never even imagined by Charles Ewer, the first president, and his associates. It completes also the latest renovation and enlargement of its facilities. Its trustees thank members for their support and confidence in enabling it to perform its great work. With the completion of an extraordinary fund drive of five million dollars and an extensive renovation of its headquarters at 101 Newbury Street, Society resources will more than meet the expectations of members and scholars worldwide.

PREFACE

On the completion of a project of such magnitude, I wish to thank all those who offered and gave their assistance to enlighten my paths of research. I interviewed many members and former officers of the Society, and most members of the staff, and have benefited from their assistance. Nathaniel Shipton and Scott A. Bartley, who are in charge of the manuscript and archival resources of the Society, helped in a special way. Both men have great research instincts and found materials that were not thought to be any longer in existence. I thank Professor David L. Greene for his sensitive suggestions as well as Mrs. Joan Ferris Curran, who has seen the Society from many viewpoints. Gary Boyd Roberts gave me his suggestions about the progress of events in the history of the Society. His editor's pen was occasionally a heavy one. My computer assistant, Paul A. Cartwright, helped me put the manuscript on diskette, Margaret F. Costello prepared it for the press, and David Ford was in charge of the book's overall design. Most illustrations, with some exceptions noted, are taken from the Society's extensive archives. Finally, I thank Ralph J. Crandall, a friend of many years, whose words of encouragement and confidence in me made the book possible.

John A. Schutz
101 Newbury Street
in the Heart of Boston

A Noble Pursuit

The Sesquicentennial History of the

New England Historic
Genealogical Society

1845-1995

CHAPTER 1

The Coming of a New Society

Long before the founding of the New England Historic Genealogical Society in 1845, Americans were thinking of their family history. Few had written anything lengthy or systematic to detail the experiences of their families, but they cherished stories handed down in the reminiscences of their grandparents and speculated about their ancestry. Some treasured a brief diary, a few letters, a family Bible, and possibly a portrait of an ancestor, often household items, and of course their inheritance of the homestead. Family, for most New Englanders, was regarded as a blessing of God, a sacred institution reaching back to "our pilgrim fathers who fled to this new world" and to some unknown village in Europe where "unchristian persecutions" had driven them to America.[1]

Most Americans in 1845 were unable to trace their families to the *Mayflower*, or some other celebrated vessel, because accurate details of colonization were not easily available. Early times were admittedly important times, but the Winthrops, Endecotts, and Bradfords were more names than personalities for them. Thomas Hutchinson, the last civilian governor of Massachusetts before the American Revolution, possessed unique documentation on his family, a collection of stories, and great personal interest, but he was imprecise in his history of Massachusetts in providing details on his family. Other New Englanders had less available family information than Hutchinson, but they were driven by the same impulse to know more about their forefathers. They sought letters, Bible records, wills, and almost anything else that would satisfy their curiosity. They extracted the letters of relatives,

1

searched their own attics for information, and speculated on what they found. The kind of difficulties they encountered may be illustrated by the experience of the Lothrop family.

Two members of that family, John Lathrop and Abiel Holmes, both clergymen and descendants of John Lothrop, wondered about their own relationship, the spelling and pronunciation of the Lothrop name, and the availability of information. John finally contacted a distant relative and granddaughter of their ancestor and received the following report: "my honored grandfather . . . who was the pastor of the church in Barnstable, deceased in the year 1653 . . . brought with him four sons, viz. Thomas, who settled in Barnstable; Samuel, at Norwich, Connecticut; Joseph, at Barnstable; and Benjamin, at Charlestown. And after he came to New England, Barnabas and John, both settled in Barnstable." Apparently he also had daughters, Jane and Barbara, whose names were later given in the minister's will. In time the family spread, reported John, into Connecticut and New York as well as locally into many Massachusetts towns. Information was so uncertain about the family, however, that John concludes:

> Thus, Sir, have I given the best account I have been able to collect of our great great grandfather; mine by my father's side, and yours by your mother's. . . . We are amazed, when we contemplate the wonderful providence of God, which brought our fathers into this quarter of the world, to turn this wilderness, into fruitful fields.[2]

Admittedly they had difficulty tracing the Lothrop family. No printed vital records existed, nor church records, nor cemetery, probate, or census listings, and there was no library filled with books and manuscripts anywhere in New England. Most families, instead, relied heavily on family remembrances and folk stories, often handed down from parents, grandparents, and other relatives. Some families happily owned a Bible record and inscribed the usual entries in it as the occasion required, often adding brief notes that reflected joy or sorrow. In most of those books a page or two would be reserved for the family history, and probably the only written memory of a dear son or daughter who died as a child. That record often accompanied the family to meeting on Sunday and had during the week a prominent place in the home. Many Bibles, however, had only stark records—a progression over generations of individuals' names, births and deaths, with little to mark the tragedy of a death from disease or accident, or the joy of a marriage or birth. In their day grandfather, father, or a son made any necessary family notation, possibly at a little ceremony as a quill pen and ink were used to record the event.

Thousands of family Bible pages have been torn from their original books, now reside in New England libraries and provide indispensable information for the identification of their former owners' families.[3] The tantalizing combination of brevity and starkness that one feels today in looking at these pages was shared by earlier observers, and they often wrote "memoirs," or reflections at the death of an individual to give posterity something additional by which to remember him. In the mid-nineteenth century, as a democratic society evolved, the memoir served to identify contributions of distinguished individuals and note conspicuous talent, and to become a kind of written monument to the founders of the republic. Certainly memoirs were a secular successor to funeral sermons still being performed, if not always published—and were regarded as an accumulation of historical information available to coming generations. These memoirs were no less patriotic and formal than the political orations of the Fourth of July, or the stone monuments then being erected in cemeteries for heroes across the nation, but they were another expression of the public desire to remember important family members.

Memoirs also competed with plans of the Mount Auburn Cemetery Association—a group of Bostonians who established a memorial park on the western edge of Cambridge. The desire for a permanent area away from the industrial and commercial encroachments of Boston was one motivation. Old Granary Burying Ground in Boston was threatened by the expansion of the city, as was the burial ground of King's Chapel. Mount Auburn permitted monuments, park-like vistas, and a restful quiet distinction for families both then and through ages to come. It was most of all a place to commemorate the deeds of a beloved relative with some expensive stone work in a beautifully landscaped park.[4]

The memorial purpose of Mount Auburn Cemetery was described by General Henry Dearborn, one of the promoters, in these words:

> The Cemetery will be a public place of sepulture, where monuments can be erected to our illustrious men, whose remains, thus far, have unfortunately been consigned to obscure and isolated tombs instead of being collected within one common depository, where their great deeds might be perpetuated and their memories cherished by succeeding generations. Though dead, they would be eternal admonitors [sic] to the living—teaching them the way . . . to national glory and individual renown.[5]

Although Mount Auburn was immensely successful as a memorial shrine, it did not completely satisfy those relatives of the deceased who wanted something more, and they liked the custom of issuing memoirs. These memoirs would be written of New England's great and near great for at least a century to come. But some organization needed to be founded to supervise this activity and publish memoirs for general circulation. Until the 1840s memoirs were selectively issued, but missed celebrating the deeds of most people. Dissatisfied leaders searched for ways to remember the deeds of beloved colleagues and were not always satisfied with their efforts.

A few people turned to the Massachusetts Historical Society (MHS), which was becoming widely influential in New England. Founded in the last decade of the eighteenth century, it was at first known as the Historical Society, but incorporated later as the Massachusetts Historical Society. The founders at first invited about 30 (later 60) New Englanders living in and around Boston to join with them in establishing a historical collection and publishing documentation on the region. It had classes of members—resident, corresponding, and honorary—which included governors, cabinet members, legislators, and the wealthy and influential citizens of New England and the nation. It was an exclusive men's club which tried to save for posterity some historical manuscripts of the nation, provide material for the writing of history, and accept anything left by Indians and nature that seemed appropriate to collect.

It was admittedly ambitious, and the members rallied to give books from their own libraries, to arouse the community to the need for a safe depository for national treasures, and to discover the existence of manuscripts secreted in the attics of New England houses. MHS irregularly published a single volume of its *Collections*, which presented a wide variety of letters, journals, official papers, histories, and news of library acquisitions. It was admittedly ambitious in what it was doing, but it was functioning, nonetheless, as an historical depository for the letters of important people and publishing selectively a few of its gems for public admiration. Occasionally, it published memoirs of distinguished New Englanders. In 1836, five men were so honored, a unique tribute in an otherwise heavy concentration upon historical materials. One of those five individuals was the Rev. John Prince. The tribute was spread over twelve pages, with little space devoted to his family and education and most space used to describe the impact of his learning, research, and influence upon the civilized world—"All the arts of civilized and social life had engaged his study. In architecture, painting, and fine arts generally, his taste was highly cultivated."[6]

In the memoir of John Pickering, William H. Prescott, the distinguished historian of Spanish imperialism, opened his essay by noting the ultimate importance of the memoir to history: "It is fortunate that in these *Collections* a place has been reserved for the portraits of those members . . . who by their exemplary lives and well-directed labors, have contributed to . . . the best interests of humanity. What, indeed, is more worthy of commemoration than the lives of such men, or what part of a nation's history can form so rich an inheritance for its children? . . . The biography of an individual . . . touches us as akin to ourselves."[7]

Pickering's noble character was well described in the memoir. Other such essays in that volume of the MHS *Collections* celebrated the contributions of John Davis as United States justice and William Lincoln as legislator and historian. The oratorical splendor of the memoir was impressive, if not overwhelming, except that little was reported on the person's family, ancestry, or business and professional connections.

Some critics asked if just the prominent, the wealthy, and the educated should be the only people to be honored? Should not the ordinary citizen also be remembered? John Farmer, the well known genealogist and antiquary, attempted to answer the query. His *Genealogical Register of the First Settlers of New England* in 1829 was an amazing departure in research, but only an incomplete attempt to rescue the founders of New England from obscurity. His illness and death in 1838 left the future of his project in doubt.

Farmer might easily be called the father of genealogy or family history. Born in Chelmsford, Massachusetts, in 1789, he was self-educated through his genuine love of books and literary discussion. In youth, he was a country store clerk, schoolteacher, and writer, in that order, but his health was always so precarious that he chose indoor work and was able in later life to publish pamphlets on the towns of Billerica and Amherst (N.H.). His large miscellany on New Hampshire life and times in the 1820s won him praise and an honorary M.A. degree from Dartmouth College. A founder of the New Hampshire Historical Society in 1823, he lived most of his life in Concord, New Hampshire, where he authored book after book on subjects relating to that state's history and institutions. His membership in MHS was followed by several articles in the *Collections*. Farmer published sketches of Dartmouth College graduates, lists of graduates of New England colleges, and a new edition of Belknap's *History of New Hampshire*, among his many works. From 1822 to 1824 he published with Jacob Moore *Collections: Historical and Miscellaneous*, which may be America's first full-fledged historical journal. His amazing energy was truly remarkable, and nowhere more evident than in the great book of his life.

The *Genealogical Register of the First Settlers of New England* was undeniably his most ambitious project, more an introduction to a biographical and genealogical dictionary than the definitive project that was actually promised. It listed prominent officials of government in all the colonies, all ministers in the colonies, members of the Massachusetts legislature to 1692, members of the Ancient and Honorable Artillery Company, and freemen of Massachusetts and some other New England colonies to 1692. It was a massive gathering of data on families. Its genealogical data was most impressive:

> It embraces many thousands of names of persons, with dates of births, deaths, offices sustained, places of residence, etc., chiefly through the seventeenth century . . . . For one who is fond of genealogical investigations, there is no treasure-house like it.[8]

Farmer's unfinished study and the contributions of many younger gentlemen who worked with him to complete it left a group of surviving scholars who hoped one day to see the fulfillment of his plans, possibly with a much-enlarged new edition. Before Farmer's untimely death in 1838, he was widely honored by societies like MHS, which recognized his unique contribution to family history.

The presence of MHS in his life was not so important as was the New Hampshire Historical Society. Both societies were part of a spreading movement that was inspiring the founding of regional societies like the American Antiquarian Society in 1812, the Essex Historical Society in 1821, the Rhode Island Historical Society in 1822, and the Maine Historical Society in 1822. Many New Englanders were likewise members of the American Statistical Society, the Massachusetts Horticultural Society, and the American Pomological Society. Farmer was corresponding secretary of the New Hampshire Historical Society for nearly fifteen years. Most of these societies shared members who gathered regularly to discuss new books, to read manuscripts, and to raise learned questions. The members were clergymen or former clergymen, lawyers, medical doctors, politicians, professors, teachers, and business people— men of education, prominence, and (sometimes) wealth. They numbered perhaps several hundred or more and lived in metropolitan Boston, Worcester, Salem, or distant Concord, New Hampshire. Their interests were as varied as their occupations, and many were often ready to found other societies to focus their avocations.

Most of these gentlemen were intensely interested in the purpose and work of their organizations. They were generally learned amateurs and quite serious about their pursuits. John Wingate Thornton, for

example, was a well-known lawyer and antiquary who enjoyed brows-
ing in bookshops. One day while looking over books in Burnham's shop
in Boston he picked up a copy of Bishop Wilberforce's history and read
some familiar writing that reminded him of Bradford's *History of
Plimoth Plantation*. He made notes of what he had read and let John S.
Barry see his work. Barry had a similar interest in the lost Bradford
manuscript. Before Thornton realized it, Barry had located the missing
Bradford manuscript at Fulham Place in London and rushed to solidify
his claim of finding it with plans for publication. Thornton felt justly
robbed of a share in the discovery and never forgave his former friend
of theft.[9]

Less dramatic were Joseph Barlow Felt's relations with this community of amateurs. An ordained Congregational minister in his younger
years, he suffered continuing ill health which forced him to dissolve his
pastoral relation with the church in Hamilton, Massachusetts, and seek
less exacting employment. Moving to Cambridge and Boston, he was
soon working in the state archives arranging documents. He next accepted responsibility for editing a volume of documents for MHS and
served ten years as its librarian. In time he joined similar Boston organizations and found time to write and read learned papers and hold
offices. For nineteen years (to 1859) he was recording secretary of the
American Statistical Association. In later life he was secretary of the
Congregational Library Association. None of this work was as fascinating, however, as that with John Farmer. Felt associated with others in
Boston who like him were former assistants of that charming man and
remained loyal to his memory long after Farmer's death.

As a workhorse for many Boston societies Felt had an equal in
Nathaniel B. Shurtleff, a medical doctor who was interested in phrenol-
ogy, genealogy, and history. Like Felt he held memberships in many
organizations—"probably no one in the community was connected
with a greater number," but in his later life he served as mayor of
Boston. His interest in local history brought forth a few short genealogies of the Shurtleff family of Marshfield and a massive involvement as
editor in the publication of the *Massachusetts Colony Court Records* (1853-

1854), followed by the first eight of the twelve volumes of the *Plymouth Colony Records* (1855-1861). When a memoir was written for him in 1873, his association with MHS was cited as a contribution, but the writer added that Shurtleff "dissipated" his energies in too many directions.[10]

Living an equally crowded life was Lemuel Shattuck, who became well known in three professions—as a teacher, bookseller, and publisher. Elected to MHS in 1830, he was a regular participant in its proceedings, but shared his energy developing plans for the Massachusetts school system and writing a history of Concord, Massachusetts. His life remained full as he worked on a genealogy of the Shattuck family, joined in the founding of the American Statistical Society in 1839, and pioneered statistical methods which led to the state's vital records law and its department of health.

While writing the history of Concord, he was disturbed by the chaos in the town's recording of vital documents and developed a system of listing data which was adopted by Massachusetts and later the U.S. government when it was planning the census of 1850. His emphasis upon the individual instead of the family brought the introduction of names, ages, birthplaces, nationality, and neighborhoods into record-keeping. His great concern for people and their origins, as seen in his history of Concord, led to an interest in genealogy and conversely to his discouragement with the historical activities of MHS.[11]

When the bookseller and businessman Charles Ewer approached him in 1843 about founding a genealogical society, Shattuck was very interested and met several times with Ewer to speak about the practicality of establishing yet another organization. Shattuck, though inordinately occupied with his many projects, liked the idea of a genealogical society and may have gone with Ewer to Samuel G. Drake, another bookseller, and John Wingate Thornton, a struggling young lawyer, to discuss the idea. They may have also visited the young Boston merchant William H. Montague, who was immediately enthusiastic and pledged support, and the learned Rev. Doctor William Jenks who liked antiquarian history. Shattuck knew Felt and Shurtleff through their relations with John Farmer's *Genealogical Register*, but both of these friends, as also Jenks, when interviewed, apparently decided to wait until Shattuck and Ewer had more concrete plans. Could a society grow around genealogy, were a sufficient number of people interested, and was genealogy a serious enough pursuit to follow? Ewer recalled criticism of genealogists in the past and wanted to launch a new society on a firm basis by gathering together a sufficiently important number of prominent individuals. Ewer was apparently suffering from ill health and had much free time. He offered, if it were agreeable, to head the new society and rally support in Boston.

This group of congenial people met socially in the autumn of 1844. Already agreeing to create an entirely new organization, they were unwilling, except for Lemuel Shattuck, to concentrate solely on genealogy as the purpose of the organization. They argued among themselves about the emphasis which the Society should take. Ewer liked the idea of a genealogical and heraldic society, while Thornton wanted to make the pursuit of history the driving core of their activities. It should be, he said, an historical and genealogical society. Only Shattuck would hold out for a genealogical society, but he was not so insistent as to delay their plans. Shattuck had worked fifteen years earlier with John Farmer and believed he could use this opportunity of founding a new society to promote a revival of Farmer's innovative work in tracing families through several generations.

The five founders now set upon their plan for a society and met in October 1844 at the home of William H. Montague at 4 Orange Street, then at the residences of Lemuel Shattuck at 79 Harrison Avenue and Samuel G. Drake at 56 Cornhill. A constitution was written in the meantime and approved. Plans were made to incorporate the society as the New England Historical Genealogical Society, and a net was cast for New Englanders with similar interests to be members. The group chose their officers at their first board of directors meeting January 7, 1845, and gave themselves all the existing offices:

Charles Ewer, President
Lemuel Shattuck, Vice President
Samuel G. Drake, Corresponding Secretary
John Wingate Thornton, Recording Secretary

William H. Montague, Treasurer
(Thornton served also as librarian)[12]

On March 18, 1845, the General Court of Massachusetts approved the petition for incorporation. The purpose of the Society in this charter was defined as collecting, preserving, and publishing (occasionally) genealogical and historical matter relating to New England families. It noted the intent of establishing a manuscript and book depository and limited the total wealth of the Society to $20,000. In the process of petitioning for the charter, with some opposition in legislative committee from Charles Francis Adams of the Massachusetts Historical Society, Thornton was persuaded to give the Society the legal name of New England Historic Genealogical Society—which then disturbed only one or two of the founders who regarded the name as cumbersome.

The officers had already ordered stationery and notebooks so that they could record the business of each monthly meeting. But they met informally, and privately too, as they laid plans for the new society. They were anxious to increase the potential membership as quickly as possible and to accomplish this task within the first year after incorporation. They were not bound like MHS by any maximum number, but wanted, of course, influential and congenial members. Each of the five officers began nominating prospective members and the monthly meetings of 1845 mostly processed these prospective members. Their success rate in securing acceptances was absolutely amazing—indeed astonishing. About 42 resident members qualified, as well as 40 corresponding and 5 honorary members in the first year. They attracted to the Society a broad representation of the historical, political, professional, and intellectual community, including John Quincy Adams, George Bancroft, John G. Palfrey, Nathaniel B. Shurtleff, William Jenks, and Lucius R. Paige.[13]

A pamphlet was also written, and published in 1846, which advertised the purpose of the Society and, of course, invited new members. The Society announced to everyone that it was interested in preserving the public documents of the towns of Massachusetts, gathering data on cemetery memorials, and forming a library. Ewer made a tour in 1846 around Massachusetts, speaking with prospective members and looking for books and contributions. With a full bag of promises, he returned without anything tangible. He felt successful, however, because he had spoken with eminent members like Harrison Gray Otis and was assured of their continuing interest.

Ewer was collecting personal memorabilia, too; for him a bust, medallion, furniture, and portraits were almost as good a gift as books and manuscripts. He had to be careful in accepting these gifts, because the Society had not been able to find inexpensive office space.[14] The five leaders had contributed almost no money to the Society, other than the three-dollar membership fee, but fees from the other new members came in slowly. So the officers rented a temporary room in the City Building on Court Square, No. 9. It had good space, with three windows, on the third floor, mostly suitable to store the gifts, books, and historical items. The public meetings of the board, however, were held at the American Education Society on Cornwall Street and at the residences of the officers, although they purchased furniture for their storage room and met there occasionally for a monthly board meeting.

By the end of 1845 the founders had organized their Society, were holding monthly programs for the reading of scholarly papers, and were entertaining an abundance of proposals to improve the Boston intellectual community. Samuel G. Drake and John Wingate Thornton felt that the Society should immediately solicit community opinion and determined the feasibility of launching a journal. A new member, the Rev. Samuel H. Riddel, was then chosen to preside over a publications committee which brought in a favorable report for a genealogical and antiquarian quarterly of 96 pages and a subscription fee of $2.00 a year, providing financial arrangements could be made with a publisher. Lemuel Shattuck, on another important matter, pressed for government action to preserve the records of towns from reported deterioration then taking place, and the board responded by submitting a petition to the General Court. Always taking center place in their discussions was the importance of genealogy in the future of the Society. Drake presented at an open meeting a paper on the essential ideas and procedures of genealogy. He liked to lay down rules as an authority, but he was insistent that genealogists must decide upon a structure for publishing their data. The board listened attentively, but the members were not ready to commit the Society solely to genealogy. They debated whether John Farmer's *Genealogical Register* should be reprinted and delayed any decision until they saw the original copy which they heard was greatly enlarged. They welcomed, during their monthly meetings, gifts of books, memorabilia, and pamphlets, and purchased a record book where they might list benefactors. Their debates, conversations, and arguments would continue into 1846, but the officers regarded 1845 as a remarkable year—genealogy and family history were being recognized as subjects worthy of scholarly study.[15]

Notes

[1] "Memoir of Hon. Joshua Thomas of Plymouth, who died January 10, 1821," *Collections of the Massachusetts Historical Society*, 2nd Ser., 10 (Boston, 1823): 1-2.

[2] John Lathrop, "Biographical Memoir of Rev. John Lothrop," ed. by Abiel Holmes, *Collections of the Massachusetts Historical Society*, 2nd Ser., 1 (Boston, 1814): 163-178.

[3] The library of NEHGS has assembled over 2500 Bible entries taken from their collection.

[4] Wilson Flagg, *Mount Auburn: its Scenes, its Beauties, and its Lessons* (Boston, 1861).

[5] Blanche Linden-Ward, *Silent City on a Hill: Landscapes of Memory and Boston's Mount Auburn Cemetery* (Columbus, 1989), 183.

[6] Charles W. Upham, "Memoir of Hon. Rev. John Prince," *Collections of the Massachusetts Historical Society*, 3rd Ser., 5 (Boston, 1836): 271-283.

[7] William H. Prescott, "Memoir of Hon. John Pickering" *Collections of the Massachusetts Historical Society*, 3rd Ser., 10 (Boston, 1849): 204-224.

[8] William Cogswell, "Memoir of John Farmer," NEHG *Register*, 1 (1847): 15-16. All references to the NEHG *Register* henceforth will simply cite this journal as *Register*.

[9] *Proceedings of the Massachusetts Historical Society, 1871-1873*, 12 (Boston, 1873): 315-316; Thomas C. Amory, "Memoir of John Wingate Thornton," *Register*, 33 (1879): 274-282. A fine picture is included in the memoir.

[10] Charles C. Smith, "Memoir of the Hon. Nathaniel B. Shurtleff, M.D." *Proceedings of the Massachusetts Historical Society, 1873-1875*, 13 (Boston, 1875): 389-395. Smith noted that Shurtleff had "acquired [a] considerable professional reputation and a fortune."

[11] "Sketches of Lemuel Shattuck," *Register*, 14 (1860): 97-99.

[12] See "Origin of the New England Historic-Genealogical Society," *Register*, 9 (1855): 9-12. The early history of the Society can be followed in the Ms Proceedings I (1845-1851); the meeting of January 1845 records the first election. Records of NEHGS, I (1844-   ) has entries for most early meetings of the Society. The first quarterly meeting, in March 1845, has the act of incorporation. Thornton apparently named the Society—The New England Historic Genealogical Society—when he submitted papers for incorporation.

[13] Within a short time of its founding, the Society began adding new members. See *Register*, 12 (1858):368-369. In 1845, 87 members were added, in 1846, 53. A decade later (in 1855) there were 449 members.

[14] Ewer's account of a trip in search of members and donations, June 24, 1846, Ewer Papers.

[15] It is not known exactly when the Seal of the Society was designed, but it has been used on most publications since the *Register* of January 1847. For the Seal's history and a description see *Register*, 17 (1863): 231.

CHAPTER 2

The First Twenty-Five Years 1845-1870

In the beginning there was Charles Ewer who served nearly six terms as president of the new society. An enthusiastic and devout man, "one of nature's noblemen," he was fascinated by the idea of family history and its impact on American culture, and, following an inclination to do good, he wanted to meet anyone interested in genealogy and enroll him as a member of the new society. Ewer was, however, an unsuccessful businessman—in fact almost everything he touched turned to financial failure for him and gain for others. He had a love for books and collected a library of 1500 volumes, but his bookstore brought no profits. So with Avon Place and South Cove Enterprise—both were inspirational schemes to develop Boston business districts and both required more money than he could command. He lost control to others and missed his chance to be wealthy.[1]

In 1845 Ewer was fifty-five years of age, with plenty of time on his hands, but was in ill health. He wanted hundreds of members to join the new society, a publishing program, a library building, and a space for meetings. Most of all he wished to republish, perhaps enlarge, John Farmer's *Genealogical Register*. For him, it represented the best genealogical project of their age. His colleagues were certainly agreeable, especially Lemuel Shattuck and John Wingate Thornton. Both were interested in history and genealogy, though Shattuck was occupied more with record-keeping and plans to make the "census an informative source for popular history."

Thornton was then a struggling young lawyer from Maine looking for a wealthy wife. In time his pursuit was eminently successful, but not before he tasted poverty and suffered much deprivation. Less interested in administering the Society as an organization than his friends, he remained an active member and spent free time outside law libraries writing antiquarian history and searching bookstores for rare books and manuscripts.[2] Ewer had to depend essentially upon Samuel G. Drake instead of his two younger colleagues. Drake was a shopkeeper with antiquarian instincts and also a founder of the new society. At times he could be sharp-spoken, strong-willed, and unusually stubborn, but he admired Charles Ewer, whose ideas and logic seemed irresistible, and he readily became Ewer's chief supporter as an officer of the Society. Appreciating the idea of publishing John Farmer's *Genealogical Register* in an enlarged edition, Drake helped Ewer secure an interleaved copy of Farmer's work, but he was enthusiastic most of all about Ewer's plans for a journal of history and genealogy.

A quarterly publication, they believed, could be used by hundreds, maybe thousands, of researchers to rescue records then being destroyed through neglect in public offices. In addition to printing such records, a journal would give members of the Society a further vehicle for research, discussion, and writing about New England's Puritan fathers. It would also fill a deficiency in historical literature by providing information on families. Ewer and Drake developed a prospectus of what they desired, and it was widely sent to sympathetic members of the Society, who often responded with pledges of support. They tried to interest Thornton in being editor, but he declined because of precarious finances.

Much discussion of these objectives then resulted in the appointment of a publications committee with the Rev. Samuel H. Riddel as chairman. This very energetic man, now Secretary of the Society and a good friend of Ewer and Drake, held weeks of meetings, interviewed unsuccessfully many publishers, sought advice from countless members, and decided finally to ask Drake to assume the financial burden of being publisher. The shopkeeper, with his eyes wide open, accepted full responsibility as publisher and the burden of paying a salaried editor appointed by the

Society. It had already chosen the Rev. William Cogswell, who would give full time to the new journal for annual compensation of one thousand dollars. Drake had great expectations of success, perhaps even immediately, with as many as seven hundred subscribers and continuing help from the Society in advertising the journal so that 1500 subscribers could be eventually secured. Certainly Cogswell was a wonderful selection as editor. Formerly an editor of the *American Quarterly Register* and lately editor of the *New Hampshire Repository* and secretary of the American Education Society, he had many friends, a bulky subscription list for the *New Hampshire Repository*, and much enthusiasm. In presenting the committee report to the members, Riddel praised Charles Ewer for his "disinterested endeavor" in these negotiations and predicted not only honor for the members in publishing the journal but also a "source of some pecuniary income" for the Society.[3] Contracts were then signed; Cogswell appointed as editor for one year; and certain guarantees by the Society were given to protect the publisher and editor against financial loss. The committee was sufficiently cautious to reserve to the Society ultimate responsibility for the journal, now called *The New England Historical and Genealogical Register*. Though the committee regarded their enterprise as an experiment, Ewer, Drake, and Cogswell thought there was a good chance of profits and success, and a long life for the journal.[4]

In the hands of Drake and Cogswell the most important business of the Society was now entrusted. Other activities conducted by President Ewer would include a lecture series, the amassing of a library, and the recruiting of new members, but the *Register* for the present would focus the energy of the Society. Drake began compiling a subscription list and reached what seemed to him an amazing number of 1600 people. He sent out the prospectus, secured a printer, and accepted the financial liabilities of the *Register*. Cogswell's work was more challenging intellectually because he had to decide what this body of historians and genealogists actually expected from the journal. A general outline of content had already been prepared for him. It included historical articles, ancient documents, epitaph inscriptions, short genealogies, and obituary notices. The lead article of each issue, however, should always be a biographical memoir of some distinguished individual, but limited to ten pages—except in "some extraordinary case."[5]

For the first issue in January 1847, Cogswell featured a memoir on John Farmer, some of his writing, and a genealogy of the Farmer family as the leading material. How could Cogswell have done otherwise? Ewer, Drake, Shattuck, and others regarded Farmer as the "most distinguished Genealogist and Antiquary of this country." There followed in the first *Register* some extracts of births in Dedham, genealogies of the Chase and Dudley families, some poetry by Governor Thomas Hinckley, and a list of the *Mayflower* passengers. The issue in April was dedicated to Samuel Sewall, his diary and letter book, with an article on "Reasons for Genealogical Investigations," family histories of the Cotton, Butler, and Minot families, and a list of first settlers of New England. Succeeding issues in July and October featured leading articles on John Endecott and Thomas Hutchinson and instructional essays on genealogy.[6]

In less than five hundred pages these four issues of the *Register* in 1847 left a great impression upon critics. It was a magnificent source of original documentation and history. Its readers were a crusty lot, however; many would not pay the $2.00 subscription fee until they had the four issues in their hands. Others decided that the first two issues did not fulfill the promise of the prospectus. Their stubborn attitude left Drake standing in quicksand because he was overwhelmed by uncertain subscription lists, delinquent payments for the *Register*, and mounting expenses. Apparently Cogswell was chosen not only for his skills as editor, but also for his possession of a subscription list of nearly 1200 readers from his *New Hampshire Repository*. Those subscribers as well as his other friends were expected to push the circulation of the NEHG *Register* to 1600 and maybe more.[7]

As the first year came to an end, Drake had discovered too many uncertainties and the outlook for 1848 seemed desperate. Circulation at 1600 was much too inflated; perhaps 1000 to 1200 subscribers would be realistic, if members re-subscribed and paid their fees. He had an overrun of 765 issues in storage and about 300 delinquent subscribers. On calculating profits he found nothing for himself—for his time and trouble—and unpaid expenses for engraving, paper, and storage. His frightening discovery was made known to Riddel, Ewer, and Shattuck of the publications committee, who seemed as surprised as he was over the financial crisis and sought an explanation. Drake provided for them the statistical information which was not generally unfavorable, if expenses could be contained and a subsidy provided. Drake remained, however, aroused. He wanted a new contract in 1848, release of Cogswell as a salaried editor, and help in building the subscription base. Plainly he desired full control of all matters of publication without the supervision of the committee, the interference of an editor, or the accountability of an auditor. For this independence he would give the Society 150 free copies of the *Register* and a share of the profits if its circulation reached a satisfactory level.[8] Circulation remained, moreover, a serious problem because not all members of the Society would subscribe.

His arguments with Cogswell over management forced the editor to resign because there seemed to be no money for salary, but Cogswell generously planned the format of the 1848 January issue. Drake reluctantly published and edited the *Register* in April, July, and October, but he became increasingly angry with the publications committee. He warned the members in his usually blunt manner that he refused to continue in 1849 bearing the heavy responsibility of publisher without ample compensation.[9] He decided, moreover, that the *Register* belonged partly to him as its creator and financier. Such claims of proprietorship were quickly rejected by Ewer, but the Society itself faced the reality of having no money and no staff to publish the *Register*. Whatever they thought of Drake, he was their only hope for a publisher and he had legitimate rights to be paid for his services. But the committee decided to look for another editor and thus control the contents of the *Register*. By March 1849, they had selected William Thaddeus Harris. The young, 23-year-old son of the librarian of Harvard College was then in precarious health, suffering from tuberculosis, and had an uncertain future. He was brilliant, deeply interested in documentary history, and had worked for the Massachusetts Historical Society; even more, he was available and unemployed. While he had little editorial experience, he readied for press the April, July, and October issues of the *Register*.[10] His congenial personality won support even from Samuel Drake and the crisis of 1848 faded momentarily. He praised Drake and, in a well written editorial in 1849, reminded his readers "that while errors, mistakes, and omissions are easily detected, and easier denounced, it would become them quite as much, were they to give due credit for the many that had been avoided."[11]

Though Harris could not endure the exacting duties of editor, he remained on the publications committee in 1850, while Nathaniel Bradstreet Shurtleff succeeded him. An acquaintance of Drake, Shurtleff agreed to edit the *Register* without salary. His appointment occurred as there was a change of command in the Society. Charles Ewer was apparently ill, or weary of disputes over the *Register*, and had decided to relinquish the presidency; some time later he moved to New Hampshire. His successor was Joseph Barlow Felt, a member since 1845 and librarian then of the Massachusetts Historical Society. Felt differed from Ewer in almost every experience of life, except that both had modest means and weakened health. Felt was a clergyman in youth and an archivist and librarian in mature life. He had written histories of Ipswich, Essex, and Hamilton, Massachusetts, and compiled the *Annals of Essex*. His business friends were members of the Massachusetts Historical Society, especially Shurtleff, James Savage, a longtime president of that Society, and a group of historians and genealogists.[12] Soon he was utilizing his close connections with the MHS to hold Society board meetings in their halls.

Felt realized as he settled into office that the *Register* needed some additional financial support, but he was personally incapable of raising outside money to subsidize it. The number of new subscriptions were not adequate to diminish the pressure on him, however, to find a solution for its deficits. In seeking that solution, he prevailed upon his good friend, Nathaniel Shurtleff, who was well known in the Boston community, to assume immediately the burdens of editor. In a short time, Shurtleff also discovered that Drake was a hard man with whom to work, even though they were longtime acquaintances. Shurtleff's arrangement as editor thus did not endure, and in 1851 Drake took over the *Register* when Felt could not find anyone else who would perform the task as a gratuity or labor for low wages. In 1851 the *Register* under Drake seemed well presented, with an excellent memoir on Hugh Peters by Joseph Felt. The memoir was published in installments over four issues and may have aroused the ire of some critics who undoubtedly objected to its length and the occasional character of some other articles. Drake took advantage of his position as editor and publisher to provide a short preface to the volume. It was an honest statement of his position regarding the *Register*'s need for more support from the entire membership if he would continue as its publisher:

> The Society, whose objects it has carried out, thus far, is large and well able to sustain the work, provided its members all patronize it, which is not now the case. And here we may be permitted to suggest, that no person should be admitted to membership, in the Society, who will not patronize its Periodical.[13]

Drake touched a sensitive chord which affected some members of the Society and was reflected first in the publications committee. Nearly half of the members of the committee soon resigned and new members also took charge of the Board of Directors. Felt responded by editing the January and April issues of the 1852 *Register*, while Timothy Farrar and William Blake Trask edited the July and October issues. Later in the year Drake lost his contract to publish the 1853 *Register* when Frederic Kidder formed a company specifically to undertake the task. Drake returned as sole editor in 1853, but reassumed full publishing responsibilities in 1854 when Kidder's company ran into difficulties. Until 1858 when Drake again rode the crest of a financial crisis, he was often an unhappy editor and publisher, but he handled problems with the U.S. post office in getting issues delivered on time and maintained a fairly stable subscription list.

Kidder, treasurer of the Society from 1851 to 1854, and a member of the publications committee with Jenks, Timothy Farrar, and David Hamblen, was a Boston merchant who dealt in West Indian merchandise and speculated in Maine lands. He and Farrar, the lawyer and judge, shared boyhood memories of New Ipswich, New Hampshire and great interest in the *Register* and undoubtedly assisted Drake.

Neither man was a warm supporter of President Felt, who was unhappy with both Drake's outbursts and the finances of the *Register*. Felt attempted to resign in the spring of 1852, but was urged to remain until January 1853 when new elections brought the well known lawyer and jurist, William Whiting, to the presidency—perhaps also as a mediator. Felt left for a position as secretary of the Congregational Library Association and dropped his membership in the Society. By 1855, tempers had cooled, and the directors elected Felt to an honorary membership.[14]

His presidential successor was preoccupied with his own legal practice. Younger than Felt by over twenty years, Whiting was the author of many legal papers and had joined the Society only in 1852. He used the opportunity of his election, however, to deliver a major address on the importance of genealogy to New England life. Every family, he said, should preserve its records and have a written history. Every town should have a history and preserve its vital records. The Society, he emphasized, should develop a comprehensive library full of histories and genealogies, vital records, biographies, and government records.

> Everyone will [then] know where to come, in order most advantageously to prosecute these researches; and, as the modes of conveyance are now so cheap and expeditious, there is no place more accessible to the people of New England than the capital. Boston itself would add to its reputation, by the acquisition of a Library, which would be useful to so many antiquarian scholars.[15]

At future meetings, Whiting was not always able to preside because of his legal practice. His 1853 message, however, was published in the *Register* and members accepted the invitation to give books to the library. For nearly every monthly meeting a list was prepared of donations like books, portraits, furniture, and historical memorabilia. Such gifts grew with the years, but donations of money were rare until the 1860s. In 1858, when Whiting retired as president in favor of Samuel G. Drake, the library was opened from three to five every weekday afternoon and at least one evening, and librarian William B. Trask was looking for additional book shelving. In June 1860, Trask reported gifts of 84 bound volumes, 488 pamphlets, and an engraved portrait of Isaac Barré, the English patriot of the American Revolution. That year gifts also came from the State Historical Society of Wisconsin and the Historical Society of Pennsylvania, while Mrs. Lemuel Shattuck gave 63 books and 1563 pamphlets in memory of her late husband.[16]

Scholarly papers on historical or public affairs were presented at almost every monthly meeting of the Society. Lorenzo Sabine shared his thoughts on the capture of Quebec in 1759 and 1760, James Spear Loring spoke on the historian William Gordon, and others presented tributes to William Hickling Prescott, an honorary member who had died recently, to Henry Bond, the great genealogist of Watertown, and to Lemuel Shattuck, a founder of the Society. Members as a group frequently attended formal lectures in Boston on statesmen like Daniel Webster and Lord Chatham or entertained with programs on Indians and patriotic songs of New England. Church music was also a favorite topic, particularly the compositions of William Billings and his distinctive style.[17]

Crowds at these cultural affairs probably ranged in size between twenty and forty people, including frequently a few wives of members. Afterward the audience entered into strenuous arguments, with favored subjects including names for the Society, the content of the *Register*, relations with the Massachusetts Historical Society, and government policies for the preservation of public records.

Sometime early in 1852 Joseph Felt, while he was still president, announced that James Savage was going to edit John Farmer's *Genealogical Register*. Possibly Nathaniel Shurtleff joined him in the inevitable discussion. As former president of MHS, James Savage enjoyed considerable prestige in Boston, was ready and willing to undertake the project, which would be enlarged to include about three generations of New England founders, and was expected to attract financial backing from his friends. This announcement was received explosively by Drake, Shattuck, and Thornton, and perhaps Ewer, then living in Portsmouth, New Hampshire. NEHGS was undoubtedly unable to assume the burden of the project and had no one as able as Savage ready to undertake it. But the founders were sensitive people who may have accused Felt of disloyalty to the Society and forced his eventual departure from the presidency. Shurtleff likewise experienced some harshness and separated himself from his genealogical colleagues—Drake never forgave him for his apostasy. In time Savage would successfully publish his genealogical study in four volumes. It became, like Farmer's *Genealogical Register*, one of the scholarly monuments of the age.[18]

Drake remained uncomfortably editor and publisher of the *Register* from 1853 to 1858 when he served one year as the official president of the Society and then left for Europe. Finances for him were not as strained as formerly because members of the Society gradually increased in numbers and the *Register* won the respect of a larger and larger group of scholars. While members of the Society and subscribers of the *Register* paid separate dues, the members were larger by one hundred (600 to 500) than the subscribers.[19]

That marginal difference made Drake angry whenever the subject of societal support arose, because of what seemed to be an insensitive lack of appreciation for the *Register* and his contribution to its continuance. Several times he would declare the *Register* finished as a journal only to be persuaded that help from the Society was imminent. Besides his responsibilities for the *Register*, he served as the Corresponding Secretary for many years and as a director for a short period, often rented rooms in his book shop to the Society, and hosted its directors' meetings. This little man in appearance and modest style of living was easily recognized. Dressed always in black suits, he surrounded himself with books and manuscripts in his shop; "he makes his library his kingdom and calls up the spirits of the Puritan Fathers from the regions of the past—and they come back in a living reality and move again in the history of New England."[20]

Somehow between 1853 and 1858 Drake withdrew from controversy, "like an erudite monk," perhaps preoccupied with editing the *Register* and assisting President William Whiting in running the Society. He was frequently the presiding officer of monthly meetings and handled ordinary business expeditiously. Instead of Drake heating tempers, it was President Whiting now who blundered into an issue that would arouse the Society and Drake himself. At first, however, Whiting was primarily interested in constitutional issues and helped sharpen the focus of the Society—"the object of the Society shall be to collect, preserve, and disseminate the local and general history of New England and the genealogies of New England families."[21] He urged new fees for members and honorary vice presidents for other states, including New York and Ohio, perhaps also California. But he was extraordinarily busy with his law practice and relied upon Drake, Timothy Farrar, John Ward Dean, and William Jenks to run the monthly directors' meetings. These meetings approved funds to buy books for the library, shelving, and binding of overused volumes. Apparently Whiting urged new quarters for the Society, to be not too expensive but large enough for a meeting place and the Society's growing library. Space was eventually found at 17 Bromfield Street, a third floor location, well lighted and 18 by 53 feet in size. The members were very pleased with what they rented, but Whiting and others realized that this would be a temporary location if the Society continued its present growth.[22]

Whiting, in attending many of the monthly public lectures, was amazed by the popularity of historical subjects. Almost no lecture, he noticed, was based entirely on family history, but the members were interested in a wide range of historical, antiquarian, and biographical subjects. Their interests suggested a change of name for the Society—a question which was raised privately from time to time: should it be an archaeological society, an antiquarian society, an historical society? Whiting, in response to popular feelings, appointed at the annual meeting in 1856 a committee to study the issue. But only four of the 31 present at the April 2, 1856 meeting wanted a name change if the Society were to be called an archaeological society. Drake was among the four who voted against that change. Others were in favor of calling it The New England Historical and Genealogical Society. This last change was precious, if not insignificant, but the members voted overwhelmingly to petition the Massachusetts legislature for this change of name in the charter.[23]

The cumbersome title of the Society had disturbed some members ever since its founding in 1845. Most members, however, gave only incidental consideration to the name, though among the founders there was continuing discussion about an appropriate one. The use of "historic" as a modifier for "genealogical," which was probably never the intention of the founders, irritated some, and they called their new journal in 1847, when it was first issued, *The New England Historical and Genealogical Register*. This name was perhaps inspired by the desire to emphasize equally history and genealogy as scholarly concerns of the journal. In its preface, written for the completed four issues in 1847, the editor affirmed the policy of the *Register* to publish the results "of Historical and Genealogical Researches."[24]

The legislative petition in 1858 for a change of name aroused an immediate protest from MHS. About one third of its resident members put their signatures on a memorial to the legislature and instructed the oldest and most eminent member, Josiah Quincy, and two other distinguished members to await a call from the legislative committee reviewing the matter. At age eighty-six the former president of Harvard College actually delivered an address explaining the MHS protest. The matter at dispute, he said, was the projected change from "Historic Genealogical" to "Historical and Genealogical." He regarded the change significant, troublesome, and unnecessary. The similarity of names currently was causing confusion in the public mind and interfering with the chosen work of both societies. Further, the redefining of names would be very harmful to them and the Commonwealth.[25]

He condemned also the offensive tactics of NEHGS in circulating a pamphlet to all legislators, calling it abusive and indiscreet. The publications committee of NEHGS, moreover, he pointed out, had the arrogance to change the Society's own name for its journal, indicating that it actually expected little opposition from MHS and ready consent from the legislature.[26]

Apparently the MHS offered a compromise during the course of this confrontation and would have agreed to call the Society *The New England Genealogical and Historical Society*. The arrogance of the MHS was too much for Drake, who left for England in 1859, and for his interim successor as president, Almon D. Hodges, who favored withdrawing their petition. Drake had stepped into the presidency when Whiting got involved in the agitation over slavery and Republican Party politics, but Drake for other reasons wanted only limited service. So it was with Hodges, a Boston merchant and banker who was deeply aroused by the mounting crisis over slavery but was ready to lead the Society until a successor for Drake was found.[27]

Too many members of both societies, including Hodges, felt the bitterness of divided loyalties. Emotions were too great over what was an insignificant change of title and for what was not a very serious reason. Surely MHS in using its title could be easily distinguished by the public from the New England Historic Genealogical Society. But matters of prestige, rivalry, and exclusiveness separated the societies. NEHGS, in trying to find higher grounds, now took steps to locate the leadership and resources to challenge MHS as a scholarly society. There lingered, however, the feeling among a few NEHGS members that a change of title would strengthen the identification of the Society with history. But such proposals, though causing debate, were easily voted down by men interested in larger issues.[28]

More energy was expanded now in another direction. Some members of the Society wanted an auxiliary organization completely devoted to publication of original—primary—historical materials. They may have had in mind the *Historical Collections* of MHS. They gathered in May 1858 and with some debate formed the Prince Society for Mutual Publication. Among those debaters and shakers were, of course, Samuel G. Drake, John Wingate Thornton, Frederic Kidder, John Ward Dean, and William H. Whitmore, and a few others who were book collectors, antiquaries, and historians.[29] All were loyal members of NEHGS, one should repeat. The only conditions of membership in the Prince Society would be a pledge to buy its publications:

No member is called on for a subscription, but when a volume is issued, the Council fixes its price, as near the actual cost as possible, and he pays and receives his copy. A limit will be placed on the number and prices of volumes to be issued in any one year. For the first year, this limit will be three dollars.[30]

Not until 1865 did the first volumes appear: William Wood's *New England's Prospect* and two of three volumes of *The Hutchinson Papers*. Printed in beautiful type-face and rag paper, the title page had a part of its lettering in red ink as well as the seal of the Prince Society in red. At first the numbers of copies of each volume ranged between 160 and 180, but the popularity of the books brought a larger printing. Until 1911 the volumes appeared almost yearly, and totaled 35. The final volume, *New England Company of 1649*, appeared in 1920. Many important historians, genealogists, and antiquarians were editors of the series—some even members of MHS. Drake was president of the Prince Society until 1870, then John Ward Dean to 1880, and for decades thereafter Edmund F. Slafter, who was also a pillar of NEHGS during many years at the turn of the century.[31]

Scholars from all New England states contributed to the Prince Society, but the driving spirit of the organization in its early decades derived from members of NEHGS. The Prince Society frequently met at No. 17 Bromfield Street, in the meeting room of NEHGS, used the book collection, and called upon Drake and Thornton for access to their great private libraries of rare books.[32]

Drake was absent in England during 1859 and until May 1860. For that period a publication committee, composed of William B. Trask, William H. Whitmore, and John Ward Dean, edited the *Register* and continued to do so until January 1861. Drake's resumption of responsibility in 1861 coincided with the continuation of earlier problems associated with the *Register* because subscriptions had fallen in numbers while he was in England and some subscribers, as was nearly a tradition, let their payments become delinquent. During 1861-1862 Drake was uneasy about the deficit, which he continued to absorb, and then took the extreme step of offering the *Register* for sale, or contemplating its discontinuation.[33]

Happily, the treasurer of the Society, William Blanchard Towne, and John Ward Dean, one of the editors of the *Register*, contacted Joel Munsell, a noted publisher of antiquarian books in Albany, New York, a corresponding member of the Society since 1857, and native of North-field, Massachusetts, and convinced him of the practicality of publishing the *Register*. Munsell was surprisingly receptive, but asked the Society to take care of editorial responsibilities. The agreement with Munsell was one of those eleventh-hour, unexpected arrangements that reflected the new prominence of both the Society and the *Register*, and maybe also the generosity of Joel Munsell, who was cautiously willing to assume the risks of financial losses. He reduced immediately Drake's press run from one thousand to five hundred copies and adjusted the number in 1862 to six hundred and fifty.[34] Some money was then made on the *Register*.

The last confrontation with Drake occurred during a serious time in the nation's history. The election of 1860 split political parties, encouraged a secession of the South from the Union, and made most people in the North ponder what they would do if a war occurred. Younger members of the Society were preparing to leave for military service. President Hodges, who hated war, was a Lincoln Republican who pledged to aid the Union in whatever way he could. He and the directors of the Society sensed the need to find other leadership to manage the Society. Hodges stood ready, in spite of his sixty years, to accept a role in the home guards and wanted to be free to volunteer. Sometime in late fall 1860 the directors contacted Dr. Winslow Lewis, who was not so determined to serve in the coming conflict, and persuaded him to stand for election as president.

In January 1861 the directors proudly introduced Lewis to the assembled members of the Society and urged his election as president. His popular reception was a stroke of genius. Not only did he enjoy prestige as a medical doctor in Boston, experience as a former legislator, and a wide acquaintanceship as Grand Master of the Freemasons, but he had the time to direct the Society. He had European education and travel as well, and most of all substantial wealth and an excellent family heritage that could be traced to the founding fathers of Massachusetts Bay and

Plymouth colonies. Further, he collected books of history, poetry, and antiquity and enjoyed the classics, translating passages from Greek and Latin as a hobby.[35]

His immediate interest was the library, not the *Register*, not the physical accommodations of the Society, and not the promotion of heraldry or genealogy. Before he left the presidency in 1866, he established new priorities. He discovered in 1861 a library of 3,294 books, 14,000 pamphlets, and some manuscripts, and during each month of 1861 he welcomed gifts of more and more books for the library. In March he gave the Society a book and an unpublished letter of Voltaire. In November other donors gave 133 volumes and 645 pamphlets. During 1862 nearly 400 books were given and Dr. Lewis appointed his first committee to raise money for a new, more spacious library to house these treasures. Time passed without much progress, but donations of books increased at a steady rate until the library committee in 1865 emphasized in its annual report that more space for books was urgently needed, and advised the Society that the present building was not a safe place to house the now valuable collection of 6,786 volumes, 20,242 pamphlets, many town histories, and manuscripts.[36]

Responsibility for supervising this overflowing library belonged partly to John Hannibal Sheppard, an Englishman who immigrated as a youth to Hallowell, Maine and then to Boston. A lawyer, longtime overseer of Bowdoin College, a freemason and scholar who also loved music, poetry, and biography, he devoted his full time to the Society, although long retired from his profession, and ten years older than Dr. Lewis, who was sixty-two in 1861. Sheppard liked books, but he enjoyed writing biography even more. In the 1860s he contributed many sketches of societal members to the *Register*.

The remarkable increase of books under Sheppard's supervision pleased Dr. Lewis very much. Besides his own frequent gifts of books, he made public pleas for donations. As president he decided to present an annual address; members could also read it later in the *Register*. His purpose was an exalted one of setting a tone for the work of the Society. The speech was a departure from the conduct of past presidents, who rarely gave formal addresses. His message in 1862 was so warmly received by his audience that he made his address an annual event until he left the presidency in 1866.[37]

Standing before an audience of fifty or more members in 1862, he confined his thoughts to the elements of biography and genealogy—"the twin hand maidens of their elder and more stately sister, *History.*" Biography, he observed, if properly pursued, "must ever be accepted as, under God's blessing, one of the most powerful means and modes of training men to be good citizens, good members of society in the present life, and fitted to enjoy the purer . . . happiness reserved for them in the life to come." Genealogy, he continued, explores the mental as well as physical qualities [that] are handed down . . . from parent to child, from forefathers to posterity, and . . . thus, pure and healthy descent is of immense importance . . . I need scarcely allude to the . . . conclusions which the philosophical genealogist arrives at, when, in watching the life of . . . America's . . . noble sons, he observes the generic seeds of those virtues, and that nobility of soul in the parents or ancestors."

The importance thus of history, through biography and genealogy, was obvious. Dr. Lewis cited some of his cherished authors. Henry St. John, Lord Bolingbroke was quoted approvingly as favoring the definition of history, given long ago by Dionysius of Halicarnassus, as "philosophy teaching by example." "Both in our own hearts within," he added, "and in all the facts and records without, ancient, middle age, and modern, we shall find ample and constant evidence of its truth. To the same effect and of equal truth is the remark of the great Roman historian Tacitus: 'Some few distinguished honorable things from dishonorable, profitable from hurtful, by their own example; but a far greater number [of people] are taught by the example of others.'" There followed quotations from Seneca, Livy, and the American Republican fathers, suggesting that history "entwined the memories of our ancestors, of Washington, Henry, and Franklin . . . and all other heroic men and women of the Revolution . . . in erecting . . . the noble edifice of a People's Power."[38]

Dr. Lewis, in spending time on the importance of historical knowledge in his long address, touched on ideas held by Ewer, Whiting, and Sheppard, who firmly believed that the essence of the past was contained in memoirs and biography, in family history and experience, and in heraldry, which he mentioned only briefly, but considered symbols for valor, courage, and heroic deeds.[39]

As time passed, his speeches "from the chair" varied in subject matter but not in tone. They occurred usually at the opening of a new year; they looked to past accomplishments and to future expectations; they were elevated in language to discuss noble ideas and convey a passionate message. Until his "valedictory address" of 1866, he presided regularly over the monthly meetings, except for some months of vacation in Europe during 1865, and encouraged financial policies that kept the Society out of debt. Members were persuaded to convert their annual into life memberships, and the directors established various funds to provide an endowment for the Society. Permanent funds in 1864 were listed at $2,500, but gifts and bequests were providing small increases annually. New Englanders in substantial numbers joined the Society, men like Governor John A. Andrew of Massachusetts; Francis Parkman, the famous historian; Edmund Farwell Slafter of the Prince Society; and many future genealogists like John Adams Vinton, Charles Wesley Tuttle, and William Sumner Appleton.[40]

In his valedictory address of 1866 Dr. Lewis saluted the large audience who had come to hear him. Already he had resigned the presidency because of poor health, but he wanted to deliver a parting address emphasizing the urgency of finding a new home for the Society. The Civil War had ended; a spirit of renewal was affecting more people as they donated to schools and colleges; and patriotic impulses were interesting people in genealogy and history. This time of renewal, observed Dr. Lewis, was the time to spread abroad the merits of the Society and to attract surplus money for the construction of new quarters.

> I am not about to advocate the seeking of legislative assistance, however much our Society may deserve it. 'God helps those who help themselves,' and so let it be with us. Let us strive vigorously to 'help ourselves.' . . . Let

not another new year find us still in this apartment so unworthy of the dignity of our Society, so unsafe as the receptacle of our valuable historic and biographical treasures; but let us erect for ourselves a modest, and yet suitable building, which shall include a fire-proof library, a hall for lectures, and other necessary accommodations.[41]

The donations should come from members, but also from the community "who have been watching our proceedings and progress with hearty interest."

While Dr. Lewis, at age sixty-seven, stepped down from active leadership, for the next two years he often served as presiding chairman of monthly meetings. John Albion Andrew, his successor, was then retiring as governor of Massachusetts. Younger than Lewis by twenty years, he was a popular, anti-slavery, Republican governor, who was a warm supporter of Abraham Lincoln and had been re-elected by huge majorities from 1860 to 1865. His willingness to serve as president of the Society was a major accomplishment of the directors, who apparently persuaded Lewis to serve as acting president whenever ex-Governor Andrew was away on business.[42] In 1867, President Andrew gave an address to the membership that could easily have come from Lewis' pen. Both men thought alike on the importance of the family record (genealogy), biography, and history; both were convinced that new facilities for the Society were absolutely necessary sometime in the near future. But similarities ended here. Governor Andrew was an energetic, dynamic man, a popular, political figure who could speak with authority on public issues and his message "from the chair" in 1867 was crisp and forceful. His words were heard or read by a large audience both within and outside the Society.

The president began with an explanation of his 1866 service for the Society. Only once had he an opportunity "to be present," he said. "Returning to the profession of the law, after five years withdrawal, you will easily comprehend the necessity which has compelled me to yield both time and thought to its exactions."

Without further explanation, he launched into an exposition on the importance of genealogy. "All of knowledge we can gather about our predecessors, their lives, their thoughts, their achievements, their daily practices . . . their industry, their worship . . . their style of speech, their sympathies and their controversies, all that we can in like manner garner up, methodize, and transmit to the future, belonging to life, character and history of our time, tend, not only to enlarge the formal stock of common knowledge, but to preserve the treasures of human experience and thought."

Much more was said in similar language, but he then turned to history as the synthesis of human experience. "History touches all human life, on every side. It instructs the individual. It gives a new tone to a community. It elevates a nation. It enlivens a generation. It inspires the human race."

History to be written and read was an objective for the Society. Its resources were "already valuable . . . for the uses of the ingenious student, antiquary or historian. It must continue to grow in richness and in volume . . . . I hope that the zeal of the members of the Society and the enlightened generosity of liberal men, will give early success to an enterprise . . . for the procurement of an appropriate and commodious building to be the permanent home of the Association."

In a peroration he called for cooperation of members and pledged his help, but emphasized again the utter importance of historical and biographical research, the inheritance the nation had received from its forefathers.[43]

The warmth of his speech, and the enthusiasm of the audience, disguised only momentarily his fatal health problems. He does not appear to have returned again to Number 17 Bromfield Place. On November 1, 1867, the members gathered for a solemn memorial service led by former president Winslow Lewis, who then became acting head of the Society until another president was chosen at the regular elections in January 1868. Full funeral services for John Albion Andrew were held in Boston, with official recognition and newspaper accounts, and a solemn procession to Mount Auburn Cemetery in Cambridge.[44]

Much sadness was felt by the directors, officers, and members of the Society. But there occurred almost by chance the publication in April

1867 of a full memoir of Marshall Pinckney Wilder by John H. Sheppard. The article, with a picture for the frontispiece, and a genealogy of the Wilder family, was immediately followed by former governor Andrew's 1867 address. It introduced the members to a major figure in Boston's intellectual life, a member of the Society, a businessman, and former legislator. Like Lewis and Andrew, Wilder was an unusual person. He came to Boston from Rindge and Portsmouth, New Hampshire, in 1825 and became a commission merchant for many years and director of a bank and insurance company for almost as long. In 1832 he bought a large estate in Dorchester where he experimented with camellias in hot houses, and other kinds of flowers, and planted thousands of pear trees—reportedly 800 varieties. As a hybridizer of camellias, he was honored with a variety named after him, the Camellia Wilderii. He drafted landscaping plans for Mount Auburn Cemetery and Forest Hills Cemetery in Roxbury. Over the years he served as president of the Horticultural Society, the Pomology Society, the Norfolk County Agricultural Society, the United States Agricultural Society, and other similar organizations. He served one term in the Massachusetts House of Representatives but was elected several times to the Massachusetts Council and Senate.

Like Lewis and Sheppard, Wilder was a member of the Grand Lodge of Freemasons in Boston and was elected for a term in the 1860s as Deputy Grand Master. He held rank for a time as colonel in the New Hampshire militia and was an officer of the Ancient and Honorable Artillery Company.[45] Admittedly, he was neither genealogist nor historian, but he had a fine library and was an early member of the Society. His family was related to the Wilders of Lancaster, Massachusetts, and to the Lockes of Woburn and Lancaster whose brightest star, Samuel Locke, was the twelfth president of Harvard College. Locke's tenure as president was unfortunately cut short just before the American Revolution by news that he fathered an illegitimate child.[46]

When Marshall Wilder gave the above information for his memoir to John Sheppard, neither man expected him to be elected shortly thereafter to the presidency of the Society. He had left for Europe in the spring of

1867 and returned in the fall when Andrew was already seriously ill. The trustees had already looked over possible candidates for the Society's new president and Andrew's death in late October hastened the search. Wilder's candidacy was nearly irresistible despite his lifelong preoccupation with growing flowers and trees and holding agricultural fairs. His national prominence as the founder and director of many organizations made him attractive. Even more notable, perhaps, was his involvement in the construction of permanent quarters for a few other societies in Boston.[47]

On January 1, 1868, Wilder was declared by Winslow Lewis the elected president of the NEHGS. No one present, in offering congratulations, could have predicted that he would remain in that office until 1886, into his eighty-eighth year of life. He began immediately to handle the tasks of his new position by calling librarian John H. Sheppard, treasurer William B. Towne, past presidents Winslow Lewis and Samuel G. Drake, Edmund F. Slafter, and John Wingate Thornton—maybe others—to his office. They discussed a wide variety of objectives, but Wilder apparently guided their thoughts to a library policy that would emphasize the accumulation of certain kinds of books consulted by most readers— "local, genealogical, or family histories," including "biographies, travels, journals, histories of corporations, and military expeditions."[48] He wanted the Society's constitution scrutinized for defects and weaknesses and its purpose to be restated in words such as these—"to collect, preserve, and disseminate the local and general history of New England and the genealogy of New England families."[49] The conferees recommended that fees be raised to three dollars per year for members and an initial fee of five dollars be imposed on admission to the Society. With Wilder's encouragement, a special committee was appointed to make plans for the purchase of new quarters and the collections of funds.

Most business of the Society was traditionally performed by committees. In preparing tributes to deceased members, a laborious affair, the Rev. Dorus Clarke and Charles W. Tuttle, both of Boston, assembled biographical materials on those who died during 1868. They tried to identify most of the deceased and to publish memoirs of some in the

Register. In 1869, twenty-four members died: memoirs of eighteen of them were read at monthly meetings during the year. Not everyone received a leading article in the *Register*, but Joseph B. Felt, the former president, was honored by a picture and long essay.[50] Length of the essays often depended upon the renown of the deceased group. Charles Ewer, however, had received a relatively short notice in 1854, but the Society later accepted for the library his personal papers and books from his estate, and still much later gave him a tombstone![51] The present committee, chaired by the Rev. Dorus Clarke (1797-1884), enlisted many other members to write memoirs, so that the Rev. Elias Nason, William B. Trask, and Usher Parsons, among others, were also responsible for these biographical records. Clarke, who in 1868 succeeded William B. Trask, the historiographer since 1862, could expect to serve for a long time (in fact, only to 1874). Clarke spent twenty years before coming to Boston at a ministerial post in Woburn. Ten years earlier he had served as editor of family religious magazines which were Calvinist; he was known as an aggressive defender of the faith. One of his friends said of him at his death: "I think of him as one of the Puritan fathers left long on earth, that this generation might know what those fathers were."[52]

Like the historiographer, the librarian and his committee provided one of the essential services of the Society and involved a large number of members as donors and users. John H. Sheppard spent nearly ten years as librarian processing thousands of books and pamphlets. During that time a committee of four or five members gave him solid support, sometimes serving several years. Men like Frederic Kidder, William S. Appleton, and Jeremiah Colburn moved through this and other committees as talented and hard-working people.

Over the years probably no group of members worked consistently for a better cause than the publications committee, which supervised the *Register* and insured its survival. Almost the same members continued to serve year after year during peaceful and troubled times, but certainly by 1871, when the society was 25 years old, the *Register* was firmly established in the policies of the Society. In 1861 the committee consisted of John W. Dean, William B. Trask, and William H. Whitmore. In 1864,

Elias Nason and William S. Appleton were added, and in 1868, William B. Towne, Frederic Kidder, and Albert H. Hoyt. In 1870, Trask was no longer a member, but was then a director of the Society. Kidder was the chairman of a finance committee for the bond fund.

While many men gave their services to the Society, not everyone served consistently in the offices. The number of members increased yearly, but there were men who dropped their membership, were delinquent in paying their dues, and provided no service. An amazing number, however, prepared papers for the monthly meetings, and some of them deposited their papers in the library. In 1868, from February to December, the readers of papers were:

The Rev. Calvin E. Stowe of Hartford, Connecticut, who spoke on the "Talmud." (Calvin was the husband of Harriet Beecher Stowe.)
The Rev. James H. Means of Dorchester, on the "First Home Missionary Society."
The Rev. John A. Vinton of Boston, on the "Rev. John Wheelwright and his times."
The Rev. Benjamin F. DeCosta of New York, on "Ticonderoga."
The Rev. F. W. Holland of Rutland, Vermont, on "Rutland Insurrection."
The Rev. Dr. W.M. Cornell of Boston, on "Notes on the Character of Mr. Matthew Newkirk of Philadelphia."
John H. Sheppard of Boston, on a "recent visit to the localities of historical interest in England."
Rev. William C. Fowler of Durham, Connecticut, on "Local Law in Connecticut."[53]

As the twenty-fifth anniversary of the Society's founding approached, certain ceremonies were planned for newspaper attention. President Wilder, in January 1870, gave an address full of patriotic praise for New England's contributions to the history of the region and world, in which speech he reminded his appreciative audience that the Society was the keeper of records to safeguard the past for the instruction of the present.

Whenever I reflect on what New England has done for the world, what she has done for the cause of education, religion, civil polity, and for the amelioration of the ills that flesh is heir to, the blood courses more freely in my veins, and my heart rises in gratitude to the Giver of all good, that He permitted me here to be born—here to live. Here let me die.

The sad fact, he said, was the loss frequently of information about these contributions. It was the duty of the Society "to treasure up these events and incidents, and to transmit them to future generations." He ended his brief discourse by paying respect to history, and to the memoirs and biographies being collected. They are "her beacon lights to warn the mariner of the rocks and quicksands that endanger his voyage."

> Lives of great men all remind us,
> We can make our lives sublime
> And, departing, leave behind us
> Footprints in the sands of time.[54]

On March 18, the membership again assembled, this time to hear the Rev. Edmund Farwell Slafter, who was commissioned to deliver the official address of celebration and commemoration, on the Society's twenty-fifth anniversary. Gathering around him at three o'clock in the spacious Horticultural Hall were Wilder, Winslow Lewis, William B. Towne, the vice presidents of the Society, and about three hundred members and their wives, plus many invited guests from the government and scholarly societies. Slafter, an Episcopal priest, was known for his personality, humor, learning, and dignity. A former Corresponding Secretary, he had been a member of the Society since 1861, and was a relatively young man (born in 1816) among the old gentlemen presiding at the celebration.

As Slafter opened his long address with a fine tribute to the founders of the Society, he faced in the audience Samuel G. Drake, John Wingate Thornton, and William H. Montague, who were presumably sitting in a place of honor.[55] They had long ago relinquished their offices to other members of the Society. Thornton, younger than Slafter by two years and known for his oratorical powers, had been just named speaker of the future celebration of the 250th anniversary of the *Mayflower*'s arrival in November 1620 and the signing of the Compact. The Society, through Thornton's address, was taking responsibility for commemorating this great event of early American history.[56]

Slafter was then celebrating this rise of distinction for the Society. "Our work," he said, over the past twenty-five years, had two elements in it. "The historical is the more prominent and engrossing, requiring broader and more diversified investigations; while the genealogical, however essential, is limited and narrow. . . . Genealogy may be compared to the golden chain that holds a collection of jewels together and keeps them in their proper order and in their due relations; while history deals with each and the whole in the largest way . . . and saying all it may of their origin, their nature, their qualities, their size, their uses, and their values."[57]

The founders and their successors, he continued, had to fight prejudice against the study of family and ancestry. But in the course of time public sentiment has changed; the "cloud of prejudice and ignorance . . . has faded from sight." Through meetings of the Society, the *Register* and other publications, and the labor of its many members in compiling genealogies of their families and friends, much progress had been made. As many as 365 family histories had been published in the United States since 1854, partly as the result of the influence of the Society, and each contained, he estimated, the personal histories of three to eight thousand people. Most of these volumes traced families to the original settlers, back 200 years, "in the records and proceedings of our towns and of our schools, in the titles of landed property, in the wills and settling of estates . . . in the journals and . . . correspondence of a social and intelligent ancestry."

This progression of patriotic endeavors over twenty-five years, through a generation of exceptional human effort, was unusual and a tribute to the members. It would reach a climax in 1871 when the Society would move into new quarters, just purchased through the efforts of its president and treasurer and the donations of its members and friends. The breaking of this news by Edmund Slafter created an air of excitement that was profoundly felt by the large audience.[58]

Notes

[1] Samuel H. Riddel, "Mr. Charles Ewer," in *Memorial Biographies of the New England Historic Genealogical Society*, 5 vols. (Boston, 1880-1894), 2 (1853-1855):

113-155. Riddel published a short biographical memoir by Ewer's sister, Charlotte, in his own longer biography. See Charlotte's comments on Ewer's business experience, p. 116. Samuel G. Drake authored the short notice in the *Register*, 8 (1854): 97-98.

[2] Thomas C. Amory, "Memoir of John Wingate Thornton," *Register*, 33 (1879): 273-282, particularly 280. Thornton served for a time as librarian of the American Statistical Association. Addressed as "John" by his friends in Maine, he later signed his name "J. Wingate." He married Elizabeth Wallace of Roxbury in 1848.

[3] Minutes of Publications Committee January 17, 1846 to 1847, Ewer Papers.

[4] Samuel H. Riddel to William Cogswell, December 11, 1846, Publications Committee to Samuel Drake, January 1, 1847, Ewer Papers.

[5] "Prospects of the New England Historical and Genealogical Register," end paper, *Register*, 1 (1848): 104. See also minutes of Publications Committee January 17, 1846 to 1847, Ewer Papers.

[6] The article on Farmer in the January 1847 *Register* inspired a letter from Samuel H. Parsons to Samuel G. Drake, March 13, 1847, Drake Papers. "I think the memoir of John Farmer is a very judicious selection for the first number, and is well prepared, but I don't like the Engraving. It is miserably done." The life and contributions of John Farmer were the lead materials for *Historical New Hampshire*, 1 (1945): 3-15—an interesting tribute to the *Register*.

[7] *Register*, 4 (1850): 291; Increase N. Tarbox, "William Cogswell," *Register*, 37 (1883): 117-128. Cogswell was already ill when he resigned his post as editor.

[8] William Cogswell to Publications Committee, December 25, 1847; Samuel G. Drake to Charles Ewer, March 31, 1848; Charles Ewer to Samuel G. Drake, April 3, 1848, Ewer Papers.

[9] Samuel G. Drake to Charles Ewer and Samuel A. Riddel, August 5, 1848, Ewer Papers. "I do not wish to make any preparations for a future volume of the work [i.e. for the ensuing year 1849] but it will be *necessary* to do so very soon."

[10] Edward D. Harris, "William Thaddeus Harris," *Memorial Biographies of the New England Historic Genealogical Society*, 2: 294-304. Apparently Drake and Harris were acquaintances, so that Drake was already willing to have Harris as editor when the latter was appointed.

[11] *Register*, 3 (1849): "Our work," iv. The preface includes Harris although it is signed by S. G. Drake. Harris to Thornton, April 10, 1849, Thornton Papers—"The article in question, before it went to press, was revised by me, with more than ordinary care, and I even took the trouble to verify several of the references therein." Harris also wrote a separate preface to the *Register*, 3 (1849), preceding the one with Drake.

[12] J.B.F. Osgood, "Joseph Barlow Felt," *Register*, 24 (1870): 1-5. In this article there is a good bibliography of Felt's publications. Felt was distantly related through marriage to Abigail (Smith) Adams, wife of President John Adams.

[13] Preface, *Register*, 5 (1851): iv. Drake recommended the memoir on the Leonard family, pp. 403-414, as "perfect and complete in every respect."

[14] Director's Records (1849-1868), I, meeting of October 2, 1855. Drake presided over the meeting in the absence of President Whiting.

[15] *Register*, 7 (1853): 107-114.

[16] Proceedings III (1859-1865): meetings of June 1 and October 3, 1860, MSS, NEHGS.

[17] Proceedings II (1850-1858) meeting of January 19, 1859; Proceedings III (1859-1865) meetings of February 2 and September 7, 1859. A musical program on June 5, 1861 apparently "thrilled the audience," both men and women.

[18] Savage's *Genealogical Dictionary* was regularly quoted or corrected in the *Register*. Some bitterness remained into the 1870s.

[19] Proceedings III (1858-1865) meeting of May 1, 1861; *Register*, 15 (1861): preface, v.

[20] John H. Sheppard, "Memoir of Samuel Drake," *Register*, 17 (1863): 211. Sheppard described Drake as a solitary man, with a "face kindly," and possessing a voice "which does one good."

[21] Proceedings II (1850-1858) meeting of December 4, 1854.

[22] Directors' Records I (1849-1868) meetings of June 2, August 11, August 19, and September 2, 1857, MSS NEHGS. See Winslow Lewis's valedictory address, *Register*, 20 (1866): 145-151.

[23] Proceedings II (1850-1858) meetings of March 5, 1856 and January 7, 1857.

[24] *Register*, 1 (1847): preface, iv.

[25] *Proceedings of the Massachusetts Historical Society, 1855-1858*, II (Boston, 1859): 266-270, 344-351. See Samuel G. Drake, *Narrative Remarks* . . . (Albany, 1874).

[26] Issues of the *Register* in 1857 and 1859 carried the revised name: The New England Historical and Genealogical Society, but the seal carried the legal name—The New England Historic Genealogical Society.

[27] Almon D. Hodges (1801-1878) became a member of the Society in 1852 and a life member in 1859. He served later on financial committees, but he was often absent, because of his activities with the Rhode Island Historical Society. See *Proceedings of the Rhode Island Historical Society, 1878-1879* (Providence, 1879): 102-103.

[28] The Rev. Edmund F. Slafter, who became a member of the NEHGS in 1861, was undoubtedly the most active member of the Prince Society.

[29] George G. Wolkins, "The Prince Society," *Proceedings of the Massachusetts Historical Society*, 1936-1941 (Boston, 1942): 240-244.

[30] See advertisement on end papers of *Register*, 13 (1859): opposite p. 96.

[31] *Register*, 61 (1907): 147-149. The Prince Society dropped its longer name in the 1870s. Edmund F. Slafter edited many of the Society's publications.

[32] See Charles H. Bell's preface, *Memoir of the Reverend John Wheelwright* (Boston, 1876), viii.

[33] Preface, *Register*, 15 (1861): iii-vi. "The experiment of an Antiquarian

Periodical in New England has been fully tried, and when, if ever, it shall be tried again, I hope the adventure will be attended with better success than the present."

[34] George R. Howell, "Joel Munsell," *Register*, 34 (1880): 239-246. See also David L. Greene, "Samuel Drake and the Early Years of the . . . *Register*, 1847-1861," *Register*, 145 (1991): 232-233. Greene has searched the archives of the Society and has written an informative account of the *Register* in its early years.

[35] John H. Sheppard, "Winslow Lewis," *Register*, 17 (1863): 1-13. Lewis was unanimously elected president of the Society in 1861.

[36] Proceedings III (1859-1865): meetings of January 2, 1861 and January 4, 1865.

[37] The addresses of earlier presidents, if they gave formal ones, were rarely published in the *Register*. William Whiting, on January 12, 1853, delivered a distinguished address; see *Register*, 7 (1853): 107-114.

[38] *Register*, 16 (1862): 119-128.

[39] *Register*, 16 (1862): 125-128.

[40] The Society issued a special publication: *Rolls of Membership of the New England Historic Genealogical Society, 1844-1890* (Boston, 1891), in which classes of membership were given: John A. Andrew, resident 1863, life 1863; Francis Parkman, resident 1865, life 1871; Edmund F. Slafter, resident 1861, life 1866. Between 1861 and 1866 180 resident members were added. Many became life members. Only 12 honorary members were added.

[41] *Register*, 20 (1866): 145-151, especially 150-151.

[42] *Register*, 23 (1869): 1-12. Andrew (1818-1867); Lewis (1799-1875).

[43] *Register*, 21 (1867): 121-124.

[44] Proceedings IV (1865-1872): meeting of November 1, 1867.

[45] Proceedings IV (1865-1872): meeting of January 1, 1868, *Register*, 21 (1867): 97-120.

[46] Clifford K. Shipton, *Sibley's Harvard Graduates*, XIII (Boston, 1965): 620-627.

[47] *Register*, 21 (1867): 114-120.

[48] Proceedings IV (1865-1872): meetings of March 2 and April 7, 1868.

[49] Proceedings IV (1865-1872): meeting of March 2, 1868.

[50] *Register*, 24 (1870): 203. The article by Dorus Clarke and J.B.F. Osgood on Joseph B. Felt (1789-1869) was published on pp. 2-5. The authors regarded Felt's volume two of his *Ecclesiastical History of New England* "the crowning labor" of his long life.

[51] *Register*, 8 (1854): 97-98. Charles Ewer (1790-1853) died comparatively young in New Hampshire, but was buried at Old Granary in Boston. A modern marker was placed over the grave in 1945.

[52] *Register*, 38 (1884): 253-261. During his years as historiographer he prepared 127 memoirs.

[53] *Register*, 23 (1869): 221.

[54] *Register,* 24 (1870): 165-168; Proceedings IV (1865-1870): meeting of January 5, 1870. The president's address was praised as "interesting and eloquent."

[55] *Register,* 24 (1870): 168.

[56] *Register,* 24 (1870): 428-429. Apparently Thornton invited himself to give this anniversary address. He called the *Mayflower* Compact "the germ of our present free institutions, civil and religious, and as such of national importance." He offered a resolution and asked for a committee to prepare for the celebration.

[57] *Register,* 24 (1870): 225-249, 430. Besides the address by Slafter, introductory remarks were made by Wilder, a prayer was offered by Rev. James H. Means of the Second Church, Dorchester, and a few appropriate songs were sung.

[58] *Register,* 24 (1870): 246-247; Proceedings, IV (1865-1872): meeting of May 4, 1870. The president gave the details of the purchase. The impression is that Slafter was premature in making this announcement.

Society Founders: President Charles Ewer (1790-1853), top left; Vice President
Lemuel Shattuck (1793-1859), top center; Corresponding Secretary Samuel
Gardner Drake (1798-1875), top right; Recording Secretary and Librarian John
Wingate Thornton (1818-1878), bottom left; and Treasurer William Henry
Montague (1804-1889), bottom right.

City Building, Court Square, Boston. Room 9 on the third floor of the hip-roofed building on the right was the Society's first home, February 1846 - October 1847. A room on the ground floor of the center building (then called the "Massachusetts Block," later the "Sherman House") was the Society's second home, 1847-1851. See the *Register* 33(1879):424-426.

5 Tremont St., Boston. A room on the third floor was the third home of the Society, 1851-1858.

13 (later numbered 17) Bromfield St., Boston. The third floor of the building next to the "19 Ford" awning was the fourth home of the Society, 1858-1871.

Winslow Lewis (1799-1875), sixth
President of the Society, 1861-1866.

Marshall Pinckney Wilder (1798-1886),
eighth President of the Society, 1868-
1886.

Reading Room of 18 Somerset St., Boston, fifth home of the Society, 1871-1913 (picture dated 1895).

Rev. Edmund Farwell Slafter (1816-1906), Corresponding
Secretary of the Society, 1867-1886, President of the Prince
Society, 1880-1906.

Rev. Edward Griffin Porter (1837-1900), 11th President of the Society, 1899-1900.

John Tyler Hassam (1841-1903), promoter of English research and the consolidated index to the *Register*, volumes 1-50.

Henry FitzGilbert Waters (1833-1913), antiquarian,
contributor of "Genealogical Gleanings in
England" to the *Register*, 1883-1899.

CHAPTER 3

Decades of Progress

On March 18th, 1871, on its twenty-sixth anniversary, the Society opened new doors at No. 18 Somerset Street and with that action celebrated the purchase of its own quarters. A fine stately mansion was lately purchased from the Solomon D. Townsend family for twenty thousand dollars and, with some substantial alterations, would be occupied in 1872. To celebrate the coming event, Marshall P. Wilder presided before an overflow crowd in the building, with evidence of new construction everywhere, and bid members to enjoy this unique occasion. His brief introductory address on this late afternoon was followed by prayer, community singing—perhaps aided by a choir singing a hymn beginning with the words "Let children hear the mighty deeds" . . . and then the address of the day by Charles Henry Bell, president of the New Hampshire Historical Society and the son and nephew of Granite State governors. The instructive message of approximately one hour still left sufficient time in the long program for a concluding hymn, benediction, and refreshments.[1]

The Hon. Charles H. Bell, lawyer, historian, and public servant, was an orator of distinction. His chosen subject was "The Future of American History," an inquiry into the importance, vitality, necessity, and popularity of that kind of research. In the last generation, he said, "many of the most intelligent, prominent, and accomplished" citizens of the business community had become historians. They shared their time with all the other pursuits of life, but they have admitted as a group that their feeling for historical research and writing was one of the most rewarding and dignified of human activities, equal, if not surpassing, that of any occupation. Bell noted the rising popularity of history, the support of government, the founding of societies, and the publication of books. Even so, he worried about popularizers of history, sloppy workmanship, prejudice, and unworthy purpose, but hoped that this new edifice in Boston would aid in the "discovery and elucidation of historic truth" and encourage "individual efforts and abilities, more earnestly and zealously than heretofore." While he did not separate genealogy, heraldry, and history—all were performing a type of research that should not be bound by class, wealth, or education—he had these further words. "Men . . . whose fathers were simple yeomen are no less anxious to trace out the branches of the family tree, than if they bore in their veins the blood of all the Howards."[2] The study of family history, in short, should be available for everyone.

This gathering of members in special celebration revealed their strong approval of the purchase of No. 18 Somerset Street, a structure solid, tasteful, convenient, and spacious. It was constructed of brick, in 1805, with stone facing in front, four stories, frontage of 29 feet and depth of 42 feet (not counting a two-story rear extension of 22 feet by 13), and was located near the heart of state government. The Society spent an additional $23,000 to arrange house space and make the building suitable as a public meeting place. Many people attending that ceremony had already pledged funds for the acquisition of the building, or gave outright gifts, so that the Society would not be burdened by a huge debt.[3]

No one was more satisfied with this move to Somerset Street than President Wilder—except, perhaps, William B. Towne, treasurer of the Society since 1861. An officer, like Wilder, of the agricultural and pomological societies, Towne was a native of New Hampshire and dry goods merchant in Boston for many decades, a supporter of William Lloyd Garrison and the anti-slavery movement, and a benefactor of many causes. Wilder and Towne called upon the wealthy members of the New England community during a three-month campaign in 1870 and raised the $43,000 which financed the purchase and renovation of the Somerset building.[4]

Just before these celebrations Towne had resigned as treasurer and was succeeded by Benjamin Barstow Torrey, the well known railroad executive and financier, who would serve until 1903. Towne continued as chairman of the "club," founded in 1864 to assist *Register* editors and publication. It especially aided Albert Harrison Hoyt, the editor since 1868. Towne moved to Milford, New Hampshire, where he was trustee of the public library, president of the Souhegan National Bank, and elected state representative in 1873 and 1874. For most of these years he managed at a distance the business affairs of the *Register* and was chiefly responsible, with a few others, for putting it upon a sound financial basis.[5]

The figure of Marshall Wilder at this time of celebration was ever to be seen in most business and social affairs of the Society. He presided regularly over its activities, enjoying the challenges of each month, but also directed his agricultural and pomological societies, and advised on the development of Boston Back Bay, the Massachusetts Institute of Technology, and the Boston Society of Natural History. Wilder was on speaking terms with the governors, legislators, and other officials of Massachusetts, and with the social leaders of Boston. His good works earned him a Ph.D. from Dartmouth College in 1877, an LL.D. from Roanoke College in 1884, as well as annual re-election as president of the Society into his eighty-eighth year.[6]

Wilder liked books not because he read extensively but because books (records and manuscripts) were essential for historical and bio-graphical work. In 1871, the Society library had a good collection, but each year it grew at an impressive rate—as the following statistics show:

	1871	1873	1875	1883	1885
books	7,653	10,498	12,337	18,381	20,200
pamphlets	6,943	34,338	44,414	59,445	62,720

Added to this collection were donations of newspapers, genealogical papers, letters, documents, paintings, and public papers. The library was becoming a repository for almost anything donors were willing to give. In 1873 the first donation of the Henry Knox Papers was received, followed in 1874 and 1876 by other items.[7] These papers were an exceptionally valuable gift by Knox's grandson, Henry Knox Thatcher, and were catalogued. Other important gifts were presented also. In 1873, the *Register* printed six pages of donations in which approximately 275 persons gave one or as many as 1200 items to the Society. The flood of generosity was equaled only by the willingness of members to place on deposit in the vault some of their family's treasures so that others could benefit from their availability.[8] In 1878, too, the Society received a major addition to its collection of portraits—those of Joseph B. Felt, John A. Andrew, Frederic Kidder, and Dorus Clarke. The hope, expressed repeatedly, was for gifts of suitable portraits of Society leaders to be placed in honor on the walls of the library and conference rooms. Wilder himself agreed to sit for a portrait by E. D. Merchant of Philadelphia; it was soon hung prominently in the auditorium.

The librarian during these exciting and busy times was John Ward Dean (1815-1902), who had a great interest in genealogy, bookbinding, and, of course, books. A member of the Society since 1850, he served as editor, treasurer, corresponding secretary, and member of the board of directors. He was also a longtime member of most other New England historical societies except the Massachusetts Historical Society. He was a large man, cautious, humorless, deliberate, and patient; above all he was an indiscriminate collector for the Society. Piles of books and newspapers often surrounded him in his office. He read voraciously from youth and acquired an unmatched knowledge of the library.[9]

Though Dean served continuously as librarian until 1889 (and as editor of the *Register* until 1901), he had only a few visitors each day in the library. It was usually open five days in the week and one or two nights, attended by part-time help and volunteers. It had ten seats at tables for readers, but a few additional researchers could be accommodated with chairs if there was an unexpected crowd.[10] Most materials for research were incomplete, but there were several thousand books with usable biographies, histories, and genealogies. The library had as its catalogue only some folders listing manuscript collections and important books. Dean was almost as good as a modern catalogue in locating books, however. His vast knowledge directed researchers to shelves apparently separated by states, regions, and countries. Most researchers supplemented library work with visits to town offices, probate repositories, and local cemeteries.

The reading room and the auditorium on the third floor were meeting places for genealogists and historians. At least once a month there was a gathering of members to hear a formal paper, eat and drink refreshments, and discuss whatever was on their minds. Almost any day the Reverend Dr. Lucius R. Paige might be in the library.[11] His massive, genealogical works surpassed those of any author then alive. Samuel G. Drake, who lived until 1875 and had a mind full of stories about people and places in Boston, Charlestown, and Cambridge, was occasionally in the library. So was the younger scholar, Rev. Edmund F. Slafter, who often presided at monthly meetings, was active in the Prince Society, and was then arranging the Knox papers.

Slafter was an unusually influential officer. He advised members of the New-York Genealogical and Biographical Society in 1869 on the fine points of founding an organization and journal similar to the experience of the New England Historic Genealogical Society. "After a free interchange of views on the subject, and an interesting statement of the plan, progress and condition of the 'New England Historic Genealogical Society' by the Rev. E.F. Slafter, it was determined that an effort should be made to establish in the city of New York, a similar organization for the State of New York." The first issue of its *Record* (January 1870) called the New England Historic Genealogical Society a sister society. Perhaps, also, it reflects the success of the New England Historic Genealogical Society as a unique experiment on this twenty-fifth anniversary of its founding. But Slafter was ever ready to serve Wilder and the Society in any way possible.

Nearly always present at monthly meetings was Marshall P. Wilder, though one wonders where he found the time to participate in all the organizations he served as a member and officer. Wilder, working with Treasurer Torrey, was ever alert to locate contributions for the library, salary for the librarian, and funds for modernization of the building. Over the years, in his annual addresses, he announced donations and reminded members of the financial opportunity to promote genealogy. In 1879 he was seriously disabled by a fall which damaged his hip. For nine months he was confined at home, but at the 1880 annual meeting delivered as usual an address which was "able, far-reaching, and comprehensive." All rose in an ovation when he finished his address. He then left the chair to Slafter who had been regularly presiding since the accident. Wilder had announced before his departure an increase in special funds, purchases for the library, and other genealogical activities. By 1885 he had raised $25,000 for the enlargement of the Somerset building. His advice upon making the announcement of a two-thousand-dollar bequest from John Merrill Bradbury revealed one way he was raising money. He urged members in his audiences to name the Society as a beneficiary in their wills.[12]

Wilder's annual appearances were often extraordinary occasions for the audience to hear an oration on the state of the nation, indeed even of the world. His sparks of personality usually aroused the audience and brought applause, standing salutes, and even cheers. As he moved deep into his eighties, the old gentleman did not lose his ability to inspire an audience. Votes for his re-election were always unanimous, and members often endorsed Dean and Torrey almost as warmly. Wilder remained the central figure of any meeting.

Wilder sat on the platform toward the back of the room in the John Hancock chair, a massive piece of mahogany with a gold, brocaded seat. Six other chairs were acquired, from past governors of New England states, so that they could take their places alongside the Hancock chair. Vice presidents of the Society would presumably be seated in them whenever members attended the solemn pronouncements of President Wilder.[13]

During his annual addresses Wilder performed a number of tasks. Most important was the recognition given not only distinguished deceased members, officers, and donors, but also state, national, and world figures he singled out as well. His solemn roll call of names, in his loud baritone voice, conferred a kind of honorary degree upon great spirits. His tribute to Ulysses S. Grant in 1886, for example, was perhaps his most exalted:

> I now mention another American hero greater than the rest, and for whose recent death the great heart of our nation still throbs with grief. Our Honorary Member . . . the great soldier, has passed on to the final Review above, where his peaceful soul shall no more be disturbed by the storms and convulsions of earth . . . . The whole nation mourns his death . . . . A sense of justice demands for him an earthly immortality. We assign him a place among the illustrious men of our age who are entitled to the gratitude of mankind . . . .[14]

Members did not wait in line, understandably, to receive this presidential tribute, but it was the custom and work of the Society to mention the deceased in reverence. The tribute for Abraham Lincoln in 1865, for James Garfield in 1881, and for Marshall Wilder himself in 1887 were exceptional marks of respect that also recalled another purpose of the Society.[15] At annual meetings it celebrated patriotic anniversaries that had occurred during the past twelve months. Through the years of Wilder's presidency the nation was noting the centennial anniversary of the American Revolution, and Wilder took care to remember these events. Special programs recalled the glories of Lexington and Concord, Bunker Hill, the French Alliance of 1778, the sacrifices of Valley Forge, the Massachusetts Constitution of 1780, and, in 1885, the completion of the Washington Monument. Here is Wilder speaking again:

> The most imposing ceremony of the year, if we except the funeral obsequies of Gen. Grant, was the dedication of the Washington Monument, the tallest structure of which we have any record in history, successfully completed under the supervision of Col. Thomas Lincoln Casey, of the United States Army, a member of this Society . . . . The crowning incident of this occasion was the oration of our associate member the Hon. Robert Charles Winthrop.[16]

Thirty-seven years previously Winthrop had laid the cornerstone, and he lived to provide the capstone in 1885. Wilder paid respect to Washington by quoting directly from Winthrop's great address, but then added that "the names of Washington and Winthrop will be happily associated in the history of this monument until it shall have crumbled into dust." His tribute included mention of the Massachusetts Historical Society, past president Winthrop, and current president George E. Ellis. "I desire to express our gratitude to the Massachusetts Historical Society, for her noble example in the good work [promotion of historical and genealogical research] and especially our thanks due to Mr. Winthrop . . . for his able and meritorious labors during a term of thirty years in which he has occupied the chair of that Society."

The spirits of Drake, Thornton, and Felt must have fluttered to hear the President's unusual praise for Winthrop and MHS. But Winthrop in 1883, while still president of MHS, had already joined community leaders in a Boston dinner to honor Marshall Wilder and George Bancroft, both octogenarians, on their birthdays.[17] And Winthrop also chose at the annual meeting in January 1883 to pay tribute to the fifteen years of Wilder's leadership of the Society: "The Hon. Robert C. Winthrop made some very interesting complimentary remarks touching the long and vigorous service of the venerable president, and stated that during all of its years he has taken a deep interest in its progress and work."[18]

The venerable president did not live to give his address in 1887. In December, just after completing his address for the January meeting, he died suddenly of a heart attack. His health had been apparently good, and the shock of his death turned the 1887 meeting into deep mourning. "The hall was draped in black, as was his portrait which hung upon the wall on the left." His customary chair was "covered with habiliments of mourning." Hon. Joseph B. Walker of Concord, New Hampshire, presided and Edmund F. Slafter, Wilder's friend of many years, read the posthumous address.[19]

The committee on nominations had selected Wilder already for another term, well aware of his eighty-seven years of age and nineteen years of continual service. But he had presided at monthly meetings even within a few days of his death and most members were shaken by the unexpected news. While he lived few members dared to be outwardly critical of his policies, but his death brought a struggle for the presidency, and perhaps a realization that changes were necessary in the way the Society was governed. Wilder had raised money easily; he moved around the Boston community with grace and good will; and he attracted a group of workers who supported the ideals of the Society. Slafter wanted to be Wilder's successor and thought of himself as the heir-apparent. In times of celebration and crisis his voice was heard. He gave the twenty-five year anniversary oration; he spoke for the president during Wilder's year of incapacity in 1879 and 1880; and he read Wilder's posthumous address. He was head of the Prince Society and a frequent presiding officer of monthly meetings.[20] His opposition, and a critic of Wilder, was Abner Cheney Goodell (1831-1914) who had served on the board of directors since 1884, was a lawyer in Lynn, a writer, a genealogist, and an advocate of heraldry. Long an active member of the Society, Goodell had also joined many other scholarly organizations, including the American Academy of Arts and Sciences, MHS, and the Essex Institute, and held responsible offices in some of them. Professionally, he was the compiler of a four-volume collection of the statutes and laws of Massachusetts and registrar of the court of probate for Essex County. A lover of poetry, history, and conversation, he put himself forward as the new leader of the Society.[21] Apparently a majority of members agreed.

The selection of the scholarly Goodell, even allowing for other personal qualifications, did not soothe the feelings of Slafter's friends nor those of the deceased Wilder. Slafter immediately resigned his position as corresponding secretary and member of the publications committee. Dean would soon leave his post as librarian. Significant as were these resignations, which should have cautioned the president, Goodell advocated and was granted many new changes in the administration of the Society. The by-laws were modified to provide a council of nine members and some *ex officio* officers. These councilors, unlike the old Board of Directors, would have rotating terms of three years and could not succeed themselves. They had the authority, moreover, to make appointments and formulate policy. The post of librarian was now directly in their hands. Under this constitution the Society would be less presidentially directed, but operated by twelve or more standing committees which would report to the whole Council.[22] The members of the 1889 Council were not new men unacquainted with Society business, but most had not served as directors on the old board. Only former governor William Claflin was a holdover for the Council and had served as a director since 1883. But Goodell also had the services of William B. Trask and John T. Hassam, who were well acquainted with daily routines.[23]

Undoubtedly the great difference between the Board of Directors and the new Council was the latter's impudent behavior, its daring language, and its insensitivity to tradition. The strong, benevolent hand of Marshall Wilder was now gone, and Goodell's was inexperienced. He and his associates wanted change, and blamed Wilder for imperfections they discovered everywhere. They focused first on the library and found books, papers, magazines, and newspapers stacked in untidy bundles, with the greatest mess in the basement. Dean had received gifts of newspapers without discriminating between potential use and the realities of space. Over a thousand different titles were counted, with holdings of single issues to runs of decades. Goodell himself was particularly shocked by the lack of order. He held Dean responsible and in his public reports branded the accumulations as rubbish. When Dean resigned, Goodell and his friends decided to handle the problem of cleaning up the mess without the benefit of another librarian. They rented a storage room in a neighboring building and emptied the basement into that room. A committee then began the process of disposing of the library's treasures, whatever their value, and at the risk of angering donors. In one report the Council accused Dean of permitting "the administration of the library [to get] . . . beyond the ability of those who had it in charge. . . . Relief has been found by a disposal of much useless trash of no value to the Library."[24] Finally they chose the Rev. Ezra Hoyt Byington as librarian. This deeply religious man, a writer and historian, readily agreed that there was a crisis, but he soon pointed to Goodell, the standing committee, building renovation, and the inadequacies of the building itself as equal culprits, and resigned his position in a struggle for authority after one year of frustration.[25]

Goodell and the Council had already concluded that No. 18 Somerset was an old-fashioned building, not really suitable for the uses of the Society. The sides were weak, floors squeaked from the heavy weight of books, halls were dark, and partitions unnecessarily divided space. They ordered much construction work—an enlarged skylight, major repairs on the roof, a reconditioned furnace, strengthening of the building's structure, some bright colors, and, of course, a complete change in the arrangement of book space. They decided to locate the principal library, about 25,000 books, on the upper floor; the second floor held the most frequently consulted books; and along the walls of the first and cellar floors were all other books. They decided, too, that there was enough book space if only the trash, nonessential books, government pamphlets, school texts, and newspapers were discarded.[26]

Many of these decisions caused arguments in the Council because they reversed or challenged long-standing practices. In the case of book selection, the choice raised issues of the Society's purpose—whether historical, genealogical, heraldic, or literary. In the end only general books were discarded, so that molding the collection was again postponed for some future day. The Council agreed that *The North American Review*, certain governmental publications printed before 1820, and school books could be given away. But there were boxes upon boxes of newspapers, pamphlets, and hard items like medals, old pieces of money, and furniture. Should these go likewise?[27]

Another issue that caused much emotion was the policy of open membership. Since the Society's founding few if any candidates were ever refused. Members prided themselves on a democratic policy of admitting anyone willing to pay the annual fee. They were not like the aristocratic MHS, they said, which only admitted a limited number of wealthy older men. Of course, if anyone became delinquent, he might be expelled. Even here, however, everything possible was done to retain members.[28]

This open-door policy kept the number of members high and considerably complicated recordkeeping. Goodell and the Council felt that the Society's records were sloppy, and its selection of members in the past erratic. They wanted potential members to be screened for character, interest, and financial backing, and proceeded to order a review of each candidate. In 1890 they required eight affirmative votes of the Council for approval of membership and began rejecting applications. The number rejected was probably not large, but some names of applicants were made public. At the same time, they searched for delinquents, warned them, and expelled a few. Thirteen were expelled in one group in 1890. A complete membership list seemed desirable, and in 1891 they published in the *Register* the names of resident, corresponding, and honorary members.[29] The list was still imperfect, but a serious continuing attempt to identify members was ongoing. The Council was not content solely with its effort to regularize the membership list; it also wanted accuracy.

Goodell and the Council had majority support for these efficiency measures, if not for imposing qualifications on accepting new members, but they apparently experienced increasing tension, nonetheless, when most issues were raised, whether controversial or not. John Tyler Hassam plainly did not like Goodell—probably because he was not so capable as Marshall Wilder in raising money. Hassam wanted money to finance ongoing research in English repositories. He had discovered Henry F. Waters, raised money in the 1880s to send Waters to London, and shared partly in Waters' unbelievable success as a genealogist.[30] As money became scarce, the project was threatened with cancellation. Financial conditions were tight, moreover, and Society expenses elsewhere needed to be guarded and employees released if inefficient or unnecessary. Goodell was plainly not attracting money in the marvelous ways Wilder had discovered. Expenses were heavy because of the modernization of the building and monthly bills were paid by dipping into Wilder's fund for expansion—a practice which irritated some members of the Council, especially Hassam.

Worse still, Goodell and the Council, in examining the Wilder fund, had found a low return on investments. They thus transferred some of this endowment to securities offered by Showalter Investment Company, which provided a high return at much risk. These properties soon became liabilities as markets became depressed by unstable financial conditions in the United States. Most of the twenty thousand dollars they had risked became frozen assets and the likelihood of substantial loss was possible.[31]

Goodell's chief opponent was Hassam, older by ten years than the president, but a man of great energy, devoted to the Society, a friend of Dean, Torrey, and the late Wilder. He was a solemn, humorless scholar who spent his whole life in Boston, except for the years he studied at Harvard College. Though he practiced law, he published many genealogies and spent much of his life researching family history. He had little respect for Goodell, although the latter's scholarly attainments were equal to Hassam's. Goodell was truly not an historian or a genealogist.[32]

Their arguments arose over council appointments, financial policy, library management, and undoubtedly anything else debated in the Council. Hassam joined Robert C. Winthrop, Ezra H. Byington (the former librarian), and John Ward Dean in this opposition and succeeded in May 1892 in raising a storm. Two or three members of the Council immediately resigned, but replacements could not be found without causing a bitter fight. Finally, the Council rented Horticultural Hall on Tremont Street for a general emergency meeting of the membership.[33]

The members had already learned of this growing bitterness from the annual meeting in January when the Council squared off against Byington, who reported angrily on the library and dramatically submitted his resignation. Byington accused the President and Council of trying to divide and conquer, of interfering through its many committees, and of taking away most of the decision-making authority of the librarian. "Our Library needs," he said, "the constant care of a gentleman of culture and executive ability." Of course the Council strongly denied these allegations of interference.[34]

Before the crisis had passed, like a powerful thunderstorm, six members of the Council had resigned, plus the recording secretary, librarian, and corresponding secretary. Goodell stood his ground against the abuse, but asked Andrew McFarland Davis, a well known historian, to find a compromise and left the auditorium. Davis hastened to appoint a committee to mediate the issues. Its chairman publicly begged the councilors to reconsider their resignations. "Honest differences of opinion," he said, "created no necessity that they should resign."[35]

While Goodell held onto his post until June 22, monitoring the negotiations, he realized eventually that they were futile. The harried president then decided to abandon his post and deliver in retreat what he called a valedictory address. It was a calm, dispassionate statement of stewardship which put the policies of his administration into proper focus. It was in no sense apologetic, but explanatory.[36]

In this acute institutional crisis, cooler heads begged former governor William Claflin to assume the presidency. Mild-natured and wise, he had supported Goodell in the Council, but had not resigned or joined publicly in the controversy. He was then aged 74 and in uncertain health when he became president. He was known as a reformer in politics, an advocate of women's rights, a bank and college president, and a participant in many movements like temperance and anti-slavery. He was "passionately fond of music" and had helped found the New England Conservatory. Over the years almost every organization he had joined soon made him its president.[37]

This most attractive, elderly man had not yet been president of the Society, when leadership was thrust upon him. Aside from his advanced age and unfamiliarity with genealogy, he was undoubtedly the most distinguished political figure at the Society's helm since its founding nearly fifty years before (with the possible inclusion of John Albion Andrew).

His hands were now extended in friendship and peace to the warriors. Ezra H. Byington was elected to the Council with the help of Hassam, and other vacancies were soon filled mostly with new people. John Ward Dean returned as librarian as did Benjamin B. Torrey as treasurer. Torrey had not formally left office during the crisis. Many members of the Society had resigned in anger, but by the annual meeting of 1893 conditions had been stabilized. Claflin was not well, and the

Council, with his assent, chose Ezra Byington as the *pro tempore* leader during his expected absences.[38]

Byington was a curious choice as temporary second-in-command of the Society. Unlike Claflin he was a publishing scholar, deeply concerned with Congregational missionary activities, but would find time for Society business. He agreed to be historiographer and a member of the Council. Over the next three years he wrote biographies for sixty deceased members and stood ready to preside at monthly meetings. Like Claflin he had uncertain health, though he was ten years younger than the president.[39]

Over the coming years, while Byington and a few other councilors presided at meetings for the president, Claflin cultivated an impression of being conciliatory, deliberative, and hospitable, so the heated tempers of former years became rare occurrences at monthly meetings. Goodell and his friends, showing realistic good sense, let Claflin and his associates take charge of the Society. Goodell renewed his interest in the Essex Institute at Salem and joined the newly organized Colonial Society of Massachusetts, partly because of the historians and lawyers who were members of both. Claflin rarely gave public addresses, and often charged others with that important duty. His vast prestige, however, drew many new members to the Society. Probably more than three hundred persons applied and gained membership between 1894 and 1899.[40]

These new members partly reflected the popularity of No. 18 Somerset Street as a gathering place, but the building itself was showing its limitations of space, even after Goodell's house-cleaning activities. Bookshelves were still packed, the reading room had thirty or more chairs, and the little staff was being professionalized to handle the increasing burdens of service. Assistants were hired for the librarian, treasurer, editor of the *Register*, and for maintenance. In September 1894 William Prescott Greenlaw was employed to help catalogue books and manuscripts, sort the mail, and distribute it. His salary was six hundred dollars in 1894, but raised a year later to seven hundred and fifty dollars. At age thirty-one, he was energetic and, possessing a great memory for detail, was fascinated by family history. He and Librarian Dean were very much alike in their interests and labored harmoniously to put the library into shape for the many new patrons.[41] Greenlaw's appointment may have been Claflin's way of relieving Dean of some burdensome duties as librarian and answering some justifiable criticism of the earlier years of confusion. Dean was still editor of the *Register*.

While Greenlaw had to worry about space in bringing order to the library, the Council was also well aware of the urgency to do something. It debated for a time about the possibility of acquiring an entirely new building, but was cautioned by Claflin to gain consensus before any decision was taken. The decision was difficult because of much feeling that the present building would never be satisfactory. In June 1895, however, a contract was let to construct two floors over the rear annex, thus extending the two upper floors by twenty-two feet. Some work on the cellar was necessary when new foundations were laid, but the work proceeded quickly and the new space was available early in 1896. Nonetheless, Dean was again ordered to reduce nonessential resources and reshelve books in order to gain space. Claflin reemphasized the need for a library policy which would automatically dispose of marginal materials. Neighboring societies, he said, should be asked to accept some books not meeting the policy of the library.[42] The suggested disposal of sometimes rare books, however, was not easy to implement. Claflin appointed a special committee to assist Dean and Greenlaw in selecting items to be discarded.

Funds were also voted from time to time to continue the cataloguing of the collection, and a few books were purchased to improve research. The *Columbian Centinel*, for example, was incomplete, but now the missing volumes would be sought. Some councilors wanted the Society to press New England towns and cities for publication of their records. No real research, they observed, could be done without an appropriate collection in print of town vital records.[43] On the outside cover of the April 1897 *Register* the librarian advertised for county histories and similar kinds of books. He particularly wanted volumes on Berkshire

County, Massachusetts, Merrimack and Belknap counties, New Hampshire, and Vermont's *Historical Gazetteer.*

As members crowded the library, they left their requests for new books and stayed for afternoon programs. The monthly lecture series year after year continued in regular fashion. Sometimes the audience was given a treat. In 1895, for example, Lucius Robinson Paige visited the October 2 meeting. At age ninety-four he was definitely infirm, but had come to see the newly completed facilities of the Society, and revealed his pleasure by waving his hand. His presence brought a standing ovation from the appreciative audience, who very much admired his tradition-breaking studies of Cambridge and Hardwick.[44]

Paige revealed to the assembled members that he was the Society's oldest living member. Joining the Society in January 1845, he had seen it grow in prominence through fifty years of service. President Claflin and the Council were well aware of this anniversary. They had already celebrated the first gathering of members on April 19, 1895 in an early morning tribute in the historic halls of the Old South Meeting House where Charles Carleton Coffin spoke of the talents of Charles Ewer and other founders of the Society. Only a few in that audience—perhaps only the venerable Senator George F. Hoar—remembered the last surviving founder, William H. Montague, who had lived until 1889, but was long confined to his home by blindness and infirmity.

Coffin was a newspaper reporter, writer, and former Massachusetts legislator who had authored eleven books and articles on popular history and public affairs and whose presence had drawn a large crowd to the celebration. No more significant day of the year could have been chosen. On the 19th of April at Lexington and Concord in 1775 had occurred the first clash of arms of the Revolution, and it was, the speaker said, the beginning of a new era of history, progress, and nationalism. Coffin concluded his stirring message with these words, which may have raised an eyebrow or two:

> The world is vastly better at this moment than it was when Charles Ewer and Wingate Thornton and their associates founded the Society. The his-

toric evolution of the past indicates that it will be better tomorrow than it is today. . . . The voices of nature, of prophecy and history, are in accordance with the longings of the world for the coming of a time when there shall be a consummate flowering of the human race. Grant, if you please, that this is optimistic; but this is the optimism of history. . . . During the eighteen hundred years that have passed since the Man of Nazareth in the month of April, rose victor from the grave, triumphant over death, the banner of progress has borne this inscription: The Brotherhood of Man; the Redemption of the World.[45]

At the first meeting of 1896 President Claflin again celebrated the anniversary of the Society. This time, instead of introducing Charles Coffin, he spoke himself on "the Life and Public Services of John Hancock," the first governor of the Commonwealth. His address, part of the annual meeting of 1896, was well delivered in the Wilder Room, the auditorium newly named for the revered former president. Both celebrations, unlike the one in 1871, were given only passing notice in the *Register*.[46]

The Society had another significant event to celebrate. For some months, perhaps years, in anticipation of the event, the members had argued over admitting women as members of the Society. Finally, in January 1897, the members voted by special ballot on this momentous issue. The ballots returned were 523, and of that number 451 were favorable and 53 were negative. An additional thirteen qualified their approval of such a forward step. Claflin and the Council were delighted with the ballot results and immediately petitioned the Massachusetts legislature for a change in the charter.[47] In less than a month the legislators and governor agreed to the change. The bylaws were quickly modified, and a membership committee began the slow processing of suitable candidates.[48] By February 1898, thirty-six women were nominated for membership, and twenty-nine accepted. One of these women, Lucy Ellen Hall, was the wife of William Prescott Greenlaw, the young assistant librarian. She was then augmenting the family income with work as a professional genealogist, but in 1898, she became the editor and publisher of *The Genealogical Advertiser*, a journal that specialized in Plymouth Colony families.[49]

Another celebration was held for the *Register*, which completed its fiftieth year in 1896. Dean was still the editor, and had discovered a format that was generally appealing to genealogists. The *Register* did not attract subscriptions from the whole membership, and in 1900 probably there were no more than 450 subscribers among a membership of 953. But it was regarded as a treasure of the Society—a bit too costly to be created again but far too valuable to be abandoned.[50]

Some members, particularly John T. Hassam, felt that a fifty-year index would be an invaluable guide to the *Register*. Claflin agreed and appointed a committee with Hassam, George K. Clarke, and John Ward Dean to solicit funds. Members were urged to pay a subscription fee of $100 and make donations. Three thousand dollars were necessary to produce the Index and three times that sum would be needed to publish it. The committee advertised on the cover of the *Register* and presented such impressive and convincing arguments that one would have readily expected members to line up and donate. Perhaps this single paragraph will give the spirit of the enterprise:

> Few people are aware that in a single volume of the *Register* there are mentioned more than 3,000 places, 4,000 family names, and 12,000 individuals. These figures, large as they are, are below the average of the later years, and the 20,000 pages of printed matter already published contain, it is estimated, more than 600,000 names of persons.[51]

The project would take much advertising and hard work before the four-volume index appeared from 1906 to 1909. But it would become an invaluable tool for complete examination of the first fifty volumes of the *Register*.

Since the early 1880s Hassam had been one of the *Register*'s most powerful supporters. He became interested in English research through a book by James A. Emmerton and Henry F. Waters, *Gleanings from English Records about New England Families*, Salem Press, 1880. He was asked by John W. Dean to review it, and he liked it so much (was in fact fascinated by it) that he wrote nearly three *Register* pages of analysis. At the end of this extra-long review he observed:

> The success of these investigations shows what may be done by a systematic and thorough search among the English records, made by a

competent and experienced antiquary. Is it too much to hope that as the New England Historic Genealogical Society grows in age and prosperity, it may at some future time be endowed with funds sufficient to enable it to maintain an accredited agent in the mother country constantly engaged in such researches as these?[52]

Hassam was not to be denied a positive answer to his question. After making inquiries, he confirmed his own opinion that Waters, then a member of the Society's publications committee, was a gifted genealogist—and he discovered that Waters was ready to undertake research in London for a few years. Hassam pressed friends, the Harvard Club of New York, the Board of Directors of the Society, and Wilder himself and collected nearly $2,500, about two thousand less than was needed for three years of service. His expectations of continued assistance were satisfied by donors from MHS and other societies in the Boston area.[53]

Waters left for London and research at Somerset House in May 1883. Over the coming decade and a half he published his research in the *Register* under the title of "Genealogical Gleanings in England." Some sixty installments of his research appeared over seventeen years. In 1887, when he was introduced to a meeting of the Society, his research was described thus: "Mr. Waters' method is to examine all the records between certain dates, seriatim, keeping a sharp lookout for everything possible indicative of the slightest connection with known American families."[54]

So Waters spent years in the gloomy cellar of Somerset House. Turning pages, looking for references to families that came to the colonies, and then posting his articles to the *Register*, he made many discoveries. He found the parentage or "origin" of John Harvard, Roger Williams, the Virginia Washingtons, and countless other less important immigrants. Another discovery was Winthrop's map of the Massachusetts Bay Colony. His research graced the *Register*, sometimes in grand articles such as the two on John Harvard. Marshall Wilder in his address of 1886 had described this work as a "remarkable achievement" and welcomed the honorary degree conferred on Waters by Harvard College.[55] President Goodell in 1887 appealed to "the lovers of American history everywhere to assist [the Society in continuing Waters'] enterprise to dispel the obscurities which have hitherto shrouded the antecedents of those men of great and good intentions" who discovered and occupied the Western Hemisphere.[56]

Hassam was ever ready to show the influence of Waters' research. He offered clippings in 1886 from a French newspaper and wrote an introduction in 1901 to a two-volume reprinting of *Genealogical Gleanings in England*. Hassam had written introductions also to the Harvard articles and again in 1894, with the help of William Claflin, collected money for Waters' research. The president, speaking through Samuel A. Green, praised the *Register* as "the oldest quarterly magazine in the United States," much responsible for the great interest in genealogy. Waters' "discoveries in relation to John Harvard, Roger Williams, and George Washington," he observed, had first been reported in the *Register* and were "great contributions to historical and genealogical literature."[57]

When Waters became too old and infirm to continue his research, Hassam was not interested in finding a permanent replacement. Money continued to be scarce and Hassam had turned to other less expensive projects. The Society was crowded with readers in 1896 and 1897 as membership was increasing and the number of books in the library was multiplying, and thoughts turned now to new leadership. Claflin wanted to leave his post in 1898, but the Council urged him to serve for another year or until a suitable successor was found. Many new men like Charles Sidney Ensign, James Phinney Baxter, and Caleb Benjamin Tillinghast, among others, had posts in the Society, but some of them barely knew Claflin, who rarely now came to Somerset Street and communicated only by letter.[58]

The candidate who received the most support in 1898 was Edward Griffin Porter, a beloved Congregational minister from Lexington who lived for some years during his boyhood in Dorchester, and graduated from Harvard College in 1858 and Andover Theological Seminary in 1864. Known as a mild-mannered cleric, he had two decades of service in Lexington at retirement and had published two scholarly papers almost every year since 1875. Some of them were published in the

Proceedings of the MHS. A member of the Society since 1870, he may have been sponsored by Marshall Wilder since both had lived in Dorchester, but he was widely connected to most scholarly associations in New England. In particular he was a member of the American Historical Association and an overseer of Harvard University. Abner Goodell, the former president, felt Edward Porter, "possessed without qualification, or flaw, all the qualities which distinguish the New England gentleman."[59]

Unlike Claflin and Wilder, Porter was not well known, but he was charming, modest, and cordial. The Society could look ahead after his election to many vigorous years of service. At age 62, he delivered in person a short but pleasant address to the membership in which his humility, sincerity, and gentility deeply affected many listeners:

> The membership of many of us dates back to Colonel Wilder's time. He was the friend and neighbor of my boyhood; and when, a little later, he welcomed me here, neither he nor I could have imagined that it would ever fall to my lot to be one of his successors in this chair. His genial and dignified features look down upon us from the familiar portrait on yonder wall like an inspiring accessory at all our meetings; and I hope we shall ever maintain the high standards which he strove to perpetuate in the Society to which he was so sincerely attached and for which he labored so many years.[60]

There was a good word for Hassam and the promotion of an index for the *Register*, for *Register* editor John Ward Dean, and for a few others. Porter was truly interested in research and also had praise for the well-known genealogists William Henry Whitmore, William B. Trask, and Albert H. Hoyt. "Our work is that of scholars, not politicians nor athletes. We are supposed to live in the pure upper air of letters, and to handle precious documents left to us by the silent dead . . . . The intelligent genealogist deals . . . with real men and women whom he is often to resuscitate and to clothe with a vigorous and picturesque life."[61]

President Porter had a dark beard, a spring to his walk, and a full head of hair. Looking younger than his age, he presided in 1899 over all the monthly meetings of the Society and most Council sessions. Not much was done that year because of the Spanish-American War; accounts of battles in Cuba and the Philippines filled the newspapers. His reelection in 1900 and his address of "spirited eloquence" were well received. This annual meeting was a time, however, of reflection. Benjamin B. Torrey was retiring as treasurer after thirty years of service. Albert H. Hoyt, the corresponding secretary, was also retiring after nearly thirty years in various offices. And John Ward Dean, librarian and editor of the *Register*, was terminally ill. Surely this year was one of those turning points in the history of the Society. The speeches of Edward G. Porter and James Phinney Baxter, who had also spoken, made their impressions and the meeting adjourned.

In early February, Edward G. Porter was suddenly stricken by a heart attack and died within a few days. The Society was now confronted again with the task of finding a leader.[62]

Notes

[1] Wilder, 1871 Address at Annual Meeting, *Register*, 25 (1871): 174-179; Proceedings of Society, ibid., 297-298.

[2] Bell, "The Future of American History," March 18, 1871, *Register*, 25 (1871): 317-328. See "Memoir of the Hon. Charles H. Bell," *Register*, 49 (1895): 9-23.

[3] Wilder, 1871 Address at Annual Meeting, *Register*, 25 (1871): 175; Proceedings, IV (1865-1872): 197, MSS. NEHGS.

[4] John W. Dean, "Sketch of the Life of William B. Towne," *Register*, 32 (1878): 13-14; Proceedings, IV (1865-1872): 225, MSS.

[5] Dean, "Sketch of the Life of William B. Towne," *Register*, 32 (1878): 13-16.

[6] Hamilton A. Hill, "Marshall Pinckney Wilder," *Register*, 42 (1888): 233-242.

[7] Proceedings, IV (1865-1872): 210; V (1872-1877): 37, 136; VII (1883-1888): 10, 45, MSS. References to Knox Papers are in Proceedings, V (1872-1877): 62, 94, 263, MSS.

[8] *Register*, 27 (1873): 200-206.

[9] Deloraine Pendre Corey, "John Ward Dean," *Register*, 56 (1902): 223-235; Ruth Wood Hoag, "John Ward Dean, M.A.," *The Genealogical Advertiser*, 2 (1899): 97-103.

[10] Josephine E. Rayne, "Report of the Librarian," *Register*, 85 (1931): 185-186. Rayne was making a comparison and noted that the seating capacity was 80 in 1930.

[11] Proceedings, VI (1877-1883): 12, MSS.

[12] Wilder, 1885 Address at Annual Meeting, *Register*, 39 (1885): 123.

[13] Proceedings, VII (1883-1888): 45, MSS.

[14] Wilder, 1886 Address at Annual Meeting, *Register*, 40 (1886): 139.

[15] Ibid., p. 142.

[16] Ibid., pp. 142-143.

[17] Robert C. Winthrop, "Remarks," October 1883, *Proceedings of the Massachusetts Historical Society, 1882-1883* (Boston, 1884): 342.

[18] Report of January 3, 1883, Proceedings, *Register*, 37 (1883): 314.

[19] Report of January 5, 1887, Proceedings, *Register*, 41 (1887): 318-319. Wilder's last address, as read by Edmund F. Slafter, ibid., pp. 141-150.

[20] Charles Knowles Bolton, "Reverend Edmund Farwell Slafter," *Register*, 61 (1907): 147-149. Slafter's age (he was born in 1816) may have also been important. In 1920 David G. Haskins, Jr., Recording Secretary from 1873 to 1890, commented on Slafter and the election: "He was eminently fitted for the presidency, and should unquestionably have been elected to succeed Colonel Wilder, but unwise councils prevailed, he was passed over, and the results were disastrous." See *Register*, 75 (1921): 68.

[21] Elizabeth T. Thornton, "Abner Cheney Goodell," *Register*, 69 (1916): 3-8.

[22] The 1888 By-Laws are reprinted in *Proceedings of the New England Historic Genealogical Society, 1886-1895*, especially bound, after the Annual Report for 1889 (Boston, 1889), pp. 51-62.

[23] See list of officers, *Proceedings of the New England Historic Genealogical Society at the Annual Meeting*, January 2, 1889 (Boston, 1889), p. 5.

[24] See Council's introductory note to the Report of the Librarian, 1892, *Proceedings of the New England Historic Genealogical Society at the Annual Meeting*, January 6, 1892 (Boston, 1892): 18-24.

[25] Ezra Hoyt Byington, "Report of the Librarian," 1892, ibid., pp. 25-39.

[26] NEHGS Council Records, I (1889-1893): 110-113, 127, 148, 149, 159, MSS.

[27] Ibid., p. 96.

[28] Ibid., pp. 94, 103-107, 109-110.

[29] Ibid., pp. 65, 88; "Rolls of Membership of the New England Historic Genealogical Society, 1844-1890" (Boston, 1891), a special publication of the *Register*.

[30] See Hassam's introduction to Henry F. Waters, "John Harvard and his Ancestry," *Register*, 39 (1885): 265-267.

[31] Abner Cheney Goodell, Jr., *Valedictory Address to the New England Historic Genealogical Society* (Boston, 1892), 12-13.

[32] Elizabeth T. Thornton, "Abner Cheney Goodell," *Register*, 69 (1916): 3-8.

[33] Council Records, I (1889-1893): 207, 211, MSS.

[34] Ezra Hoyt Byington, "Report of the Librarian," 1892, *Proceedings of the New England Historic Genealogical Society at the Annual Meeting*, January 6, 1892 (Boston, 1892): 18-24.

[35] Hassam was quoted in the Council Records, I (1889-1893), 224, that Goodell's presidency "has been disastrous, financially and otherwise." Report of the Proceedings of June 1, 1892, meeting, *Register*, 47 (1893): 222.

[36] Abner Cheney Goodell, Jr., *Valedictory Address to the New England Historic Genealogical Society* (Boston, 1892), 7-15.

[37] Charles Sidney Ensign, "Hon. William Claflin," *Register*, 61 (1907): 112-116.

[38] Council Records, I (1889-1893): 256, 258, 265, 276, 280, MSS.

[39] George M. Adams, "Rev. Ezra Hoyt Byington," *Register*, 56 (1902): 115-121. Byington apparently died suddenly in 1901 of a heart attack.

[40] Council Records, II (1893-1900). For the period 1888-1894 the Council admitted 333 and 227 accepted.

[41] Florence C. Hawes, "William Prescott Greenlaw," *Register*, 100 (1946): 81-84. Council Records, II (1893-1900): 91, give his official appointment as assistant librarian as April 29, 1895. His salary is given on page 127.

[42] Council Records, II (1893-1900), 35, 43, 53, MSS.

[43] Ibid., March 2, 1896, p. 124.

[44] Report of October 2, 1895, Meeting, Proceedings, *Register*, 50 (1896): 227.

[45] Quoted by George M. Adams, "Hon. Charles Carleton Coffin," *Register*, 50 (1896): 295; the Boston newspapers gave good coverage to this celebration. See the Boston *Transcript*, April 16, 18, and 20, 1895.

[46] Report of January 1, 1896, Annual Meeting, *Register*, 50 (1896): 228.

[47] Meeting of March 3, 1897, NEHGS Proceedings, IX (1896-1905): 45, MSS; Report of March 3, 1897, Monthly Meeting, *Register*, 51 (1897): 229.

48 The petition was accepted by April 7, 1897. See NEHGS Proceedings, IX (1896-1905): 448, MSS.

[49] Meeting of February 2, 1898, NEHGS Proceedings, IX (1896-1905): 69, MSS. Her advertisement ran in the January 1896 *Register*, 50 (1896), cover.

[50] See Report of the Treasurer, December 31, 1900, Supplement in *Register*, 55 (1901): xxxvii; Edward Griffin Porter, Annual Address, in *Proceedings of the New England Historic Genealogical Society*, Annual Meeting for 1899 (Boston, 1899), 10. The Council found the deficit balance from 1901-1907 at an average of $323.05 per year. See ibid., 22.

[51] *Register*, 50 (1896): January cover.

[52] Hassam's review is printed in *Register*, 34 (1880): 422-424.

[53] See Albert Mathews, "John Tyler Hassam," *Register*, 58 (1904): 13; James Kendall Homer, "Henry Fitzgerald Waters," ibid., 68 (1914): 9-16.

[54] Abner C. Goodell, Jr., "Remarks on Mr. Waters's English Researches," *Register*, 42 (1888): 40-41.

[55] *Register*, 41 (1887): 144.

[56] *Register*, 42 (1888): 44. Waters' research into the English origins of Great Migration immigrants was continued in the twentieth century by the widely acclaimed reports of the Committee on English and Foreign Research, contributed largely by Joseph Gardner Bartlett; Elizabeth French, later Mrs. Bartlett;

and George Andrews Moriarty. Major twentieth-century English-origins scholars who published in the *Register* independently of the Committee, or after its dissolution, have included Walter Goodwin Davis, John G. Hunt and Walter Lee Sheppard, Jr. (who all also published under the aegis of the Committee), plus Arthur Adams, George Walter Chamberlain, John Insley Coddington, Meredith B. Colket, William Prescott Greenlaw, Myrtle Stevens Hyde, Paul W. Prindle, Douglas Richardson, Milton Rubincam, John B. Threlfall, Sir Anthony R. Wagner, and Robert S. Wakefield. At least five editors of *The American Genealogist* contributed English-origins data to the *Register*—Donald Lines Jacobus, George Englert McCracken, Robert Moody Sherman, David L. Greene, and Robert Charles Anderson. All such pre-1983 articles were reprinted in *English Origins of New England Families from the New England Historical and Genealogical Register* (two series, 6 vols., Baltimore, 1984-1985).

57 Samuel A. Green presided at the 1894 annual meeting and gave a short speech on being chosen president *pro tempore*. *Proceedings of the New England Historic Genealogical Society at its Annual Meeting, 3 January, 1894* (Boston, 1894): 14-15.

[58] Charles Sidney Ensign (1842-1917) regularly substituted for Claflin during 1897 and 1898. Claflin's last appearance as chairman was on October 6, 1897. Ensign was a most talented presiding officer. A lawyer and legislator, he served many terms on the Council.

[59] Goodell's estimate was published as part of the 1900 memorial for Porter, *Register*, 55 (1901): 19.

[60] "Address of the President," *Proceedings of the New England Historic Genealogical Society at its Annual Meeting*, January 11, 1899 (Boston, 1899): 10-11.

[61] Ibid., 10.

[62] Report of Annual Meeting, January 10, 1900, Proceedings, *Register*, 54 (1900): 220-221; ibid., Meeting of February 14, 1900: 221-222.

CHAPTER 4

Taking Responsibility

A change of guard occurred in the Society with the coming of the new century. Dean, Hassam, Torrey, and, alas, Edward G. Porter, whose sudden and premature death shocked everyone, now made way for many younger leaders. Happily, for Porter's place a successor was already evident to most members. James Phinney Baxter, then serving as the Society's vice president from Maine, had been well received in January 1900 when he spoke at the Annual Meeting. An accomplished speaker, most distinguished in appearance, he had good height and a strong, deep voice and was well known as the successful founder and manager of a Maine corporation. Besides, he was an editor of documents on Maine and a recognized historian.[1] His reception as vice president was most favorable.

Only a few members, however, had met him before he was presented as Porter's successor. Most of his life until age seventy was spent in Portland, Maine, as industrialist, mayor of the city, president of the Maine Historical Society, and officer of various organizations like the Portland Public Library, the Freemasons, and the Portland Society of Art. His homes were in Portland and Mackworth Island, with farms in Gorham and elsewhere in Maine. He did not expect to move into Boston as president of the Society. In 1904 and 1905 he would again be elected mayor of Portland. Almost every day when he was in Portland, he spent his morning at his desk in the Portland Packing Company, a pioneer processor of canned foods, or conferred with sons who were managers in family enterprises. He budgeted his time at the office, or a library, or at meetings, and expected his associates to do likewise. Several assis-

71

tants were usually at his side taking dictation or helping with his historical research.[2]

His first address before the Society in 1901 was brief, though he expressed a genuine pleasure at being chosen its president and paused momentarily to observe the significance of this change of centuries. It was a momentous time for civilization, he said, and for the Society. "A new day has dawned for the world, and when . . . [the century] closes, the race will probably have achieved more than it has [accomplished] during the preceding ten centuries." For genealogy and history, he observed, much awaited researchers as they applied new techniques in their analysis of original documents. Baxter was impressed with graduate work at Johns Hopkins University and predicted that through its influence, most history written during the past century would need to be rewritten. He sensed a greater interest in historical and genealogical research and the enthusiasm of people in libraries as they assumed the burden of scholarship. Looking over his audience of Society members, he flattered them, and sincerely so, by observing that they were not second in intellectual ability to any group then gathering in New England. Like the scientists, medical doctors, and business people assembled elsewhere, they had an important task to do and would gradually achieve recognition for their accomplishments in the new century.[3]

The audience was well aware of Baxter's great reputation as an historian, but few members realized that he was profoundly interested in family history and would concentrate the attention of the Society upon developing its genealogical resources. He and Edward G. Porter, the lamented former president, had apparently agreed upon this direction for the Society when they met in Portland, shortly after Porter had assumed the presidency in 1899. Their deliberations had a strong effect upon Baxter, who often referred to Porter as his friend and was convinced that focusing on genealogical research was a desirable policy. Porter had undoubtedly reminded him that a president was only as strong as his support and a majority vote of the Council was essential in administering the Society.

At his first presidential address Baxter was accompanied by his wife, Mehitabel Cummings Proctor, and other family members whose presence surely revealed his own priorities. Baxter was indeed a family man. Eight of his eleven surviving children by two wives were educated with ideals of public service and sent to excellent colleges. Rupert Henry and Percival Proctor went to Bowdoin College, from which Baxter himself had received two honorary degrees, while Emily and Madeleine attended Wellesley. Percival took his law degree from Harvard University in 1901; later in life he would be elected to the Maine House of Representatives, the Maine Senate, and the governorship. Rupert Henry was a corporate executive, banker, and for some years an official of Sagadahoc County. Emily "devoted herself to College Settlement work on the East Side [of New York]" and later was engaged in personnel work in Portland where she also used her talents as a linguist and organist. James Phinney Baxter, Jr., graduated from Williams College and entered the firm of H. C. Baxter and Bros. as one of the managers. His son James Phinney Baxter III was particularly his grandfather's favorite (in later life this grandson was an historian and president of Williams College). The remaining sons of the Society president, Hartley Cone, Eugene Raddin, and Clinton Lewis, were involved in family or allied businesses in Maine.[4]

Northern New England and eastern Canada was Baxter country. When President Baxter came south by train, he conducted Society business and participated in the affairs of other scholarly organizations and then returned to his family in Portland. The administration of the Society was conducted during his absence by the other officers and the councilors. Until advanced age, he regularly presided over monthly and Council meetings, often held on the same day. He liked to engage in discussion, read papers, offer observations, and point to new research. But he insisted that the meetings adjourn on schedule and be conducted in harmony and good will. His amazing ability to end monthly meetings in two hours or less was shown year after year.

Baxter worked well with his associates, but had his favorites and relied upon them to carry out the tasks of the Society. His closest associate was Caleb Benjamin Tillinghast (1843-1909), State Librarian since 1893 and the Society's senior vice president. One critic observed that Tillinghast "knew more things accurately than any man I ever knew." With a good memory and a devotion to work, he was ready to undertake any task Baxter assigned. One might add that he hated the small talk of public dinners and brushed off warnings of friends that he was working too hard. Nevertheless, he was recognized with honorary degrees from Harvard and Tufts and respected by his colleagues.[5]

When Baxter was not able to attend meetings of the Council, for whatever reason, Caleb Tillinghast presided. The deliberate, good-natured procedures instituted by Baxter seemed to be the order of the day with Tillinghast. Their personalities were certainly different, however. Tillinghast was involved with public education, book collecting, and government policies, while Baxter was interested in fine points of history and literature, the authorship of Shakespeare's plays, painting, and poetry; Baxter was even given at times to quoting a few lines of his own verse and permitted a family publication of his poetry. He nominated Tillinghast as chairman of the Publications Committee, and together they planned how the generous bequest of Robert Henry Eddy would be administered. Eddy had given the Society a magnificent gift of $56,500 for the publication of the vital records of Massachusetts. With support from these funds, the Society would ask the Commonwealth to join in the publication of these vital records by buying five hundred copies of every volume for library distribution. Other organizations like the Essex Institute in Salem would also participate with their own vital record projects. A vast number of town vital records would now be saved from destruction through the labor of Henry Ernest Woods, Dean's successor as editor of the *Register*, and several women assistants.[6] Baxter and Tillinghast gave Woods their support in the Council and monthly meetings.

Over the coming forty years, these tan cloth-covered volumes would be issued year after year. Sometimes the Commonwealth of Massachusetts, as in the First World War, would discontinue its subsidy, but the continued support of the Society and of other societies made this unique and valuable set possible. With the legislative help of Charles Sidney Ensign, a fine lawyer and member of the Society, the 1902 law was passed, and Ensign occasionally appeared before legislative committees to battle for its continuance. In 1903, Baxter spoke at the annual meeting about the project and gave it his blessing in these words: "it is impossible at this time to realize fully the importance to the Society of this undertaking."[7]

These volumes represent a unique experiment in how to present and publish vital records as public documents. But many members immediately asked whether only the records of the town clerk's office should be used. Woods and his assistants found that local graveyards contained inscriptions that added about twenty percent to the data collected by town clerks. Others checked records of the local churches, surviving Bible entries, and local diaries and discovered even more information about former residents. So, as the vital records appeared, volume after volume over the years, more and more data from more and more sources were included. Inaccuracies were not a major problem, but the inclusion of the best available information was the objective, so that the researcher could make his judgment from a wide collection of documents. In the years since 1970 editors of vital records have tried to transcribe data verbatim, a form that gives the researcher most information that appeared in the original records (town, church, or Bible) without artificial arrangements. Society members earlier debated which was the better record—Bible or tombstone? And the Council ruled that the Bible was better.[8] Since 1970 debate has occurred over the appropriateness of exact duplication.

For years the Society, under Baxter's leadership, sponsored a committee to copy cemetery records. Most actual work was done by volunteers, but the Society sent letters to town clerks, church groups, and members urging that they take charge of local projects to gather tombstone inscriptions. Baxter spoke in 1904 on the urgency of doing the work because tombstones were being destroyed or damaged at a frightening rate. There was some humor at the meetings when speakers referred to members being sent to cemeteries, but Tillinghast and

Woods hastened to affirm the value of such data for the vital records being produced. Thousands of these graveyard surveys were completed and filed in the archives of the Society.

In 1903, the *Register* published two substantial reports from Ethel Stanwood Bolton of Shirley, Massachusetts, the wife of Charles Knowles Bolton, director of the Boston Athenaeum, who copied over a period of months all inscriptions from the cemetery at Shirley Center. That same year *The Essex Antiquarian*, a well-known journal that published vital records as a matter of policy, featured a leading article on the Chebacco (Essex) burying grounds. Both journals were supplying the genealogical community with all sorts of vital data as eager individuals hastened to save town vital records for posterity.[9] Reflecting upon this activity, the Society's Committee on Epitaphs made this report in 1903:

> The importance of the preservation of inscriptions is shown by the fact that out of 700 inscriptions in the two older graveyards in one town, Concord, Mass., 164 (23 per cent) are of deaths which are not noted in the Town Records. The Committee again submits that the preservations of the inscriptions is a matter of public interest, and should therefore, to the extent of that interest, be under the care of the State, as are other records of a public nature.[10]

One cannot exaggerate the popularity of graveyard transcribing by members of the Society, but along with this activity they also copied ministerial records—baptisms, marriages, and deaths at local churches. In the *Register* of 1903, George Kuhn Clarke, cited above, published the baptisms of the First Church in Needham, 1720-1821. A year earlier his transcription of births and deaths in Needham had also appeared.[11] Both were well received by researchers. Also important in this regard was the work of the Massachusetts Society of Mayflower Descendants, which published in its journal, *The Mayflower Descendant*, the vital records of many towns in Barnstable and Plymouth counties, Massachusetts.

The Society was certainly not premature in taking responsibility for publishing town records. But the popular insistence on including more sources forced Henry Ernest Woods and his colleagues to expand each volume. The legislature, however, warned the Society not to depart radically from the format used in earlier volumes.

The Society was slower in adjusting to the financial problems of publishing the index to the *Register*. The inspiration for the index came from John Tyler Hassam, who waged a drive for subscriptions in the 1890s, but age and infirmities lessened his energy. He raised about $2400, but Baxter, Tillinghast, and Woods found nearly three times that amount of additional subsidy. While the project benefited by increased popular support, it was slowed by a rise in costs.[12] Hassam, feeling the anxiety of old age, spent time consolidating the indices until his death in 1903. In his place Tillinghast worked to solicit enough to subsidize the index, but those most thrilled by the project retired or died with the passing years and the burden of proofing fell upon Josephine E. Rayne and Effie Louise Chapman of the library staff, who saw the job to completion in 1909. Its value, as Hassam had repeatedly said, was indescribable—it unlocked the treasures of the *Register*.

Production of the index was a burdensome project. The fiftieth volume of the *Register* was completed in 1896, the full index in 1909. Hassam had never realized the laborious nature and cost of the project and even advocated an expanded index, through perhaps volume 60. Unfortunately, cost and other projects became excuses for delaying the extension. Not until 1994 would the next general inclusive index be published, and this recent index was made possible with the application of advanced computer technology.

Though Baxter wanted the index completed, it was costly, nearly $15,000 to print. He was frankly more interested in the library and its development than in the index.[13] When Dean died of old age in 1902, the Society had already on staff an associate librarian who was ready to assume his responsibilities. Two women assistant librarians and editors, Rayne and Chapman, joined the staff about this time. William Prescott Greenlaw had visited the Society first in 1891, attracted by its books on genealogy and history, possibly also by the likable qualities of the librarian. When an opening in the library staff was made for Greenlaw in 1894, he readily accepted and served as assistant librarian, then as acting librarian in 1902. Born in Bristol, Maine, in 1863, he was a salesman for some years, then a foreman in leather goods factories, and finally an insurance agent. Greenlaw liked books, read widely, enjoyed conversation, and cultivated a knowledge of languages, architecture, and navigation. His love for the sea was well known among members of the Society who saw him on coastal cruises and enjoyed his salty stories.[14]

Greenlaw and Baxter may never have been warm friends, but they agreed on library policy. In his address of 1903, Baxter endorsed a book-buying program which would make the library a "centre of genealogical knowledge not only for New England, but for the whole country." He then noted purchases of "over six hundred genealogies" in 1902. "It is intended," he said, to buy "every American genealogy which has been published." These additions should not be limited to American resources, but should also include English family histories, parish registers, and local histories. As if to emphasize the determination of the Council, he observed that "such works are indispensable in a library like ours, and every effort should be made to make our collection of them as complete as possible."[15]

When Greenlaw later spoke to this audience, he added further specifics to Baxter's book figures. "There have been added to the Library six hundred and twenty-five genealogies, many of which are rare, some exceedingly so, and several are unique copies." He cited the books donated and purchased, the number of pamphlets and manuscripts, and then added: "If the Library is to maintain the foremost position among American libraries in its own special field, a broad policy for the acquisition of genealogical books and manuscripts must be pursued with vigor."[16]

Greenlaw then stressed the need for more funds to bind books, to catalogue the collection, to buy additional books and manuscripts, and to hire personnel. All of these improvements required money, but Greenlaw refused to be troubled by such matters. Those were problems for Baxter, the Council, and the membership. Part of his spacious report is worthy of rereading:

Nearly ten years ago a new card catalogue was begun, and from time to time small additions have been made to it until it now contains about twenty thousand cards, three thousand of which have been written this year . . . . The present Library staff, besides attending to the ordinary routine work, may not be able to catalogue the greater part of the current accessions. With sixty thousand volumes and pamphlets in the Library and only twenty thousand cards written it is evident that additional help will be needed to bring this division of the work up to where it should be maintained.[17]

The tedious labor of processing the flow of new books continued in 1903 and Greenlaw and his assistants added over 4000 cards to the catalogue. Baxter, in his annual report for that year, mentioned with pleasure this work, but also the 800 town directories, many issues of the *Boston Evening Transcript*, and substantial numbers of genealogies. The Council, moreover, gave the total number of acquisitions to 1904 as 30,545 books, 33,470 pamphlets, and many manuscripts and some gifts other than books. "The Library was thus becoming more useful as well as larger." Soon the stacks would not be able to house these increased resources. Everyone agreed with Baxter that "we are building not for our own day, but for the future" and the collection would soon be a unique archive of "family history."[18]

If we are building for tomorrow, Baxter concluded, then plans should be developed immediately for a new library, land should be purchased, and funding should begin. The Council agreed and imagined a library building five stories in height, or sixty feet high, with frontage on Somerset Street, and a depth of 142 feet, to Allston Place. The cost, they calculated, could be as high as one hundred thousand dollars. To think in terms of such a magnificent edifice required both imagination and planning, perhaps courage. The Council reacted by ordering the purchase of neighboring property costing about $52,000— property that could be presently rented or used for the storage of books until the plans for a library were developed in the coming five or six years.[19] Greenlaw reacted by urging the Council to move forward with the project as soon as possible. His boldness, although not appreciated by everyone, was one characteristic of his personality.

Baxter remained cautious for a time but announced gifts of some twenty thousand dollars in 1904 and 1905 and three thousand from the estate of Robert C. Winthrop in 1906. Generous as these gifts were, he said, they would not go far enough in paying any major expenses of construction and expansion of facilities. While the Council also hesitated, a committee investigated the Society's building at No. 18 Somerset Street, possibly hoping that a new library could be delayed for a decade or two by improving the present structure. The firm of Wheelwright and Haven was engaged to study what might be done to improve the building, provide for space needs, and allow for library expansion. It would also look into the desirability of the current location. The architects got busy almost immediately and submitted their official report, brief as it was, in the form of a letter to the officers and Council. For the architects the outcome of their investigation was obvious. The building was never intended for public use, much less the storage of books. It had been a luxurious, private home for near half a century. The walls—12 to 16 inches in thickness compared with the city code of 20 inches—were not thick enough to withstand the weight of heavy floors, and the walls on the north side of the building were actually bulging. The upper rooms lacked sufficient bracing and vibrations in the floors indicated too much weight from the books. The ceilings on the lower floors were uneven. The furnace was not well insulated from gas pipes and the plaster walls in the building did not provide adequate fire breaks. The building, in brief, was not worth renovating for use as a library.[20]

The architectural report evidently removed all thought of staying at No. 18 Somerset, which was now regarded as a fire trap that endangered the uniquely valuable library. Baxter and the Council reacted by taking steps to accumulate a building fund. The Society owned widely scattered pieces of property in Massachusetts, and the Treasurer, Charles Knowles Bolton, was ordered to sell these properties for cash as soon as possible. The Council studied plans to raise membership fees and the subscription rate of the *Register*. An advertisement was placed in the 1907 *Register* describing the financial needs of the Society and an "Appeal" for donations was later broadcast.

The advertisement laid out plans for a fireproof library building in the rear of No. 18 Somerset Street, to be five stories high, with book stacks for 250,000 volumes, and a reading room to accommodate 80 researchers. The cost was set at $60,000. When the Council added costs for fixtures, furniture, etc. for the library, it discovered the need for approximately another $30,000 which would then take care of the purchase of the site. Other less urgent sums included funding for additional research for the vital record series ($10,000); an endowed book fund ($75,000); the completion of the catalogue ($8,000); genealogical research in England ($15,000); and other projects ($21,000).[21]

The "Appeal" which appeared in the 1911 *Register* revealed a considerable maturation of Society plans. The Council had already purchased lands on Ashburton Place, midway between the State House and the new Court House on Beacon Hill. It had decided to erect the new building as soon as possible and make it as safe as modern construction would permit. The building would be fireproof and use metal fittings, be spacious and well equipped. The "Appeal" was a call for financial help based on the Society policy of free access to all researchers, men and women, members and non-members, young and old. It gave "an opportunity for sons and daughters of New England, no matter where they lived, to help in preserving and publishing the records of their sterling ancestors." They had a chance to provide a memorial plaque, endow a special room, or provide money for equipment and publication. In short, it assured readers that "sums in *any amount* will be welcome."[22]

Funds for the new facility came into the treasury slowly. Edmund F. Slafter and William B. Trask left bequests of five hundred dollars apiece, sales of numbers 16 and 18 Somerset Place brought nearly forty thousand dollars in mortgages, and pledges of financial help rose to almost another forty thousand dollars. The most gratifying developments were the increase in members from 1,081 to 1,133 (between 1907 and 1912) and participation of members and their friends in monthly lectures. Pilgrim Hall on Beacon Hill Street was rented for these gatherings which sometimes attracted over 300 people to an illustrated lecture, music, and refreshments. Topics were less serious than previously, often travelogues like Ninna Eliot Tenney's on "Beautiful New Brunswick and Historic Quebec."[23] The excitement of these gatherings, it was hoped, would increase pledges for the new building.

Like many other societies full of mature and aged people, the membership changed at times dramatically. Caleb Tillinghast died suddenly in 1909. His death was deeply felt by Baxter, who was nearing his own seventy-ninth birthday and depended upon Tillinghast as ever for advice and majority support in the Council. Old George Gordon, the Recording Secretary, resigned that same year because of Parkinson's disease. Baxter was never very warm personally toward Gordon, perhaps because the latter fought for the Confederacy, but he was secretary for seventeen years and absolutely reliable. Baxter considered his records "a model of order and completeness."[24] Another who died during these years was William Carver Bates (1838-1910), who served briefly on the Council and many years on the Committee on Papers and Essays. His energy and good will may have been largely responsible for the resurgence of the monthly meeting as a genuinely popular gathering. George Sumner Mann (1834-1909) contributed to many activities of the Society. Retiring early in life as a dry goods merchant, he engaged in real estate and the care of trusts. At his own death in 1909, he bequeathed to the Society two thousand dollars.[25]

The places of such men were rarely filled, but new men came along and made other contributions. Charles Sidney Ensign (1842-1917) served for several decades as a councilor, a vice president of the Society for Massachusetts, and in posts like the Library Committee. His long experience as an attorney brought practical knowledge of business and government to discussions, but his greatest asset to Baxter was availability to serve on any commission that needed dependable leadership. Like Ensign, Frank Ernest Woodward was ready to help the Society whenever he could. A member of the Library Committee, the Council, and the membership committee, he had expert knowledge on heating and ventilating buildings. Most of all, he was born in Damariscotta, Maine, in Baxter country, and published a genealogy of the Woodward family. Both Ensign and Woodward were exceedingly valuable advisors to Baxter as he turned to problems of financing a new building for the Society.[26]

One feels the excitement of these years. Many men and a few women flocked to Baxter's side to serve on important committees. Many visited the library as researchers. In fact, the library was often crowded with more non-members than members, and some of these inspired genealogists applied for membership. Almost every monthly meeting admitted from ten to twenty-five new members, and some gave books from their own collections in appreciation of research they accomplished in the library.

Greenlaw had developed in 1910 an impressive manual for operating the library. Typical of his love for detail, it gave instructions on almost every aspect of library management from reader registration, use of books, cataloging, and maintenance of a quiet reading room, to the specific details for separating library collections through his own system for classifying books and shelving them. He used devices like colors of ink in registering them, which surely tested the patience of his assistants. Of course, Greenlaw did not have the benefit of computers and the Library of Congress classification system.

His colleague, John Albree, became Recording Secretary in 1910, bringing a youthful spirit to a time of heavy labor for his office. The work of Francis Apthorp Foster was even more important. His appointment in 1908 as editor of the *Register*, after only one year of service as treasurer, coincided with the rapid expansion of circulation and modest profits for the journal. He also supervised the publication of vital record volumes. Henry Winchester Cunningham succeeded Tillinghast as the Society's vice president for Massachusetts in 1910 and was prominent on committees which supervised the early planning and financing of the new building. He withdrew as an active committee member when he was not elected vice president in 1912. Continued membership in the

Society thereafter kept him involved in its affairs, but he decided later not to serve on committees or bequeath any of his vast fortune to its endowment in 1930.[27]

Whatever the real cause of his anger, Cunningham shared the tension among leaders which should be expected at this time of great decisions. Baxter, Bolton, Cunningham, Albree, and Greenlaw were especially active in Society business. Contracts were let for the new building in late 1911 and early 1912, with the expectation that it could be occupied in 1913. Most meetings of the Society were then shifted to Pilgrim Hall and No. 16 Somerset was sold to the Boston Architectural Club and No. 18 to Simmons College. Books were stored in a temporary location and the editorial activities of the *Register* moved into the business offices of a member. Some lending of books to members was possible, but the library was generally closed for a six-month period beginning in the late spring of 1912. During this interruption of services, books were cleaned, rebound, and processed, and portraits were examined for wear, cleaned, and repaired.[28]

The financial operations for the Society were generally conducted by borrowing money from the Boston Safe Deposit and Trust Company. A letter of credit, or open account, provided $80,000 of ready cash, while the mortgages of Simmons College and the Architectural Club were held as long-term investments. Other investments were continued without disturbing the dividends or interest and were pledged, instead, as security for loans to finance the new building. In general the officers used available money, down payments from its recently sold properties and the redeemed pledges of donors to pay for construction. The plan was to carry a long-term debt on the new building of $44,000 and let investments pay the interest.

Since the library would have enough space for a hundred years of normal growth, Baxter and the Council hit upon the marvelous idea of leasing unused space to other patriotic and genealogical societies, such as the Daughters of the American Revolution, the Sons of the American Revolution, and the Society of Colonial Wars. Goodspeed's Book Shop agreed eventually to lease and renovate one of the Society's buildings.

The idea of using the new building as a center of patriotic activity had much appeal to Society members, who also made available to their renters the auditorium and meeting rooms.[29]

As ideas for the new building were being collected by William P. Greenlaw, the grounds were cleared by order of a special building committee composed of the President, John Albree, Charles K. Bolton, Thomas Minns, Francis Apthorp Foster, Henry W. Cunningham, Henry E. Woods, and Nathaniel J. Rust. Greenlaw had apparently interviewed librarians of neighboring institutions while gathering information on space distribution and met from time to time with interested members of the Society to solicit their suggestions. His recommendations were generally incorporated by the committee and contractor into plans for the new building.[30]

Construction began early in the spring of 1912 and the basic structure was completed by early December. Much decorating then needed to be done in 1913 and 1914, but the staff moved books into the building in December 1912. The dedication of the structure was held on March 18, 1913, the sixty-eighth anniversary of the Society's charter.

No. 9 Ashburton Place was a reinforced concrete and steel building, sitting upon sloping ground so that visitors entered at the center of the building with two stories below to the basement and auditorium and two stories above to the library and some offices. On Alston Street was a rear entrance which lead immediately to the auditorium and its spacious area for 325 seats. On the street floor there was a council chamber, a few smaller rooms for the editor and assistants of the *Register*, and the librarian. Finally, and most importantly, there was a vault forty feet long, seventeen feet wide, and twenty-one feet high. Eventually its three tiers of stacks would provide fireproof safety for the entire collection of priceless manuscripts and documents at the Society. The building had space for books, offices, and meetings, but it had space also that could be converted into a museum.[31]

Although the building was stark at first, members looked forward to the time when portraits of past presidents would be hung on the walls, and memorials, plaques, and flags would enliven the rooms. Most members approved of the Society's venture as they walked through the building. The painting of some walls disturbed a few, possibly women members, and they asked the contractor to find suitable colors and better workmen. The officers were most disturbed by the building's mounting expense. It cost the grand sum of $127,801.88, but gifts of $75,382.35 and some unpaid pledges would shrink the deficit. Still there were furniture to purchase and increased maintenance costs to anticipate, and the officers were sobered by these heavy expenses now facing the Society. Baxter would soon announce that there was still $12,000 of necessary construction expenses to pay before the building was finished.[32]

On dedication day, March 18, 1913, a capacity crowd gathered in the new Wilder Auditorium. Marshall P. Wilder's daughter and other surviving members of the family donated flowers for the occasion, and former Governor John Davis Long was the speaker for the day. Delegates from the Massachusetts Historical Society, the New Hampshire Historical Society, the American Antiquarian Society, and the Essex Institute joined representatives of fraternal and patriotic societies, Commonwealth and city officials, and distinguished members of the Society. Long gave a relatively short, but strong address. His tribute to the work of historians and genealogists warmed the hearts of many present:

> The soil is rich with the ashes of the good and great; and our tribute goes out to them the more warmly because it goes not to the few, to an illustrious warrior here or a great benefactor there, but to the whole body of those plain, sturdy, God-fearing, and self-respecting men and women, whose names and memories you are so wisely and loyally preserving, and who so raised the general level of the ordinary life of their times that any distinction among them which they made was often the accident of circumstances and any distinction which we should make would be an injustice.[33]

Music, congratulatory remarks, and refreshments ended a full afternoon that began with James Phinney Baxter calling the meeting to order at 3:00 P.M. The overflow crowd of members and visitors included a generous number of women and was probably the first of the anniversary meetings in which wives and women members together totaled over half the audience. Mrs. Nancy Jewett Bigelow, the daughter of Marshall Wilder, enjoyed the celebration, but was distressed at the condition of her father's portrait, which the family offered to have rehabilitated. It hung in a prominent place in the auditorium and his deeds in raising the first money for this new building were praised during the ceremonies.[34]

With the festivities concluded, the Council and officers immediately had to face problems of appointments and finance. Both the editor of the *Register*, Francis Apthorp Foster, and the Society's treasurer, Charles Knowles Bolton, had resigned and new appointees had assumed their duties. Several eminent members had died, including William Sanford Hills, a major donor to the new building, and Henry F. Waters, the noted genealogist.[35] Miss Mary Ellen Stickney, the assistant librarian, was leaving the Society in May 1913 to marry a reader. Transitions had often occurred, but the Council and officers were disturbed by so many key changes in such a short time. Happily the new editor of the *Register* was Henry Edwards Scott, previously assistant editor, a middle-aged man of considerable knowledge and enthusiasm.[36] Baxter was then eighty-two, still presided over most administrative meetings, but depended on Charles Edward Lord, the new treasurer, to assist with financial negotiations, and William Greenlaw to maintain library efficiency. Baxter's majority on the Council was as loyal as ever though he lost in death some of his closest friends.

Baxter was then unduly worried by Society finances. The new building cost much more to maintain than the older one—lighting, heating, and cleaning charges were taking larger slices of the budget. Almost every office of the Society had more staff than in years past, and salaries were inching higher. Annual interest on the mortgages was over two thousand dollars. Book sales of both the *Register* and vital records were lagging and inventories were growing. In 1914 Baxter recommended some ways to raise money—a membership drive, advertisements of services, and an adjustment in rents for the learned societies with space in the building. A full-page announcement to members first appeared in the January 1914 *Register*, urging all people interested in American genealogy to support the activities of the Society. It provided almost a catalogue of the Society's accomplishments for the past 69 years of its history and offered the services of its staff to members "desiring to create memorial funds by gift or bequest, the income of which shall be used to promote the objects of the Society."[37] Several times Baxter reminded the membership that a healthy society must be one with substantial endowment.

Baxter was seriously reacting to budget deficits that seemed to be mounting, to a drop in donations, to the cost of repairs on its older rented buildings, to the rise in telephone expenses, and, undoubtedly, to the depression that was affecting dues payments and publications sales. In 1914 the first World War broke out in Europe and had an immediate effect in the United States on wages and prices. The staff was denied a salary increase and a few unlucky employees were discharged as unnecessary, but wages actually rose year after year. Baxter and John Albree, the Recording Secretary, secured lists of members from other organizations and solicited membership in the Society. In a mailing of one thousand letters they secured favorable replies from forty-three individuals who were welcomed with much enthusiasm.[38]

In his report to the Annual Meeting in 1916, Baxter tried to describe what he and the Council were experiencing. Our expenses, he said, grow "like Jack's bean stalk . . . night and day, [and] are troubling your Finance Committee."[39] The worry was essentially the overhead expenses in maintaining the debt and operating the Society's headquarters. The endowment portfolio of $176,470.00 was not paying sufficient dividends or interest and the treasurer was forced to borrow money on short term notes to take care of some operating expenses. Many dedicated funds were not available for other uses.

As members researched in the library, however, they saw much progress. Holdings increased yearly with new genealogies, reference works, pamphlets, and manuscripts. Greenlaw was always alert to suggestions and tried to accept gifts that fitted into the general collection. In his report of 1915 he estimated that the library now had 78,000 books and pamphlets, not counting manuscripts and other resources on deposit at the Massachusetts Historical Society and the American Antiquarian Society. Visitors in some years were surpassing even the numbers of members. Many of those attending the monthly meetings and addresses were not members, but were drawn by outstanding speakers and programs. In January 1917, Mary Antin spoke on "The Promised Land," a story of Jewish immigrants and their adjustment to American conditions. "The young Jewish immigrant not only is very early made conversant with the history of this country, but is thoroughly awakened to the manifold opportunities that it holds out to him and as a result, becomes in a surprisingly short time one of the most ardent and patriotic of American citizens." The address attracted probably over 400 people "by far the largest [audience] of the present season, completely filling Wilder Hall and overflowing into the adjacent corridor."[40]

In March 1917 Governor Samuel W. McCall spoke briefly and a fellow worker of Alexander Graham Bell read a paper entitled "The Birth and Babyhood of the Telephone."[41] Over four hundred people came to hear Mary Boyle O'Reilly's experiences on the French war front in March 1918. Hers was not the only report of a war experience. A Canadian grenadier, "with ingenious, boyish, and direct manner," spoke of his service.[42] In April 1919 George William Tupper of Brookline used lantern slides to illustrate his thoughts about current immigration. The talk inspired much discussion, and Baxter, who was presiding, gave his views on the seriousness of so many undesirable aliens in New England and urged the audience to contact their representatives about this dangerous situation.[43]

Most of these monthly meetings, however, were joyous affairs. In December 1918, John Albree, the former Recording Secretary, spoke on "the Art of Singing in the Old Bay Colony." With him on the platform was a quartet who illustrated his major points with hymns old and new. He brought hymnals presumably for use in community singing.[44]

Since for many of these years the nation was faced with threats of, or engaged in war, these meetings often provided for the sale of Liberty

Bonds and included soldiers visiting from the war front in Europe. Frequently Baxter and others spoke on the curse of war and the justice of the Allied cause.[45]

Some of the people who crowded into Wilder Auditorium each month were seriously interested in heraldry and proudly displayed coats-of-arms in their homes, even sometimes on their carriages and automobiles. A regular committee was appointed each year to advise members on coats-of-arms, but a committee in 1898 had taken a distinctly hostile view toward any initiative the Society might adopt in ruling on the ownership of a coat-of-arms. It held that coats-of-arms originated in Europe and no one in America was competent to rule on their legitimacy. In 1913 Greenlaw urged the Committee on Heraldry, now chaired by Robert Dickson Weston, to restudy the custom of heraldry in the United States and make some practical recommendations. After months of discussion Weston and his committee finally agreed that a reversal of the 1898 policy was wise. They believed coats of arms enlivened history, increased interest in family origins, and added artistic and sentimental qualities to the past. Further they were uncertain how many coats could be authenticated, and if they were, what then was accomplished. They urged the Society to perform the function of a registry and review liberally evidence of claims for coats-of-arms. "If, for example, the first settler in this country brought with him a real piece of silver or painting displaying arms rightfully borne by a family of the same name in England, we should hold that such evidence taken by itself was amply sufficient to make a good *prima facie* case of descent from some unidentified member of that family."[46]

The committee hinted that it liked the use of coats-of-arms, but wanted members to realize that coats were a human creation and should be treated in like manner. In short, there was nothing divine, nothing truly noble about the origins of most, but something beautiful, something exciting about their use. Weston believed the Society was undoubtedly acting within its charter authority in stimulating this practice, but it wanted simply, "to put the whole business [of ruling on the legitimacy of coats] on a basis of reason and common sense."[47]

Baxter agreed with Weston, but he was fully aware that many members were sensitive about their right to use coats-of-arms and were alarmed when others, without much justification, attributed arms to their families. He did not speak out for or against the wide use of arms, but he liked collecting old watches and Indian pottery, books, and manuscripts and appreciated the attraction of the old and ancient to Society members.[48] These trinkets had similar qualities to coats-of-arms—they touched the past and gave it excitement and reality.

"The venerable president," as he was now described, presided for the final time over a monthly meeting in May 1920, a few weeks past his eighty-ninth birthday. Hearty as ever, he next spoke at a commemorative meeting in Portland, Maine, and met regularly with his large family during the summer. In the fall he became ill, but in February 1921 he was reelected president by a very large vote. Though he was unable to attend the Annual Meeting, the members extended their best wishes for his recovery. His failing health for some years had kept him for long periods away from Boston, and during those absences he was represented by John Carroll Chase, Society Vice President for Massachusetts since 1917. Over the years Chase was chairman of the Library Committee and the Special Committee on Endowment and Members. He had much charm as a leader.[49]

In 1918 Baxter, Chase, and the Council created a new type of membership for the Society in celebration of the 300th anniversary of the Pilgrims' landing at Plymouth. Members would pay three hundred dollars for this special membership and be able to leave it to an heir. Never in the history of the Society was a fund-raising idea so popular. Baxter and Chase found in it a golden method to develop an endowment and ease the financial strains of the Society.

Baxter's twenty years as president ended with his death in May 1921.[50] Although ninety years old, he remained a forceful, yet modest, businessman-scholar whom age treated gently even into his last year. His death in Portland, Maine, amid his large family brought many tributes of respect from his adopted genealogical community—who realized that one of his greatest achievements was the transformation of the New England Historic Genealogical Society into a major research institution.[51]

Notes

[1] Alfred Johnson, "Hon. James Phinney Baxter," *Register*, 75 (1921): 163-175; Myron Samuel Dudley, "Memoir of the Reverend Edward Griffin Porter," *Register*, 55 (1902): 11-19; Deloraine Pendre Corey, "John Ward Dean," *Register*, 56 (1902): 223-235.

[2] Johnson, "James P. Baxter," *Register*, 75 (1921): 163-175.

[3] *Proceedings of the NEHGS, Annual Meeting 1901* (Boston, 1901): Baxter's Report, ix-xi. Supplement for April 1901 *Register*.

[4] Baxter did not complete his family genealogy, but accumulated much information on his children and their wives and careers. See Baxter, "The Baxters of New England, A Family History," 1921, NEHGS. Johnson, "James P. Baxter," *Register*, 75 (1921): 172-175.

[5] Edward S. Sears, "Caleb Benjamin Tillinghast," *Register*, 64 (1910): 3-6; Records of Council, III, 17, May 1, 1901, MSS.

[6] *Proceedings of the NEHGS, Annual Meeting 1902* (Boston, 1902): Baxter's Report, xi-xii. Supplement for April 1902 *Register*. Tillinghast (or Baxter) was undoubtedly responsible for changing the subscription policy of the *Register*. Until 1903 one could be a member of the Society without being a subscriber. Dues were raised from three to five dollars and all were then supplied with copies. The press run of the *Register* was increased to 1500.

[7] *Proceedings of the NEHGS, Annual Meeting 1903* (Boston, 1903), Baxter's Report, x. Supplement for April 1903 *Register*.

[8] Records of the Council, V (1915-1920): 54, January 3, 1917, MSS.

[9] Ethel Stanwood Bolton, "Inscriptions from the Cemetery at Shirley Centre, from 1754-1850," *Register*, 57 (1903): 68-75, 200-207.

[10] *Proceedings of the NEHGS, Annual Meeting 1903* (Boston, 1903): Report of the Committee on Epitaphs, xxiv. Supplement for the April 1903 *Register*.

[11] George Kuhn Clarke, "Baptisms Recorded by the Ministers of the First Church in Needham, 1720-1821," *Register*, 57 (1903): 21-30, 141-153, 252-263, 370-381; see George K. Clarke, "Needham Marriages," *Register*, 56 (1902): 30-39; "Deaths Recorded . . . Needham," 265-270.

[12] Records of the Council: III, 57 (December 3, 1902): 66 (March 4, 1903): 144. (February 1, 1905), MSS. See *Proceedings of the NEHGS, Annual Meeting 1905* (Boston, 1905): xii. Supplement for the April 1905 *Register*.

[13] *Proceedings of the NEHGS, Annual Meeting 1904* (Boston, 1904): xxii. Supplement for the April 1904 *Register*. See presidential report in this supplement, ix-xiv.

[14] Florence Conant Howes, "William Prescott Greenlaw," *Register*, 100 (1946): 81-84.

[15] *Proceedings of the NEHGS, Annual Meeting 1904* (Boston, 1904): ix-x. Supplement for the April 1904 *Register*.

[16] Ibid., pp. xxvi-xxvii.

[17] Ibid., p. xxvii.

[18] *Proceedings of the NEHGS, Annual Report 1904* (Boston, 1904): Baxter's Address, ix, xiv; Council Report, xix. Supplement for the April 1904 *Register*. One of the crucial problems of the library was the number of city directories given annually.

[19] The Society had already purchased No. 16 Somerset Street for $30,000, Nos. 3 and 4 Allston Place for $14,000, and No. 7 Allston Place for $8,000. Records of Council, III: 90 (December 15, 1903), MSS. A map is enclosed showing plans to buy other lots in the same area. Resolutions were passed in Council, III, 90, December 15, 1903 and III: 127 (November 2, 1904), MSS.

[20] The architect's report was published in the *Proceedings of the NEHGS, Annual Report 1906* (Boston, 1906): xx-xxii. Supplement for the April 1906 *Register*. The architect did not pronounce the building unusable, but thought a minimum of $15,000 would be necessary for a new roof, electrical insulation, and replacement of wooden bookcases.

[21] See end pages of *Register*, 61 (1907): iii. The advertisement ended with the following advisory: "The Treasurer, Nathaniel C. Nash . . . and all other officers of the Society, will be glad to advise persons intending to give or bequeath money to the Society."

[22] The Appeal was part of the end papers of the *Register*, 65 (1911). The message of the appeal is stated thus: "A modern, fireproof building with metal fittings is needed *at once*."

[23] Proceedings, X (1905-1914): 207 (February 1, 1911), MSS. She spoke about one hour. Mrs. Anna D. Hallowell of West Medford, in 1900, was the first woman to address the Society.

[24] Proceedings, X (1905-1914): 247-249 (October 2, 1912), MSS. Gordon was Recording Secretary for seventeen years. He was born in Dover, New Hampshire, in 1827 and died in Somerville, Massachusetts, on May 5, 1912. See *Register*, 67 (1913): 85-86.

[25] Marquis Fayette Dickinson, "George Sumner Mann," *Register*, 64 (1910): 103-105. Although he left a large estate, most of his money went to other institutions. The Society received $2,000.

[26] Lewis Wilder Hicks, "Frank Ernest Woodward," *Register*, 75 (1921): 243-246.

[27] Henry Edwards Scott, "Henry Winchester Cunningham," *Register*, 85 (1931): 243-246. His anger endured for many years. In his will MHS received $50,000, the American Antiquarian Society $100,000, and other beneficiaries included hospitals, educational institutions, and the Animal Rescue League.

[28] Records of Council, IV (1909-1915): 116-118, 125-138; (March 6, April 3, May 1, 1912), MSS.

[29] Records of Council, IV (1909-1915): 96-97, December 6, 1911, MSS. Baxter and his colleagues voted that the Society's "building be recognized as a headquarters for historical, patriotic, and kindred societies."

[30] *Proceedings of the NEHGS, Annual Report 1913* (Boston, 1913): Report of the Council, xvi-xvii. Supplement for the April 1913 *Register.*

[31] *Proceedings of the NEHGS, Annual Report 1912* (Boston, 1912): Report of the Council, xxxii. Supplement for the April 1912 *Register.*

[32] Records of Council, IV (1909-1915): 191-198, (March 5 and March 18, 1913), MSS.

[33] *Proceedings of the NEHGS, Annual Report 1914* (Boston, 1914): exercises at the Dedication, xlviii-liii. Supplement for the April 1914 *Register.*

[34] Records of Council, IV (1909-1915): 197-198 (March 5 and March 18, 1913), MSS.

[35] Thomas Barnes Hitchcock, "William Sanford Hills," *Register*, 68 (1914): 308-309.

[36] Henry Edwards Scott (1856-1944) served as editor until 1937 and held for long periods posts as Corresponding Secretary and Recording Secretary. He was a linguist and faculty member at several colleges.

[37] The advertisement appeared several times in 1914, often as end papers. *Register*, 68 (1914).

[38] Baxter reported a budget deficit of $5,000 in 1914 and urged that an enlarged committee of ways and means be appointed to consider this crisis. See Records of Council, IV (1909-1915): 337 (February 20, 1914), MSS.

[39] *Proceedings of the NEHGS, Annual Report 1916* (Boston, 1916): xi. Supplement for the April 1916 *Register.* Baxter wanted members to ask their friends to join the Society.

[40] Alfred Johnson, "Proceedings of the New England Historic Genealogical Society," *Register*, 71 (1917): 187.

[41] Ibid.

[42] Proceedings, 11 (1915-1928): 83 (March 6, 1918), MSS.

[43] Ibid., pp. 105-106, April 2, 1919.

[44] Ibid., pp. 91-92, December 4, 1918.

[45] Ibid., pp. 85-86, May 1, 1918.

[46] *Proceedings of the NEHGS, Annual Report 1898* (Boston, 1898): 20. Supplement for the April 1898 *Register.* Ibid., *1915* (Boston, 1915): xvi-xxii. Ibid., *1917* (Boston, 1917): xix. The Chairman anticipated in 1917 that "the number of coats-of-arms recorded will be at least double during the coming years."

[47] *Proceedings of the NEHGS, Annual Report 1915* (Boston, 1915): xxi. Supplement for the April 1915 *Register.*

[48] Baxter, will of 1919, on file NEHGS.

[49] Robert Lincoln O'Brien, "John Carroll Chase," *Register*, 40 (1936): 211-225.

[50] *The Boston Evening Transcript*, May 8, 1921, p. 5. The obituary noted that Baxter was author of "many poems distinguished by a vein of mysticism and imagery. Since he was twelve years of age, he also followed a reading course that included most writers of 19th Century fiction and many of Shakespeare's plays. In later life he enjoyed painting as a hobby."

[51] Baxter was memorialized by his son, Governor Percival P. Baxter, in 1925, in an appreciative biography (*James Phinney Baxter: Historian*): "To have his children about him, to read and talk to them was his delight. Though occupied with business, politics and literary work, he never neglected his boys and girls. He, with my mother, two sisters and myself made three trips together to Europe, on one of which we remained there more than a year while we children attended school in London. He and I went on many journeys and voyages together. It was all a part of our education. He always rejoiced to get safely back home and often remarked, "the home is the foundation of happiness. I am sorry for those without one."

(Marshall P.) Wilder Hall at 9 Ashburton Place, sixth home of the Society, 1912-1964 (picture dated 1914).

The John Foster Memorial Council Room at 9 Ashburton Place, named and donated in memory of John Foster (1817-1897), a Society director (1871-1889) and philanthropist. Foster's portrait, by Frederick Porter Vinton (1846-1911), is at right.

Stair hall at 9 Ashburton Place, showing memorials to *Mayflower* passenger
Mrs. Susannah (___, not Fuller, as per the tablet) White, later Winslow (bottom
right); Thomas Munson and Richard Lyman (top center); Captain Thomas
Leigh, Humphrey Chadbourne, and Edwin Leigh (bottom center); Rev.
Samuel Fish and his son Rev. Henry Clay Fish (top left); and Roger Williams
and his wife Mary Barnard, and Thomas Angell and his wife Mary Ashton
(bottom left). The second, third, and fourth of these plaques were dated 1922,
1920, and 1921 respectively.

Another view of the stair hall at 9 Ashburton Place. The Leigh-Chadbourne, Fish and Williams-Angell memorials are on the right of the landing. On the left are plaques honoring Edward Converse and John Cogswell (facing banister); Barnard, Joan and Captain John Capen (top, facing stairs down, dated 1920); and Edward Sturgis and Samuel, Sarah and Governor Thomas Hinckley (bottom, facing stairs down, dated 1921).

Bronze bas-relief of President
Abraham Lincoln, sculpted by
Frederick W. Allen and given to the
Society by Robert Todd Lincoln, the
President's son, in 1922 (sold in 1989).

Part of the Atkinson-Lancaster collection — Bombay side table and arm chairs, Chinese bronzes, Florentine pictures (including a nineteenth-century copy of the head of Beatrice Cenci, 1577-1599, by Guido Reni), and pier glasses — as displayed in the Atkinson-Lancaster Museum at 9 Ashburton Place (from the *Register* 89[1935]:opposite p. 50).

James Phinney Baxter (1831-1921), 12th President of the
Society, 1901-1921.

John Carroll Chase (1849-1936), 13th President of the
Society, 1921-1936.

William Prescott Greenlaw (1863-1945), Librarian of the Society, 1902-1929 (assistant librarian from 1894, assistant treasurer 1918-1945), for whom the main building at 9 Ashburton Place was named in 1944.

The Robert Henry Eddy Memorial Rooms at 9 Ashburton Place, with *Register* editor Henry Edwards Scott (1859-1944) and, at back desk, assistant editor Florence Conant Howes (1875-1958), later curator of the Atkinson-Lancaster Museum. In the foreground is Mabel Chapin of the staff (picture dated 1913).

Librarians Diana Benson Small (left), Edith Eliza Hazelton (center), and Mildred Evelyn Leavitt (right) beneath portraits of Dr. Noah Martin (1801-1863, left, Society vice president from N.H., 1855-59), William Whiting (1813-1873, center, third President of the Society, 1853-1858), and librarian and *Register* editor John Ward Dean (1815-1902, right) (picture dated November 1959).

Library scene, 1960, at 9 Ashburton Place (third floor, north side).

Revering Our Heritage

Through his whole life James Phinney Baxter revered New England's Pilgrim and Puritan ancestry, which he shared and loved, in his writings and speeches. "Never in the history of any country," he said, "has so remarkable a body of men . . . been so providentially brought together to build a nation; . . . history makes evident the fact that the spirit of New England is the true Americanism which is today the spirit of the nation, for it has been aptly said . . . that God sifted the best seed of Old England for planting New England."[1]

Baxter proposed the erection of a Temple of Honor during an address given on March 18, 1920, at the celebration of the seventy-fifth anniversary of the Society—a temple, he emphasized, "to commemorate [the deeds of the Pilgrims] . . . on this tercentenary of the landing at Plymouth." "You will agree that such a structure should be of imposing character, emphasizing the worthiest expression of strength, dignity, and simplicity; that it should be built of material from New England quarries, wrought by the hands of New England people, and adorned by the skill of New England artists; and that upon its walls should be pictorially recorded the chief events in New England history—the landing at Plymouth, at Cape Ann, at Salem, at Boston, the genesis of Rhode Island, Vermont, New Hampshire, Connecticut, and Maine." The building should be not only a memorial to benefactors of the past, but also a monument to the skill and artistry of New Englanders in the twentieth century.

To underscore his feelings of patriotism, Baxter bequeathed in 1921 fifty thousand dollars to the City of Boston in the expectation that the gift would multiply over the years and the city would sometime before 2025 have one million dollars to erect a suitable building. Otherwise, if the city were unwilling to undertake his project, he bequeathed the money to Portland, Maine, where parks, charitable and educational foundations, and humane institutions would be the beneficiaries.[2] His breathtaking vision of a monument to the New England founders still awaits materialization by Boston or the help of federal courts to be realized.

The tercentenary of the Pilgrim landing inspired the creation of a membership in the Society which would eventually draw 533 individuals. Each donated $300 apiece to become a Pilgrim Tercentenary Member. The opportunity was available from February 5, 1919 to January 1, 1921. In that period $168,300 was given to the Society in payment for these memberships, while $41,194.74 was also received from new life members. Total membership, including honorary, residential, corresponding, life, and Pilgrim Tercentenary, had now reached 1847.[3] The power upon the mind of New Englanders of the *Mayflower* passage, the founding of Plymouth Colony, and the ceremony of Thanksgiving is well illustrated by the popularity of tercentenary memberships. John C. Chase summarized this tribute to the Society in these revealing words:

> It is believed that there can be no more fitting or useful memorial to the Pilgrims than the continued maintenance of the work of the Society.[4]

Chase was undoubtedly thinking of the massive genealogical library that housed hundreds of family histories of *Mayflower* descendants. The almost endless research both in England and America concerning *Mayflower* descendants inspired librarian William Prescott Greenlaw to recommend "a complete and comprehensive guide to genealogical data in print," an updating of the Durrie-Munsell indexes that "are very incomplete."[5]

Family history research was indeed popular after the war. Greenlaw reported in 1923 that visitors to the library had reached 355. Many genealogists almost made the Society their headquarters. *Register* articles by G. Andrews Moriarty, Jr., a Society Vice President for Rhode

Island, on English ancestors of colonial immigrants were making an impression of the kind created by Henry F. Waters in the 1890s. Gilbert H. Doane of Fairfield, Vermont and Tucson, Arizona, a young genealogist in search of a job (somewhat later he became a librarian and bibliographer and capped his career as editor of the *Register*) was occasionally in the library. Donald Lines Jacobus, who worked mostly in Connecticut, also contributed to the *Register* and was occasionally in Boston. By critics he is regarded as "America's foremost exponent of scientific genealogy," the leader of many scholars who wrote for *The American Genealogist* (*TAG*), which he founded in 1922. But none of these men resided as long in Boston as Clarence Almon Torrey, a retired school principal and librarian of the University of Chicago, and a successful corporate investor, who moved to the city in 1921. His "careful, and even meticulous" listing, with references, of over 37,000 "New England Marriages Prior to 1700," has become a monument to his memory.[6] As with Torrey the presence of George Ernest Bowman was also important for research. He developed during these years a biographical listing of all known descendants of *Mayflower* passengers into some 20,600 pages of documents. The Society was, in short, becoming an important center of research—but even more a place for professional genealogists to work and gather. For others it was regarded almost as a shrine.

Along the halls of the Society's headquarters were portraits of past leaders, memorial tablets, glass cases of trinkets, coins, miniatures, and signed letters of George Washington, John Hancock, and Henry Knox, and many, many examples of rare books of law and history. Members were opposed to the creation of a museum, but they liked to see the display of period furniture and old portraits. Most historic maps were deposited in the American Antiquarian Society, almost all of the Henry Knox papers were lent to the Massachusetts Historical Society, and a small collection of theater programs was given to Harvard College. Members wanted, like Baxter, to line library halls with portraits of heroes and patriots and to be reminded of American national greatness.

Baxter's death in 1921 brought an easy succession to the presidency of the Society, though Baxter, even at age ninety, was missed as a man of rare nobility and scholarship. His successor was John Carroll Chase, who had been frequently acting moderator in his place and was unanimously elected as president in late 1921. Chase would continue Baxter's spirited direction of the Society for the coming fifteen years. Though seventy-two when he became president, Chase was still unusually active in business as president and treasurer of the Benjamin Chase Company, a wood processing firm in Derry, New Hampshire. Interest in genealogy drew him into the Society in 1899; he was a vice president from 1912. He had traced his family to Aquila Chase, who immigrated to Hampton in 1640 and became, he proudly wrote, one of the first mariners of Hampton and the northern area of Massachusetts Bay. In 1924, Chase placed on the stair hall of the Society a commemorative tablet of a ship in full sail dedicated to Aquila.[7]

Chase spent most of his professional life as a civil engineer. He was educated at the Massachusetts Institute of Technology; engineering projects took him to various parts of New England, to New York City, and to Wilmington, North Carolina, where he spent fifteen years as an engineer at the Clarendon Water Works. In 1897, he accepted an offer of his aging uncle to become manager and treasurer of the family business in Derry, New Hampshire. A decade later he succeeded to the company's presidency and remained at its helm until his death in 1936.[8]

Possessing the qualities of a Southern gentleman in his soft accented speech and in deference towards others, he was generally admired. He collected statistics and information as a hobby and was, as a biographer wrote, "one of the most comprehensively informed men I have ever seen . . . nothing that pertained to humanity was foreign to him." An exaggeration, perhaps, but he was widely considered an authority and his opinions were sought by associates.

Like Baxter he had business obligations outside of Boston and was frequently absent from the Society. His residences near Boston were in Wellesley until 1930 and in Brookline later, but his principal home was in Derry, New Hampshire. Almost every summer he traveled in the western United States, met with suppliers of wood products, visited with his daughter in Coronado, California, and enjoyed the luxury of the open spaces in the West. Only in 1932 did he journey to Europe on an extensive vacation. His second wife, Florence Anne Buchanan Ogilvy, had genealogical interests when he married her in 1928, and Alice, one of his two daughters, and her husband, Samuel Prescott, were members of the Society. Samuel was a faculty dean for a time at the Massachusetts Institute of Technology.

Again like Baxter, Chase was interested in monuments to his New England forebears. His tribute on the Society stair hall to Aquila Chase was no emotional whim. His major genealogy on the Chase family, published with the assistance of George Walter Chamberlain in 1928, was followed with other published research on family branches in the *Register* and a short history of the Society in 1935. His regard for the Society approached the sacred as years passed. He cited its library, its cultural treasures, and its facilities for research as creating an interest in family history that was "spreading over the whole country."[9]

While Chase was the head of a devoted group of leaders, he would have been the first to share credit for directing the Society with Henry Edwards Scott, the Recording Secretary and editor of the *Register*, William Prescott Greenlaw, the venerable librarian, vice presidents like G. Andrews Moriarity, Albert H. Lamson, and Alfred Johnson, and a council composed in part of Florence Conant Howes, James M. Hunnewell (also the Treasurer), and Robert D. Weston. Many of these officers had already served several decades, and Chase himself was pleased that he was surrounded by devoted, loyal, and experienced people. On the thirteen committees were equally experienced members who gave their time gratuitously to important Society matters.

Age was always the foe of leadership, because officers were frequently elderly. Except for Edward G. Porter, who died unexpectedly, most presidents entered office after a career in business, the ministry, or law and flourished into their late eighties. So too did officials and committee members. President Wilder in the 1870s and 1880s had a curious habit of averaging the ages of the deceased members of the Society when he reported deaths at annual meetings.[10] Members lived not only a long time, but they also contributed much to the history and culture of the nation in their later lives. The Society historian in the 1920s was still publishing obituary notices so that deeds of important members could be a record of the New England heritage. In 1927 one hundred thirteen memoirs, covering over ninety pages, were published in the *Register* and Annual Proceedings of the Society. These memoirs detailed careers of recently deceased members in business, education, politics, and the church.[11]

In May 1922 Chase and his colleagues assembled in Wilder Auditorium to pay tribute to an immortal of the nation, Abraham Lincoln. Robert Todd Lincoln, his son, had commissioned Frederick W. Allen, the noted sculptor, to undertake a bronze bas-relief of the late president for the Society. Lincoln was regarded as one of New England's own, whose family had migrated from Hingham to the frontiers of Pennsylvania, Virginia, and Kentucky. The tablet was to be placed in the stairway hall of the building, where everyone who entered the library was reminded of Lincoln's contributions to the nation. The hall would also become in future years a place to commemorate the deeds of the nation's other heroes. Already thirty tablets were affixed to the walls, but some fifty more were planned. The deeds of John Alden, the Mathers, Thomas Dudley, Anne and Simon Bradstreet, and Roger Williams, among others, were celebrated along this hallway of fame; no memorial was as impressive, however, as the Lincoln tablet.[12]

The ceremony of May 31 brought together former President Charles W. Eliot of Harvard College, Charles E. Park, minister of the First Church in Boston, and several hundred visitors. Robert D. Weston, the well known chairman of the Heraldry Committee, was in charge of a long, impressive program which ended happily with refreshments in the late afternoon. Chase, in the course of the ceremonies, introduced the speaker of the day by reminding the audience that they were following the national dedication of the Lincoln Memorial in Washington, D.C., with a New England dedication by means of a noble portrait "in this Historic Genealogical Hall of Fame."[13]

No one could escape the patriotic feeling of this occasion, as Dr. Charles Edwards Park spoke, with impressive voice and gestures, and enchanted his audience with descriptions of the martyred Lincoln. While the Society had often chosen world and national figures for honorary memberships, they were usually alive. It conferred honors upon James, Viscount Bryce in 1890 and Warren Gamaliel Harding in 1921, only to lose both in death in 1923. The past roll of honor included Daniel Webster, Henry Clay, Millard Fillmore, Louis Adolphe Thiers, Ulysses Simpson Grant, Chester A. Arthur, and William Ewart Gladstone, among others. More recently King Albert of the Belgians, Calvin Coolidge, Thomas Woodrow Wilson, Charles William Eliot, Herbert Clark Hoover, and Henry Cabot Lodge were chosen. For ordinary mortals the Society created in 1918 the Pilgrim Tercentenary Memberships and a right of succession which was claimed with extraordinary zeal when the original holder died. Names of these members were inscribed on tablets. In 1927, another class of life members was created which attracted in 1928 and 1929 a rush of candidates who wished to be enrolled as new Colonial Members.

Over these years to 1941 Chase, the Council, and their successors did everything they could to give members opportunities to use the Society to immortalize their families and promote genealogy. At the sesquicentennial of American Independence (1926) the Society used gifts to pay off the mortgage of $44,000 and gave members an opportunity to donate additional furniture, chairs, and tables (purchases that were deferred when the costly building was constructed in 1912). But the leadership was ever alert to find more ways to satisfy these patriotic instincts and improve the facilities at the same time. Nearly every room in the building over the years was named for a donor, many of whom bequeathed their historical libraries, handwritten notes of their research, and modest surpluses of unsold books on their families.[14]

One of these donors was Seymour Morris of Chicago, who bequeathed a massive collection of books, mostly genealogical, to the Society in 1931. At first there appeared to be many duplicates. But on opening the packing boxes, the staff found many more books and pamphlets than they had anticipated, some of fine binding and many in better condition than similar editions in the Society's stacks. The total gift—6,403 items in 267 boxes—was worth an astonishing $39,923. The Morris gift understandably brought great cheers from librarians Josephine Rayne and William Greenlaw. At their recommendation, the beautiful reading room (which had been awaiting a name) was now declared by the Council to be the Seymour Morris Reading Room. Morris's portrait was soon appropriately hung on the wall, to join those of earlier benefactors of the Society.[15]

In another important room of the Ashburton building were the impressive gifts of Council table and chairs. The table was extra long in size and black in color, with many fine leather cushioned chairs around it, fittingly solid and large enough to accommodate the councilors. The room was named in 1912 for John Foster, an early director, whose daughter Fanny doubled her father's gift of $5000 and secured this memorial in his name. At her death in 1934, she gave an additional $5000 and a portrait of her father.[16]

Many of these gifts of chairs, portraits, and plaques were admittedly modest, but when joined with regular monthly gifts of books, pamphlets, and miscellaneous items, they became a remarkable number of yearly donations. In May 1931, at the last meeting before the regular summer recess, only twenty-nine books were given, but at the October and the November meetings 195 and 246 books, respectively, were reported—and appreciation extended.[17] The problem, however, throughout the 1920s and 1930s, was the paucity of monetary gifts. Only two or three donations reached five thousand dollars, a few more the thousand dollar level. Members preferred instead to buy life memberships, colonial memberships, or annual memberships for themselves and friends. These living memorials increased the membership roll to over three thousand, but lacked the substantial size of a bequest.

The most significant gift of these two decades occurred in 1934 when the Society was amazed by the Atkinson-Lancaster bequest, a generous gift of furniture, carpets, portraits, shawls, fans, vases, dishes, and a piano which had belonged to Lizzie Daniel Rose Atkinson, M.D., of Newburyport, Massachusetts, and Calcutta, India. The furniture was finely carved in mahogany and rosewood, and had been part of her family treasures for a century. Her will provided about $67,000 in securities, a gasoline station, and rental properties.[18] The return from investment was sufficient to employ a librarian or curator and hold a series of monthly lectures or exhibitions. The Society was responsible for providing space for a museum and administering the fund. The only proper space in the building for the museum had been rented to Good-speed's Book Shop as a storage area, but it was now retrieved to make room for the new museum. Mrs. Florence Conant Howes, an assistant librarian, was named curator.[19] A charming, talented woman of un-usual energy and imagination, she immediately prepared the room, unboxed the furniture, and announced a formal opening ceremony. The room had good height, a balcony, stairway, and space. It had only a few windows which permitted wall space for carpet hangings and portraits. Newly installed electric lights helped to enhance the beauty of the art objects.

One floor away was the Wilder Auditorium and adjacent to the museum was the John Foster council room. Both could be used for unusually large gatherings for programs—when crowds were attracted by display changes in the Atkinson-Lancaster room, visiting exhibitions of handiwork like shawls, embroidery, and period clothing, and the presentation of lectures on architecture, colonial music, furniture, and New England travel. Since Dr. Atkinson lived in Calcutta during the years of her youth, Indian culture was often the theme of programs. The collection represented five generations of family collecting on India and was shown in many arrangements, but always as a family heirloom, which often touched the sentimentality of genealogists.[20]

Mrs. Howes' many programs were scheduled to avoid interference with other Society events. Sometimes in the forenoon on Tuesdays fifteen or twenty men and women met in workshops with experts. In the *Morning Globe* of September 18, 1938 a series of programs was listed which proved to be popular. The first session, on "silhouettes," dis-played 7000 items from a collection of these artistic creations owned by the Rev. Glenn Tilley Morse of West Newbury. Then, Heirlooms of Orleans; Changing Fashions of Women's Dress; Bags, Parasols, Fans, and Collars; Jewelry and the Craft of Movement; and Oriental Rugs filled part of the remaining program. These Tuesday lectures were subscribed by patrons and held in the combined quarters of the museum and council chamber. The names of subscribers, one might add, were given equal space in newspaper reports with announcements of the speakers.[21]

The Society continued to hold through the years its own monthly lectures. The topics were not much different from those of past decades, but many speakers were features in the society columns of Boston newspapers. In May 1934, Stephen Vincent Benét lectured on "How to Read Poetry," when Marion Lyndon, a writer for the *Boston Herald*, attended the event. Lyndon described the dresses and hats of the women in the audience as "leaning strongly toward flowers and feather trimming, a vogue heralded by all fashion bulletins and dear to many feminine hearts who have suffered tortures of repression during the past era of hats adorned with no more than ascetic band of ribbon."[22]

Benét did not disappoint his overflowing audience of nearly 400 listeners. Vice President James Parker Parmenter presided, but Mrs. Roland Gage Hopkins, who presented the speaker, was described as "charming in a smart print of black with small daisies in capuchin colors and a wide black hat trimmed with daisies of the same colors." Benét, with grace and humor, read a variety of poetry, but observed, "Poetry will never become one of our major industries, but better verse and more of it is being written and printed in our country now than was the case twenty years ago."[23]

Many of these monthly meetings were described by Pauline Warren of the *Boston Herald* and Margaret Ickes of *The Boston Evening Transcript*, often in language that made readers envy the style of clothing and the beauty of the gathering. Mrs. John Edward Kincaid of the Society's hospitality committee gathered social figures from Boston and neighboring towns, and they, pouring tea from a fine silver service, were cited as examples of attractively dressed Boston fashion leaders.

When the great scholar George Lyman Kittredge spoke on "Witchcraft" in February 1938, two dozen roses, three bunches of sweet peas, and some laurel and baby breath fern adorned the serving tables. Pauline Warren of the *Boston Herald* listed the names of the servers as Carle Read Haywood of Quincy, Mrs. William Crowninshield Endicott of Boston, Mrs. Harry Farlane Percival of Fitchburg, and Alice Thorndike.[24] Miss Thorndike was often asked to pour, but her social engagements in Bermuda, New York, and in the city took her frequently to other events. One may add that Professor Kittredge's address was nearly ignored as newspaper space was given instead to the local social figures who "graced the event with their presence."

The newspapers carried the names of many Society leaders as events one after another were held in Wilder Auditorium or moved to town locations like the Club of Odd Volumes, No. 17 Mt. Vernon Street. President Chase and his wife had fine newspaper coverage, with portraits which revealed a distinguished and eminently photogenic couple. In 1937, his successor, Frederick S. Whitwell and his wife, were given similar coverage in a story of Society events held in the library.[25]

Clearly in the 1930s the Society received much publicity in Boston newspapers. A group of social reporters, especially Marion Lyndon and Pauline Warren, found the artistic gatherings newsworthy events. These programs were a change from political events to costume affairs, artistic displays, and societal teas that drew the elite of Boston. Harvard University professors were frequent speakers, as were museum directors and curators. Members liked illustrated lectures, dances, music, slides, and art objects. Even Samuel Eliot Morison, the well known professor of early American history at Harvard University, brought slides when he spoke on the "Founding of Harvard College." Little genealogy, however, was featured in these monthly lectures, although G. Andrews Moriarty spoke once or twice before sizable audiences.[26]

The decision to publicize Society functions was obviously a conscious one by John C. Chase and his advisors. The exciting events surrounding the Atkinson-Lancaster Museum were remarkable additions to the interesting things taking place in the Society's building. Winifred Kincaid (Mrs. John Edward) of Cambridge was the Chairman of Hospitality between 1935 and 1939 and personally chose the pourers of tea and coffee for these events. The widow of a shoe manufacturer, she was active in the Republican Party Club of Boston and in genealogy. Long after advanced age had curtailed her activities, she was seen in the library working on her family genealogy.[27]

These community-inspired events disguised the internal conditions of the organization, but left a major favorable impression upon visitors. Chase lived until 1936, enjoying robust health until a few months before his death. A rather serious person, he provided very little excitement to the Society and relied heavily on Greenlaw, Parmenter, and Scott. They were all good officers but never pushed Chase into an active program of his own. Greenlaw served until 1929 as librarian and many years before and afterwards as assistant treasurer. Restless and talkative about the inflexible budget, he favored salary raises for the staff, expansion of the library, and various kinds of memberships to attract new money.[28] He remained impressed over the years by the success of the Pilgrim Tercentenary memberships of 1919 and 1920 and proposed to duplicate this success with a tercentenary membership for Boston in 1930 and a sesquicentennial membership for the United States Constitution in 1937. In 1938, moreover, he suggested fellowships at $10,000 for wealthy persons.

Colonial membership did attract many people, but was no substitute for a fund drive. Greenlaw sent hundreds of letters as part of one membership drive and asked associates to enlist the help of friends in getting applications in the hands of prospective members. Almost every month as a result many new people joined the Society. The statistics are extraordinary:[29]

	Annual	*Colonial*
May 7, 1930	67	10
October 1, 1930	26	28
November 5, 1930	63	5
December 3, 1930	37	3
March 4, 1931	30	0

Annual dues from these memberships rose steadily in the 1920s; by 1929 the estimated revenue was well over twelve thousand dollars. The problem of keeping dues up-to-date needed constant attention, but the attraction of Society programs, book lending privileges, and the enrichment of the library collection were well regarded by most members. Herbert C. Hoover, James Truslow Adams, and Ray Lyman Wilbur accepted honorary memberships. And the Committee on Heraldry, still chaired by Robert Dickson Weston, pronounced on the authenticity of coats-of-arms. His fine artistry and good humor added substantially to the committee's influence.[30]

The Society was still regarded as a patriotic body. It became as well a collection center for books on New England families. Every month the librarian reported gifts of many new books. Frequently more than half of them Greenlaw classified as genealogies. Members gave their family research, Bible records, letters from kinsmen, and cemetery inscriptions. Donations like these continued month after month in both the 1920s and 1930s. The librarian felt restrictions on space as a result and took steps to move city directories to another building and sell items in the general collection that seemed to be surplus. The Harvard Business School was asked to accept, on deposit, manuscript papers associated with the family of John Hancock. Greenlaw, who had resigned as librarian in 1929 but remained as assistant treasurer, agitated for a new building program to house these acquisitions. Sometime within the coming decade, into the 1940s, he said, funds should be available for a major addition. He suggested that 1945, the one hundredth anniversary of the Society, be set as the completion date for the building. Few members took his recommendation seriously, but many continued to give books and manuscripts.[31]

On the building, however, the Society had paid the remainder of its mortgage in 1928 when it received an unusually large bequest from Charles Deering. The original $44,000 mortgage had been carried into the 1920s, but gifts had helped reduce the amount to $25,000 by 1928.[32] In the meantime, the Society held mortgages on Numbers 16 and 18 Somerset Street from the Boston Architectural Club and Simmons College, respectively. The interest from these bonds was used over the years to take care of the society's own debt. After the Deering bequest that interest was added to the general funds of the Society. During these years James Melville Hunnewell was the treasurer, assisted by William P. Greenlaw when Hunnewell was busy. Hunnewell was a member of the Massachusetts House of Representatives and active in Boston religious, legal, and fraternal societies. Greenlaw usually prepared annual budgets and regularly monitored expenditures. He liked to raise salaries by small amounts, estimate expenditures on the *Register*, and calculate revenue from subscriptions. Greenlaw was a busy little man, impressive as a reservoir of knowledge and influential in a Council which relied on his advice. Ever ready to speak up in discussions, he was invited to sit on the Council when he left the post of librarian and was always more visible than Hunnewell, who was treasurer from 1921 to 1943. Both men liked railroads and utility stocks as they planned the Society's portfolio. Neither man felt the growing crisis in the stock market as they bought stocks of the Chesapeake and Ohio, Santa Fe, Union Pacific, Southern Pacific, and Lake Shore and Michigan Southern Railroads. As late as 1931 they were buying shares of the United States Steel Corporation and Chase National Bank.[33]

The threat of depression was partially felt in March or April 1931, but even then Hunnewell reported that the "Society's investments as a whole were sound, only a few stocks had reduced their dividends." He continued to buy railroad stocks and admitted at the same time that the nervous market was making safe purchases difficult to find. In January 1932 he placed stock orders for $15,000, but withdrew a March order to buy shares of the General Electric Company until the market direction was clearer.[34]

Already in 1928 the annual budgets were showing slight imbalances. But Greenlaw and Hunnewell could not be certain whether these figures were accounting errors or actual deficits because the payments of annual dues were poorly spaced. They noted that deficits appeared regularly during the 1920s, but discovered that a recalculation of the budgets showed an average surplus of $228.67 per year. New money was also realized from the increasing numbers of annual memberships and from transfers to life memberships. And a steady number of small gifts paid for unusual needs for repairs and improvements in the building. At the same time salaries increased slowly, new staff were appointed, and when Greenlaw retired as librarian, his pension of $3300 was approved providing he serve as assistant treasurer. Repairs in the building were regularly budgeted, and the *Register*'s press run was allowed to go over 3600 copies and its size to approximately 140 pages an issue.[35]

Anyone walking into the Society's headquarters in 1930 would have seen a rather busy library staff and a large, working group of genealogists. In good weather fifteen to twenty researchers daily were examining books and manuscripts, generally obeying regulations to refrain from conversation and loud talking. The facilities were improved yearly with purchases of new chairs and gifts of tables. Almost all the old furniture of the Somerset library was replaced, and interested members were donating their services to repair books and help reshelve books used by readers. To greet members and keep the library functioning Miss Josephine Rayne had served in the library many years under Greenlaw and succeeded him in 1929. She was a kindly, efficient person, who knew the library's resources and worked well with Greenlaw. Her advice to members introduced them to the mysteries of genealogy and made the experience pleasurable. Her assistants, who catalogued books and helped readers, included at various times Pauline King, Florence Conant Howes, and Edith Greerson MacBrine, all veterans in the Society's service.[36]

Since the Society was known for its aged leadership and the loyalty of its employees, year after year the same people administered the Society. Greenlaw had been a member of the staff since 1894; Henry Edwards Scott, editor of the *Register* since 1912; and John Carroll Chase, president since 1921. An exception was Harold Clarke Durrell, a retired businessman interested in the Society, who became associate editor of the *Register* in 1929, but was available earlier for all sorts of tasks like indexing, editing the vital record series, and undertaking contract work for researchers. As historian and associate librarian, he wrote obituary notes for the *Register* and kept under his supervision the Society's archives. Many visitors to the library also met James Parker Parmenter, the senior vice president, who substituted for Chase on many occasions and presided at some monthly meetings. A retired justice of the Boston municipal court, with twenty-eight years on the bench, he appeared the distinguished man that he was, but was also a friendly and charming person.[37]

These proven leaders awakened to the crisis of the depression in early 1931—none so sharply as Hunnewell and Greenlaw, the two men in charge of finance. Still they were uncertain about its seriousness and about the measures they should initiate to safeguard the Society. The first indication of crisis was the wholesale resignations of annual members who returned renewal notices of their memberships. Each day the postman brought three or more notices and soon more members were resigning than were accepting memberships. For the leaders who depended upon the an increase of members this reversal was bewildering. It was a vital threat to the finances of the Society, but even more it reflected upon the importance of the Society's mission. Greenlaw tried to stem the tide and rallied the library staff to recruit members. His efforts were at first partially successful, but failed over the coming years. He tried to advertise the resources of the Society in the *Literary Digest* and concluded that he was not reaching the right audience through journals and newspapers.[38]

In this crisis salaries were cut and positions eliminated. Greenlaw reduced his own pension from $3300 to $2327, and asked other members of the staff to take less severe reductions. Even so, reference librarian Helen Stone refused to take any change in salary or responsibilities and left her position in anger.[39] The scrub woman, Mrs. Paige, refused to work additional hours and was fired. In general, the women staff members held on to their jobs in spite of the sacrifice. They offered to raise money from library acquaintances and rejoiced when they collected a few hundred dollars in cash each year. Josephine Rayne helped Greenlaw in 1937 to prepare a mailing of four thousand letters in an experimental drive to inspire endowment.[40] Only $1500 was returned in gifts.

Undoubtedly Chase and Parmenter, and perhaps the other officers and councilors, were reluctant to conduct a fund drive among people of means. They were too ready to admit failure without much exertion. Both Chase and Parmenter, men of wealth, were old and inexperienced in soliciting money. Both willingly accepted cuts in staff salaries, library services, and book purchases, but neither ever admitted that the Society's mission should be changed. They welcomed the extensive social program of Mrs. Howes for the Atkinson-Lancaster Museum and the creative programs of the monthly meetings. Unfortunately these activities were no substitute for annual giving that would reduce mounting deficits of four to eight thousand dollars.[41] Younger leadership was urgently needed in the mid-thirties. Chase had reached his late eighties when he suddenly died in 1936. Parmenter, his designated heir, was old and infirm and died in January 1937. The Council turned to Frederick Silsbee Whitwell, then aged seventy-five, a wealthy lawyer, businessman, and real estate investor in cattle ranches, some in California. His long service on the Council gave him an insight into the Society's problems. His connections in Boston, moreover, were excellent. Like many of the great presidents before him, he belonged to a variety of Boston clubs, fraternal societies, and scholarly organizations. He was honored by France for distinguished service in the first world war, for his relief and humanitarian services on behalf of suffering soldiers and civilians. In short, he was an elder statesman of the Boston community who agreed to extend a helping hand.[42]

By the end of 1936 the library had a new head, Howard Dakin French, who was recruited as part of a New England-wide search. Josephine Elizabeth Rayne received an annual pension of five hundred dollars. In 1937, Henry Edwards Scott, editor of the *Register*, resigned after twenty-five years of service.[43] Continued at his present salary, Scott was succeeded by Harold Clarke Durrell, associate editor since 1929. Scott had undeniably raised the quality and importance of the *Register* since 1912, increased its scope, and refined its standards of scholarship. The press run had reached 3800 copies and most members of the Society were receiving the journal. But the depression had forced economies. Both the size and press run of the *Register* were gradually reduced, and the Publications Committee hastened to re-negotiate contracts to get cheaper paper and press costs. In 1940, after many years of negotiation, it changed printers—from the Record Printing Company to Rumford Press of Concord, New Hampshire. The *Register* would continue for years at approximately one hundred pages per issue.[44]

The retirement of the kindly "Mr." Scott in 1937 was a happy event. In spite of advanced age (he was born in 1859), he was a major asset to the Society as linguist, historian, antiquarian, and genealogist, and would be available for consultations. Ever ready to give advice to readers in the library, he was at the same time a devoted editor, meticulous and conscientious, and a recluse. He liked mountain climbing and astronomy, and seemed almost ageless until he decided to retire. Then age seemed to catch up with him. The Council brushed aside the budget deficit to give him a pension equal to his salary.[45]

Whitwell arranged a fine reception for Scott upon his retirement, and took comfort in the thought that Durrell, the longtime associate editor, would continue Scott's policies. Whitwell was less pleased about Society finances as the deficit increased yearly. By 1939, the deficit was $12,011 and the treasurer was dipping into the endowment to meet expenses. Whitwell and the Council had shifted some investments out of railroads to F. W. Woolworth and Parke, Davis and Company. But most of the investments had depreciated so sharply since 1929 that their sale was regarded as foolish. Happily, some gifts in 1937 and 1938 eased the impact of budget deficiencies.[46]

Moreover, Whitwell was a hopeful man, thanked God for little favors, and enjoyed a modest appreciation of returning prosperity in 1938 and 1939. Although this prosperity was tentative compared to the 1920s, he urged expenditures for necessary repairs. The phone system was integrated, the flagpole repaired, the vacuum cleaner reconditioned, and much painting contracted. A new Ways and Means Committee was chosen to study ways of cutting unnecessary expenditures. The committee recommended a cut in the retirement stipend for Greenlaw, Rayne, and Scott, a reduction of 10% in weekly salaries of those making over twenty dollars, and a cut in the hours that the library was open. The library was ordered to sell surplus books and release one of its assistant librarians.[47]

In these gloomy times, the attitude of the women employees was most supportive. They raised well over a thousand dollars in 1940 and nearly tripled that sum in 1941. Some members also showered the Society with precious documents. Lucius Barnes Barbour of Hartford, Connecticut, gave 139 volumes of vital records for that state's towns. Many members gave genealogies, local histories, and pamphlets to the Society. Librarian Howard French, a particularly energetic man, finally brought all city directories together in January 1937 and opened a separate library in No. 7 Ashburton Place. Over one thousand researchers visited that library during 1937. The Commonwealth of Massachusetts gave over six hundred directories in 1940, making the new library a significant center of research.[48]

Greenlaw interpreted these signs of improvements in the Society's welfare as an appropriate time for plans to expand the library building by an expenditure of five hundred thousand dollars. He urged a campaign to raise the money among wealthy members, and reminded the president and council that the hundredth year of the Society was approaching in 1944. Something dramatic, like the addition, should commemorate this event. There was need, however, of a history, of quiet reflection on the Society's mission, and of a re-evaluation of its resources.[49]

The depression was the single greatest problem affecting the Society. Survival was never a problem, but the availability of resources to carry forward its mission as a center of history and genealogy was a serious matter. In 1939, the outbreak of war in Europe was a new source of worry because it confused the future. The librarian worried about the safety of the collection if the United States were drawn into the war. The president and treasurer worried about finances and ways to find resources in wartime. Whitwell's concern for the future of the Society— possibly also his advanced age and growing infirmity—suggested his resignation as president immediately after his reelection in 1941. A fellow lawyer, Frederic Alonzo Turner, recently elected as vice president, was favored by Whitwell as his successor. Turner was a law partner of Treasurer Hunnewell. The Council, likewise, believed Turner was a good choice. In his farewell address of February 5, 1941, Whitwell had generous praise for his associates of the past five years. The event was regarded as unusual, but festive. No one could remember when a sitting president had resigned his post and gathered to hear his words. Whitwell's speech touched on many topics, but he selected the *Register* as one service of the Society on which to shower special praise. It was, he said, "a quarterly magazine far superior to anything of its kind in the country." Few realized on this winter afternoon that this speech contained Whitwell's last words to the membership. Within three months of this reception Whitwell was dead, and most of his friends on that February afternoon traveled to Mount Auburn Cemetery for his burial.[50]

Most successions to the presidency of the Society occurred at times of change in other strategic offices. In 1940 Librarian French had resigned because of ill health, but his place was immediately filled by Mrs. Franklin Earl Scotty who was serving as acting librarian. Both Durrell and Hunnewell were also thinking of retirement but agreed to remain at their posts for two more years. Turner and the Council as they faced the events of 1941 had the depression behind them, but the war in Europe was threatening American security. They sought now to safeguard the New England heritage in a time of international crisis.

CHAPTER 5

1921-1946. Value of Bonds and Stocks

	Bonds	Stocks	Total
1921	$160,994.58	$36,031.15	$197,025.73
1922	$133,418.57	$39,449.52	$172,868.09
1923	$143,364.00	$33,197.02	$176,561.02
1924	$139,389.08	$50,444.19	$189,833.27
1925	$139,358.51	$52,192.98	$191,551.49
1926	$142,561.38	$48,264.53	$190,825.91
1927	$106,518.11	$34,055.59	$140,573.70
1928	$93,310.70	$49,349.70	$142,660.40
1929	$100,064.91	$64,931.26	$164,996.17
1930	$93,078.39	$89,139.15	$182,217.54
1931	$81,660.64	$93,164.06	$174,824.70
1932	$74,711.54	$93,948.02	$168,659.56
1933	$69,916.67	$98,404.10	$168,320.77
1934	$80,483.20	$98,834.58	$179,317.78
1935	$114,961.19	$153,688.39	$268,649.58
1936	$105,970.40	$158,497.75	$264,468.15
1937	$103,383.91	$163,915.30	$267,299.21
1938	$82,004.80	$156,003.79	$238,008.59
1939	$72,071.33	$158,247.08	$230,318.41
1940	$57,950.70	$161,142.89	$219,093.59
1941	$54,312.69	$170,048.74	$224,361.43
1942	$53,242.74	$177,246.81	$230,489.55
1943	$53,416.49	$178,160.10	$231,576.59
1944	$50,142.87	$181,640.84	$231,783.71
1945	$45,281.46	$193,579.78	$238,861.24
1946	$95,333.57	$160,738.66	$256,072.23

1921-1946

Funds:	Unrestricted	Restricted	Nonparticipating
1921	$375,132.21		
1922	$589,121.84		
1923	$535,457.32	$49,747.07	
1924	$540,081.76	$55,576.33	
1925	$549,466.04	$59,763.02	
1926	$552,112.32	$59,810.25	
1927	$556,156.82	$59,905.92	
1928	$584,416.69	$50,040.63	
1929	$624,046.43	$60,195.99	
1930	$660,368.27	$60,195.99	
1931	$660,946.43	$61,061.71	
1932	$663,135.30	$61,165.75	
1933	$662,388.08	$61,278.27	
1934	$727,158.44	$61,219.30	
1935	$729,579.25	$61,375.06	
1936	$781,080.28	$61,375.06	
1937	$771,447.68	$61,446.95	
1938	$750,584.81	$68,250.67	
1939	$69,732.85	$425,828.41	$270,143.37
1940	$69,828.32	$426,368.41	$270,152.92
1941	$69,944.16	$432,769.66	$270,169.92
1942	$71,050.28	$439,384.19	$269,609.47
1943	$73,151.72	$440,264.19	$269,633.49
1944	$79,253.66	$441,201.19	$269,649.99
1945	$73,473.49	$461,733.90	$269,663.49
1946	$73,630.34	$465,433.90	$269,680.49

Notes

[1] James Phinney Baxter, "A New England Temple of Honor," *Register*, 74 (1920): 121-124.

[2] Baxter, will, copy on file, NEHGS.

[3] *Proceedings of the NEHGS, Annual Meeting 1920* (Boston, 1920): Report of Council, xiv. Supplement for April 1920 *Register*. See Annual Meeting 1922 (Boston, 1922): Report of Treasurer, p. xxvi.

[4] Ibid., for 1920, p. xiv.

[5] Ibid., for 1920, p. xvii.

[6] Donald Lines Jacobus, "Clarence Almon Torrey, 1869-1962," *Register*, 116 (1962): 158-159. "For forty-two years he was a familiar figure in the rooms of the Society where he worked almost daily." See also Frederic C. Torrey, *The Torrey Families* . . . , 2 vols. (Lakehurst, New Jersey 1924-1929), II, 275-276.

[7] Robert Lincoln O'Brien, "John Carroll Chase, 1849-1936," *Register*, 90 (1936): 211-225.

[8] See John Carroll Chase and George Walter Chamberlain, *Seven Generations of the Descendants of Aquila and Thomas Chase* (Derry, N.H., 1928).

[9] Chase gave one of the two major addresses at the ninetieth anniversary of the Society. See *Register*, 89 (1935): 171-172.

[10] Marshall P. Wilder, Address, 1878, *Register*, 32 (1878): 137-138.

[11] *Register*, 81 (1927): 45-106, 186-206, 323-357, 453-485. The Council worried about the length of memoirs and discouraged excessive tributes.

[12] "The Lincoln Memorial Tablet," *Register*, 76 (1922): 163-170.

[13] Ibid., 164: "we assemble to add our bit of silver to the golden tribute of yesterday, feeling assured that no more noble portrait can adorn a panel in this Historic Genealogical Hall of Fame."

[14] Wilder Hall was the most impressive of these rooms. By the 1930s approximately seventy-five funds were provided in a donor's name for special purposes. See the 1934 Report of the Treasurer, *Register*, 79 (1935): 142-143.

[15] Council Records, 1927-1933, pp. 264, 285, 324, MSS. NEHGS. All Council records hereafter cited are from manuscripts at NEHGS.

[16] Council Records, 1934-1941, pp. 91, 96.

[17] At almost every meeting of the Council books, pamphlets, and manuscripts were given to the Society. These small donations were a significant and constant source of support. Unfortunately, many of these books duplicated library volumes and were then sold to Goodspeed or other dealers.

[18] Council Records, 1927-1933, p. 390.

[19] Mrs. Joseph Curtis Howes (Florence Reynolds Conant), 1875-1958, served fifty years in various posts in the Society. She was an assistant librarian at the

time of her appointment as curator in 1934. See Elsie McCormack, "Mrs. Joseph Curtis Howes, *Register*, 112 (1958): 242-244.

[20] Harold Clarke Durrell, "Lizzie Daniel Rose Atkinson, M.D.," *Register*, 89 (1935): 47-53. At its opening in 1934, the museum was "decorated with dark green fir trees, which formed a diminutive forest and filled the air with fragrance from the top to the bottom of the building." Mrs. Frederick S. Whitwell was in charge of the festivities.

[21] *Morning Globe*, September 18, 1938 and *Evening Globe*, September 22, 1938. The clippings are in the NEHGS archives.

[22] *Boston Herald*, May 3, 1934, NEHGS archives.

[23] Marion Lyndon was the society writer who covered the social event for the *Boston Herald*.

[24] Professor Kittredge's lecture was a nice affair. It followed the Annual Meeting on February 2, 1938 and was given full newspaper coverage. See 1938 clippings folder, NEHGS.

[25] *The Boston Evening Transcript*, November 30, 1934. Most newspapers published a feature on the Atkinson-Lancaster collection and a few pictures of Society officers.

[26] See Report of the Committee on Papers and Essays, 1936, *Register*, 91 (1937): 137. Frederic Alonzo Turner was chairman. Nobody from the Society was a speaker and there were no recognizable genealogists. Most lectures were illustrated and treated faraway places and travel.

[27] Mrs. John Edward Kincaid (Winifred Weld [Batchelder] Lasell, 1869-1948), was elected an annual member in 1905. See *Register*, 102 (1948): 230-231.

[28] Florence Conant Howes, "William Prescott Greenlaw," *Register*, 100 (1946): 81-84. Greenlaw was a man of ideas and was constantly offering proposals. When he left the Council upon his retirement in 1929 as librarian, he was invited back to sit and participate in Society affairs. Tribute to Greenlaw in Council Records, 1927-1933, pp. 100-102. All citations of Council Records are to MSS records in the NEHGS archives.

[29] Council Records, 1933-1941, pp. 137, 39, 42, 44, 52, 58.

[30] Arthur Adams, "Robert Dickson Weston," *Register*, 111 (1957): 81-83. Weston (1864-1956) was appointed in 1911 as chairman of the Committee on Heraldry.

[31] Council Records, 1927-1933, p. 390.

[32] Council Records, 1927-1933, pp. 17, 22.

[33] Council Records, 1927-1933, pp. 241, 280.

[34] Council Records, 1927-1933, October 6, 1931, p. 262.

[35] Council Records, 1927-1933, pp. 102-103. Rayne received $2500 for her new salary. Apparently Judge Parmenter was Greenlaw's influential supporter.

[36] Council Records, 1934-1941, p. 165.

[37] G. Andrews Moriarty, "Harold Clarke Durrell, *Register*, 97 (1943): 303-306.

Tribute to James P. Parmenter, February 2, 1937, Council Records, 1934-1941, pp. 181-182.

[38] Council Records, 1927-1933, pp. 303, 311.

[39] Council Records, 1927-1933, pp. 298, 351. Eventually, in 1939, Greenlaw's stipend fell to $1500.

[40] Council Records, 1934-1941, p. 206.

[41] The Membership Committee admitted on May 4, 1937 that it was "still in the doldrums." Budget estimates were missing target and deficits were mounting. See Council Records, 1934-1941, pp. 213, 217.

[42] Harold Clarke Durrell, "Frederick Silsbee Whitwell," *Register*, 95 (1941): 307-312. Whitwell was born in Boston in 1862 and died there in 1941.

[43] Florence Conant Howes, "Henry Edwards Scott," *Register*, 98 (1944): 212-214. Actually his successor, Harold Clarke Durrell, died before he did, in 1943.

[44] Council Records, 1934-1941, p. 350.

[45] Council Records, 1934-1941, pp. 223-224.

[46] Council Records, 1934-1941, pp. 84, 297.

[47] Council Records, 1934-1941, pp. 304-305. A special Committee on finance presented a major list of economies including reduction of library hours.

[48] The new directory library was opened January 13, 1937. It was exceedingly popular with researchers.

[49] Durrell first made the suggestion in 1933. See Council Records, 1927-1933, p. 380. Greenlaw and others were well aware of the approaching anniversary and wanted something suitable like a library addition to mark the occasion.

[50] Council Records, 1934-1941, p. 367. Whitwell did not preside at the February meeting, when he gave the prepared speech, because he was possibly too ill to handle business.

CHAPTER 6

Times To Worry

High atop Beacon Hill, within the shadows of the county and state office buildings, the New England Historic Genealogical Society had its headquarters at Number 9 Ashburton Place, a reinforced concrete and steel building of five stories. Though the Society's main building was relatively new in 1941, the library stacks were already packed with books and a special, separate library for city directories had been founded at Number 7 Ashburton Place in 1937. Further expansion of facilities was urgently discussed in the Council from time to time, with the result that some rooms of Number 9A were cleaned and painted, particularly its large first-floor room, where duplicate copies of books were stored on wooden stacks. Officials from nearby government offices regularly used the libraries, and the state frequently deposited accumulations of city directories in them.[1]

Members of the Society liked this proximity of public offices to their headquarters. Only steps away were Suffolk County probate, land, and court documents, and state-wide births, marriages, and deaths since 1841. At a little greater distance were the State Library and State Archives; both were wonderfully rich repositories of books and manuscripts regularly used for research. The fraternity on the hill of attorneys, judicial and civil officers, and other public servants often held meetings in the Society's halls. Many of them lived and worked within a mile of the library, and some did work in the directory library. It was only natural that they would occasionally use rooms in the building as informal meeting places. Over the years the Society drew many officers from the judges, legislators, and attorneys who frequented the libraries.

Two of its former presidents were governors of the state. Its current president, Frederic Alonzo Turner, was an attorney and law associate of Society Treasurer James M. Hunnewell, a former legislator.[2]

Relations with state and county governments were cooperative and cordial on all levels. But neither planned to adopt the Society as an auxiliary or provide for its future on the hill. Their attitude was clear in the 1930s when construction of a new office building brought dirt and noise, and deep shadows over the Society's buildings hid the sun for the better part of each day. The encroachment was disconcerting. The Society had much land, an expensive headquarters, and auxiliary buildings. It had as well a known history of service, but the state and county had greater investments and were expanding each decade. The threat of eminent domain was only whispered in 1941 because everyone was concerned about the serious war in Europe. Would the United States be able to escape involvement? When librarian Mrs. Franklin Earl Scotty attempted on September 30, 1941 to alert the Council to the perils of military attack, her plan was called nebulous and premature. She had wanted to buy cartons for books and manuscripts so they could be taken to a place of safety off the hill. Her plan, if enacted, might have handicapped research before any actual crisis, but Turner, in the Council, responded by urging delay until developments in Europe were clearer.[3]

Frederic Alonzo Turner, the Society's new president, had been a senior vice president since 1936 and presided at meetings when Whitwell was absent. Turner was a specialist in probate law and a Boston resident for almost all his sixty-four years. For nearly thirty of those years he was treasurer of the Arlington Street Church, a Unitarian congregation, and held memberships around Boston in fraternal and social clubs. He was active as well in choral groups, a sailing club, and a music association. Though unmarried, he maintained a full social schedule; one friendly critic noted that his charm, wit, and twinkling eyes set him apart as a gentleman and conversationalist.[4] He liked to speak about his twenty-one ancestors on the *Mayflower*.

While Turner enjoyed the hospitality of his friends living on Beacon Hill, he well appreciated that the Society looked far beyond the Charles River. Although many members like Davenport Brown, John Kermott Allen, and Mrs. Henry Endicott also lived in Boston, others had homes in nearby Brookline, Belmont, and Arlington. Indeed, former presidents Baxter and Chase came from Maine and New Hampshire, which had provided many members and officers, as had western Massachusetts, Connecticut, and Rhode Island.

Although Turner was a probate specialist, he prepared only a few wills for Society members and rarely, if ever, solicited for gifts from possible donors. For him, as for Frederick S. Whitwell, the presidency was primarily an honorary position; his presence around Boston reminded people of the Society. He welcomed gifts, but active solicitation fell to the Society's women employees. Under the leadership of Mrs. Scotty they collected from readers, friends, and members hundreds, sometimes thousands, of dollars each year.[5] The money was seriously needed, for Treasurer James M. Hunnewell's announcement in the April 1941 *Register* had urged friends of genealogy to recruit one thousand new members to pay part of the average annual deficit of $7,500. "If each member would secure at least one new member, our present problems would be solved."[6] Before Whitwell's final illness in late 1940, he had urged the Council to engage the New York firm of Tamblyn and Brown to organize a major fund drive. The firm secured lists of names from such clubs as the Chilton, Union, Somerset, and Odd Volumes; such institutions as the Bostonian Society, Society of Colonial Wars, DAR, and Sons of the American Revolution; and such special groups as patrons of the Boston Symphony Orchestra, members of local Chambers of Commerce, and members of lawyer and trust officer associations. Tamblyn and Brown then screened these names for those "who might be especially interested" in genealogy. Lists were "compared with the [lists of] large donors . . . [to] the Community Chest," holders of large life insurance policies, and those receiving good salaries from distinguished Boston and New England firms. This extraordinary effort included mailing a booklet describing Society activities (and a letter from an important member) to many thousands of people. Interviews might follow if the response were favorable.[7]

Much hard work was performed by a sponsoring group of 46, chaired by Davenport Brown. It had the "very active and valuable cooperation of Mrs. Ralph Hornblower, Mrs. William Atherton," and Miss Eleanor H. Jones. Weekly meetings were held, a dinner for 192 people was scheduled, and case booklets and special letters were distributed to prospective donors. By December 26, 1940, five thousand appeals were ready to be mailed, and the committee sat back to hear its chairman report to the Council.[8]

Alan T. Smith read a summary of their work. He repeated the truism that "it takes a good deal of time to get interviews" with prospective donors, but he had in hand a file of 702 names of wealthy people who were yet to be interviewed, and expected much success. The Hattie M. Strong Foundation of Washington, D.C., however, turned down a request for funds. Both the Hyams Foundation and the George Robert White One Million Dollar Fund were delaying action until 1941. The total amount of money collected thus far was $1,175 in special pledges, while there was no appreciable increase in new members.[9] It was not an encouraging report, but it showed the expenditure of much labor. Perhaps it revealed mostly an amateur approach to the way money was collected for genealogical causes.

Apparently the observant Turner, as he succeeded to the presidency in the spring of 1941, decided that this solicitation for funds was a failure. Some time later even the usual membership drives were abandoned as costly and useless in a national crisis. He and the Council turned instead to an increase in dues. They eliminated various classes of life memberships and assessed a uniform rate of $10.00 for annual members. The library was now open only during day-light hours on week days. Researchers protested, and the librarian restored the longer hours, but Turner and the Council held their ground and insisted upon the limited schedule.[10] Some cuts were made in personnel, but, in general, salaries were raised slightly each year and efforts to hold loyal employees—in spite of the temptation of better salaries elsewhere—were generally successful.

The tensions of near-war conditions in 1941 and then the outbreak of war on December 7 had their impact on the Society. The devastation in London and other English cities and the bombing of Pearl Harbor caused fright and apprehension. Mrs. Scotty finally received permission to box collections of rare books and manuscripts and store them in the New England Mutual Life Insurance Building on Boylston Street. The Council negotiated for war damage insurance, and the librarians prepared the buildings for the emergency. Fire shutters were installed on fifteen windows.[11] Some book collections were given to local libraries to make necessary room for safety equipment.

The crisis slowed down repairs, limited part-time work for the staff, and delayed upkeep on the buildings. The Council eventually secured permits for minor painting, some roof repairs, and library purchases of necessary supplies. But it had trouble paying employees for overtime work. The National War Labor Board resisted any modification of wages to allow pay for additional services like rebinding books, undertaking contract research for clients, or cleaning the building.[12] The Council also wanted to change the method of heating the buildings and had contacted the Boston Edison Company for steam heat. But materials and labor were in short supply, and the company advised the Society to continue using coal and oil until the war was over.[13] Even the installation of natural gas was not possible because of shortages of labor and supplies. Fuel shortages were often critical and forced the closing of the Directory Library during some winter months.

The war thus mostly brought aggravation and interference with initiatives. Librarians were confronted almost daily with shortages of supplies, while the officers felt a huge loss in memberships. In January 1943, 62 persons were dropped from Society rolls; a year later, 57. Happily, many potential members were anxious to join and a group of 36 new members qualified in January 1944. Membership rolls were unstable, nonetheless, because of travel restrictions and preoccupation with war service.[14] Many library readers were service personnel at home on leave or waiting for reassignments.

As the war years passed, the Society approached its one hundredth anniversary in 1945. It was an occasion for ceremony and speeches. Tributes were paid to Charles Ewer, the first president, and a group of members gathered in Old Granary Burying Ground to inspect a new tombstone placed over his grave and pay homage to the memory of an insightful leader.[15] Other great men were mentioned, but William Prescott Greenlaw was especially honored for his many years of service. He first entered the Society in 1891 as a researcher and joined the staff as an assistant librarian in 1894. He became Librarian in 1902 and Assistant Treasurer in 1918. When he retired as librarian in 1929, he continued as assistant treasurer and was repeatedly elected to the Council. Most of the annual budgets until 1945 passed his inspection, and he participated monthly in the business of the Council. To celebrate his fifty years as a staff member and officer, the Council named the Ashburton library building Number 9 in his honor. A plaque was erected to commemorate the event. The old gentleman, aged eighty-two in 1945, when the building was formally rededicated, spoke briefly of his long experience as a genealogist. Infirm from the illnesses of advanced age and deeply affected by the tribute, he spoke about his life-long ambition to make the "Genealogical Society . . . the headquarters of American family history" and to house the documents in a fireproof building. "As you are aware, my dream came true and further, that land was secured on Ashburton Place where the building may be extended in the future when some benefactor is found who will erect a memorial to his family."[16]

Greenlaw claimed credit at this ceremony for the architectural design of the building that was then named in his honor. Few people had survived to dispute his claim; a few, however, may have been surprised. His library service had begun under William Claflin in 1894, and continued under Edward Griffin Porter and James Phinney Baxter, the latter of whom ratified his appointments as librarian and assistant treasurer. Greenlaw was a bibliographer of distinction (his life's work, *The Greenlaw Index of the New England Historic Genealogical Society*, was published in two volumes by G.K. Hall in 1979), and a statistician of rare ability who gathered data on memberships, acquisitions, and salaries. He liked railroads, apparently, and convinced Hunnewell to place some Society investments in them. Rails were among the nation's greatest industries, but in the late 1920s and 1930s they represented highly speculative investments and the softness of their dividends affected the growth of the Society's portfolio.[17]

Shortly after this ceremony, Greenlaw grew increasingly immobile and died in December 1945. His passing certainly ended an era in Society history. But it occurred within a period of other changes that were nearly as dramatic. Hunnewell retired in 1943. He had been the Society's treasurer for twenty-two years and served as well as member of the Library and Finance committees. His Boston associations were varied and included membership in the Massachusetts Historical Society and the American Antiquarian Society. He was a vestry man at Trinity Church and a member of the Massachusetts Bar. Those who visited his home were always impressed with his great library of rare bindings, unique treatises, and genealogy.[18] Although he was succeeded as treasurer by Alexander Bigelow Ewing, Ewing died suddenly within a year of his election and Everett Jefts Beede succeeded him. Beede was a businessman and town accountant of Belmont when he was chosen treasurer; fortunately he was able to work a bit with Hunnewell, who remained on the Council a short time.[19]

The death of former editor Scott in 1944 was not unexpected. Aged eighty-five at death, he retired as editor of the *Register* in 1937. His twenty-five year editorship (from 1912) was much admired for both genealogical standards and literary style. He had studied at the Universities of Berlin and Leipzig, was an expert linguist, and traveled extensively in Europe and east-coast America. After teaching Greek and the classics at various institutions in New England, he enjoyed the relative freedom of being editor. An avid reader of ancient and medieval history, he liked mountain climbing and association with members of the

Society of Colonial Wars, the Maine Historical Society, and the Society of *Mayflower* Descendants.[20] His successor as editor of the *Register*, Harold Clarke Durrell, served only six years (to 1943), but managed in that short time to inspire the respect of many members, particularly that of the highly critical Moriarty, who praised him for "placing the *Register* among the recognized publications upon early English genealogy and topography." Moriarty believed that Durrell widened the genealogical coverage of the journal and gained an international reputation for it. The men were lifelong friends, however, so that the tribute was affected by Moriarty's emotion in having lost a "brother antiquary of broad views. . . . I shall carry and cherish the memory of his inspiring friendship until it is my lot to follow him into the Great Unknown, where all good antiquaries will foregather."[21] Durrell's death was mourned by many genealogists, but the Council quickly persuaded William Carroll Hill, a retired newspaper editor who enjoyed genealogy as a hobby, to assume the editorship.[22] Hill was also soon commissioned to write an anniversary history of the Society.

Probably none of these deceased genealogists gained wider respect than Mary Lovering Holman (1868-1947), who spent her long life in the library and in town and county depositories all over New England. A forceful woman with decided opinions, she worked with original materials and was a pioneer in abstracting all wills and deeds for anyone she was researching. Her manuscript collection, now at the Society, covers 1200 New England families. Ill health had confined her to her home since 1945. Her association with Moriarty and Torrey, however, long gave the library a trinity of very able and skilled researchers, completely dedicated to their work. Their efforts, along with Greenlaw's before them, were redefining the purpose of the Society and setting new standards for genealogical research. Her well organized typed notes have become the basis for much future research by other scholars, including her talented daughter Winifred.[23]

The worst constraints of the war were relaxed in 1945. The Council reacted immediately by contracting for necessary repairs and painting the main library, both inside and outside, but was less concerned about its three other buildings. Money was always a consideration, with few gifts and annual deficits troubling officers. Many people were not renewing their memberships. In December 1945 the Council dropped 52 members from the rolls; in December 1946, an additional 72. A special committee was appointed in 1945 to combat these losses, and during 1945 it sent letters to ten thousand potential members. In March 1946 the committee sent second notices to nine thousand. The cost in time and exertion was a burden, but Treasurer Everett Beede, an optimistic person, reported a net profit of $7,040.47 and the recruitment of 34 colonial members.[24] Over 200 new applicants were processed in 1947. The Society received in both 1946 and 1947 bequests that totaled well over fifteen thousand dollars.[25]

Expenses remained heavy, however, and the Council investigated ways to cut printing costs for the *Register*. It negotiated a new contract with the printer and reviewed advertising rates. Its effort was not entirely successful. Economic conditions in postwar America, under Harry S Truman, were affected by rising inflation, labor disturbances, and political uncertainty, so the Council made little progress in its measures to improve finances. Some of its employees were going elsewhere for better-paying jobs, and others were pressing for salary adjustments.[26]

During these critical years the Society made major repairs on its buildings. The outside of the Greenlaw Library was sandblasted, broken plaster in the main library was replaced, the whole interior of the reading room was painted, and the Wilder auditorium was redecorated. Linoleum was installed on the library floor, and negotiations with the Boston Edison Company finally succeeded in getting steam heat for numbers 7 and 9 of the Ashburton buildings. Costs for all these renovations reached almost $20,000, but the plant was pronounced in good shape.[27] Then, on November 20, 1947, a fire broke out in the mezzanine above the reading room. Quick work by the Boston fire department put it out, but smoke, water, blackened walls, and burnt chairs made the damage look more costly than it actually was. The rooms of the Mayflower Society were most seriously damaged, because the fire originated there from defective wiring or possibly a cigarette. Damage was placed at $10,000. As a result smoking in the buildings was prohibited and twelve fire extinguishers were purchased. Happily the financial burden of the fire was met by donations from members who contributed almost eight thousand dollars in a few weeks. A new round of repairs, painting, and investigations were ordered.[28] These measures were hardly completed when another fire broke out in the alley behind the Directory Library. It spread into the basement and burnt some floor beams of the library. While the fire caused minor damage, it reinforced Council determination to make the buildings safe. Eventually wiring was checked, storage areas cleaned, and unused coal and oil (because of the conversion to steam) were sold.

In March 1948 Turner decided he had served as president long enough. He gave his support to Colonel Walter Merriam Pratt of Boston and Brattleboro, Vermont, a retired national guard officer. An energetic person, Pratt wanted an office in the building so that he might oversee day-to-day operations and undertake some research. His first task was to find a replacement for Mrs. Scotty, who asked to retire after over thirty years of service in various positions. Her decision seemed precipitate, and entailed a substantial search for a replacement. Pratt preferred Pauline King, the assistant librarian, who returned in 1947 after five years of war-time service, but the Council eventually chose Arthur Adams of Trinity College, in Hartford, Connecticut, the retiring college librarian and professor of English, who enjoyed a good reputation.[29]

The council's decision was influenced in part by the sudden death of William C. Hill, editor of the *Register*. A sober man of limited imagination, he was sharply criticized after his death by genealogists who liked Adams's wider interests. Walter Goodwin Davis called Adams a "genealogist of first rank,"[30] but not everyone was so enthusiastic. Walter M. Whitehill of the Boston Athenaeum thought his friend Richard W. Hale, Jr., was a much better choice than Adams because he could "strengthen the position of the *Register* in the historical field."[31] Whitehill liked Hale's histories of Milton Academy, the Roxbury Latin School, and the French Third Republic. Perhaps Adams's age was also a factor. Already sixty-five, he would need to perform efficiently in two important positions—as both librarian and editor of the *Register*.

Nothing much was said about combining these positions. The librarian was also traditionally in charge of the housekeeping functions of the entire building. The editor was responsible for the *Register*, but a publications committee handled some business matters. Adams, nonetheless, now became the most powerful official in the Society and was generally welcomed.

Colonel Pratt was undoubtedly willing to let Adams manage the routine affairs of the Society. Pratt enjoyed presiding over monthly meetings and receiving members in his office, but his own business obligations often took him to Chelsea, Needham, and around Boston. As president of the Pratt Paper Company, the Sagamore Real Estate Trust, and the Needham Motor Company, he was widely known as a businessman. But he had many other interests as well. He had served in the U.S. Army in the First World War as an intelligence officer and later in the Massachusetts National Guard and maintained connections with veteran's groups. He enjoyed foreign travel, and published impressions of unusual sights in distant places. His many books, mostly light and casual in tone, covered a wide variety of interests, and he also belonged to social clubs, fraternities, and sports organizations.[32]

Pratt's tall military figure gave the impression of dignity at monthly meetings, but the meetings were usually routine. One urgent item of business was the acoustics of Wilder Auditorium, which was noisy and had echoes. An expert from the Massachusetts Institute of Technology recommended the installation of draperies to dampen the echoes.[33] Another item of business was the mounting cost of the *Register*. Pratt suggested in an editorial to readers that those not interested in keeping it or who could consult it in the library ask the editor to remove their names from the mailing list. "In this way," Pratt explained, "a substantial saving would be made by the Society." This curious request, nonetheless, was a reflection on the general lack of donations and mounting deficits.[34]

By 1954 Walter Pratt had decided to relinquish leadership to Thomas

Temple Pond, a younger man by nearly twenty years who was senior vice president. Interested in finance, Pond spent almost his whole mature life in the insurance business, but served as well as a director of the New England Merchants National Bank and a trustee of Massachusetts Memorial and Faulkner hospitals. Like many of his associates in the Society he was a member of various social, historical, and antiquarian organizations; those of abiding interest to him related to King's Chapel, Harvard University, and Masons. Pond first joined the Society in 1944. A lover of history and books, he had already collected a huge library, which may have drawn him to Turner and Hunnewell.[35]

Pond had a genuine interest in the Society, mostly because it was an association of scholarly people. With Arthur Adams, the librarian-editor, he helped organize the collections and welcomed a cataloguing grant of $10,000 from the Theodore Edson Parker Association. He and Robert H. Montgomery, the senior vice president, secured a renewal of the grant for an additional $2000 in 1959.[36]

Almost every year Pond announced modest gifts from foundations or individuals. The Arthur Thomas Galt Fund, for example, was established in 1954 and received grants from the donor that reached $65,000 by 1959. Apparently Adams, Montgomery, and Walter Goodwin Davis encouraged bequests and helped Pond raise money from members. Former president Turner also heard their pleas and listed the Society for a major bequest in his own will.[37]

The financial ledgers of the Society changed, too, when the New England Trust Company was engaged to supervise investments and advise the treasurer. Everett Jefts Beede retired because of ill health in 1953 and Kenneth S. Domett, the assistant treasurer, died prematurely in 1957; but Frederick M. Kimball long survived these changes and gained the trust of the Council. His tenure as treasurer continued into the 1970s. After nearly five years of supervision by the New England Trust Company, in 1960 the Council returned full financial responsibility to the treasurer.[38]

Pond's amazing success in attracting money was no accident. A pleasant person, popular with associates and staff, he was blessed with many good friends and acquaintances in Boston. The Council shared power with him, however, and may have initiated some internal reforms which he supported. The first microfilm machine was purchased in May 1955; sometime afterward a water cooler (fountain) appeared; and an inter-office telephone system was installed to aid communication among the staff.[39]

Pond and the Council in June 1956 also decided that they should chart the future course of the Society—to evaluate its present position, study relations with neighbors on the hill, and develop a formal plan. Pond turned to Lawrence E. Bunker, a councilor, and a select committee, and instructed them to draw up a statement of purpose, direction, and future initiatives for the Society. The committee took its time, but Bunker reported in February 1958 that in the next several decades the Society would need no less than $400,000. The committee envisioned an addition to the library building, a general improvement in library facilities, demolition of the old, little used auxiliary buildings, and the launching of a fund drive to assure ample financial resources. On the Society's location, high upon Beacon Hill, the committee advised that "No other location can possibly offer anywhere near equal advantages and prestige; a move from this area where it has served the public generously for well over a hundred years would be a misfortune of incalculable magnitude." Everyone agreed.[40]

Further, the Council recommended the appointment of an architect who would design an attractive entrance to the building, find space for future expansion, and advise on the location in the library of an elevator and air conditioning system. Lastly the President and Council were urged to seek the support of governmental authorities in securing the Society's place in a master plan for the hill. This exciting statement of plans for the future apparently at no time incorporated the advice of any government officials. Even Pond, a wise and knowledgeable businessman, never contacted friends to ascertain the plans of the Government Center Commission for the hill.[41]

When Pond and Council members finally interviewed government officials, they were shocked to learn that the state was ready to seize their property. The news seemed so final that Pond thought at first that petitioning for a change of state plans was futile. Instead, he appointed a new committee, manned by Robert H. Montgomery (its chairman) and consisting of Charles M. Storey, Frederick M. Kimball, and himself, to study the availability of new sites. The question of location haunted them, particularly President Pond, who had consulted real estate agents for vacancies of suitable buildings. They were unable, perhaps unwilling, to think of a location other than one near Ashburton Place—near state and county offices.[42]

Soon after receiving this overwhelmingly serious news, Pond was informed that Mrs. Howes of the Atkinson-Lancaster Museum, an employee of fifty years, had fallen and broken her hip. Worse still, Arthur Adams, then in his late seventies, became infirm and needed forcibly to be retired as librarian.[43] The Council moved quickly to award Adams termination pay of $500, but then individual members questioned the paucity of the gift. Adams died a year after retirement, probably from cancer which threatened his life. Pond had already accepted the need for better salaries for the staff, especially better separation grants, but was particularly disturbed at agitation from the staff on low salaries at this time of crisis. He agreed to a Christmas bonus in 1959, if there was a surplus in the budget, and money was eventually found. In April 1960, he faced a divided Council and a vote of 4 to 4 on giving bonuses every six months; once again money was found. In December, he and the Council promised salary raises as well as a bonus for 1961.

In the meantime, Pond consulted with members of the legislature, spoke with important people in state executive offices, and met with the planning commission for the hill. Members of the legislature were formally invited to visit the Society's library, but with no success in changing anyone's mind. Apparently, the issue of seizing the Society's property was settled. Nothing more could be done except challenge the amount of the condemnation award.[44]

Pond and the Council faced a dilemma. Some of their buildings badly needed repairs for the winter of 1959-1960, but should scarce funds be spent on buildings about to be seized by the state? Other questions were equally puzzling. What should be done about the Directory Library, expanding dramatically in size, even as changes in genealogical research much increased its number of patrons? Should the Society continue to accept directories from publishers and the state? The library then had nearly 30,000 volumes.

The Council was able to settle one financial matter. It involved lending books to members living at a distance from Boston and unable to come into the main library. The lending library, taking form since the early 1940s, had grown in size and was used each year by nearly half the membership. In 1960 over 250 volumes were mailed each week, or nearly 12,500 for the year. The cost of this service was over $700 per month. The lending library was regarded by some people as a privilege of membership, long cherished as a major help to individual research. The Council, nonetheless, decided to charge two dollars for each bundle of books mailed. The fee only covered costs, but risked irritating some members.[45]

Another controversy occurred over the replacement of Arthur Adams as librarian-editor. Adams was much admired—perhaps loved, and no one wanted to offend the old gentleman. Not only had he given his large library to the Society, but he had provided for a $5000 bequest in his will. Death, however, removed Adams as a voice in his own succession. The Council first decided to separate the positions of editor of the *Register* and librarian, giving Pond authority to make decisions on the library during this crisis. It thus passed over many eminent candidates for the dual position, including genealogist John Insley Coddington, and chose as editor the bibliographer Gilbert Harry Doane, author of *Searching for Your Ancestors*, a well known primer. A long-term library administrator at the University of Wisconsin, Madison, he was willing to spend a few weeks in Boston before each publishing deadline of the *Register*.[46] The Society would provide an assistant editor in Boston to handle office correspondence. Assistant librarian Pauline King was appointed acting librarian. She had been employed by the Society for several decades, but was passed over earlier in favor of Arthur Adams.

In early April 1961 the Society's property was formally seized by the

State. Vice-President Montgomery was presiding when the brief announcement was read in the Council.[47] Pond was ill and had been in poor health since December. The pending removal of the Society to another location had affected his health, and in late April he died suddenly of a heart attack. The news of his death shocked many people. Two past presidents of the Society joined in spontaneous tributes on May 3rd. These emphasized his boyish optimism, his genuine interest in the Society, and his devotion to its financial solvency. Pond once remarked that he would like to find, before he left the presidency, sufficient money to end the budget deficits that had plagued the Society for nearly thirty years. As fortune decreed, there were budget surpluses in 1960 and 1961.[48]

Pond's death at age sixty-two created a momentary crisis of leadership in the Society. Vice President Montgomery himself was suffering from uncertain health, but felt that an interim president who could assist with legal problems and prepare the Society for its move to a new location should be appointed. He wanted a manager and leader. Gilbert Doane, then in Boston, was asked to take charge, but refused because of commitments in Madison.

The Council brushed aside Montgomery's words of caution and turned to Charles Moorfield Storey, who became acting president. At seventy-two years of age, Storey was one of the state's most prominent lawyers and the son of noted author Moorfield Storey. Charles Storey was undoubtedly not the person Montgomery had in mind, but the new president was known for his judgment, his work in corporate and utility legislation, and his experience as a negotiator. He was described in his 1980 obituary as a "genial but still very sharp patriarch who like a doctor made his round of morning calls, who knew everyone . . . secretaries, messengers, accountants and the clerk in the mail room as well as his fellow lawyers."[49]

The Council, probably acting on Storey's advice, immediately sent letters to the governor and legislature telling them of the great potential harm condemnation proceedings would inflict on the Society. It also authorized the president to file for damages under Chapter 79 of the

General Laws and issue a public statement to the press.[50] The Society prepared for an eventual challenge of the financial award for its property, which the state valued at $390,000, probably only a third of market value—at least in the opinion of the Council. The award, it said, did not include moving, the costs of a new building, damages for the loss of a familiar place of business, or, most of all, an appropriate sum for its property.

In the meantime, the Society received some remarkable bequests. In 1961, the estate of Marion Porter Wales of Chicago bequeathed $14,848 and in 1964 Gerald F. Sheppard's bequest totaled $136,136. In the intervening years annual estate receipts averaged approximately ten thousand dollars.[51] The Society conducted a campaign to collect funds for the eventual move and received some gifts used to pay architects and attorneys. Such drives, however, met with only limited success.

In this time of uncertainty the Society acquired the manuscript collection of Walter E. Corbin, 26 cartons of unpublished materials, mostly compiled genealogies and copies of church, cemetery, and vital records in western Massachusetts.[52] Winifred Lovering Holman Dodge was instrumental in raising funds to purchase this material, which gave the Society unique documentation for families of that area. The Corbin Collection was published by the society on 55 reels of microfilm in 1982. Mrs. Dodge herself almost every year added to the collections given by her mother nearly two decades previously; a final gift in 1974 included virtually all manuscript notes, covering over twelve hundred families, that she and her mother had compiled for clients.[53] The library continued to report annually other significant acquisitions. In 1963, the Waldo C. Sprague estate gave the Society his extracts of Quincy, Braintree, and Randolph vital records, genealogies of the Thayer, Wales, and Curtis families, and 6100 cards with full genealogical data on all pre-1850 residents of "Old Braintree." These cards were also later published on microfilm by the Society.[54] Another collection of exceptional value was bequeathed to the Society by Clarence Almon Torrey, who died in February 1962 at age 92. Long known for his meticulous research, he had developed nearly a complete list, with thousands of references to printed sources, of New England marriages prior to 1700 which is a monument of documentation and unusual scholarship. It was published as a book in 1985.

Pauline King, the acting librarian, continued to welcome city directories. In 1962, the library accepted the amazing number of 839 volumes. The Greenlaw Library that year received 1,368 books, 1,117 pamphlets, and 634 miscellaneous items. More important still, membership reached 2,956 in 1961 and 3,004 in 1962. The Society was flourishing, except that it no longer had a headquarters.[55]

In 1962 the Council decided that the Society could no longer depend upon its aging president to handle all pending business and should hire a manager. After consultations with various local friends, Council members received the name of Edgar Packard Dean as a possible candidate. Walter M. Whitehill of the Boston Athenaeum knew Dean during World War II and later at Cambridge. They were now good friends. Perhaps Walter M. Pratt, the former president, added his support. So endorsed, Dean secured an undefined position. It would be part-time at first—at a salary of $6,000, but carry the title of librarian. Actually he was immediately addressed as the director of the Society, while Pauline King soon returned to her daily routine as acting librarian.

Dean in 1962 was someone in search of a position. His credentials seemed excellent—he may have been underqualified as a librarian, but he wanted to be in charge of the day-to-day routines of the whole Society, so that he could use his talent for organization. In 1962 Dean was 56, held a doctorate in European history from Harvard University, had been an editor of *Foreign Affairs* for nearly a decade, and had served as an army intelligence officer for five years. He was discharged as a colonel in 1947. After the war, he longed for a prestigious position, but became instead a member of the Mid-European Center. Immediately prior to his joining the Society's staff, he was director of the Associated Harvard University Clubs and toured the United States promoting their activities. Dean left a curious impression upon his associates—he was not energetic, nor hungry for reputation or honor, nor always prepared for the duties expected of him. He appeared too relaxed, perhaps too lazy, to perform well in difficult situations. Some of these observations were undoubtedly true.[56]

Dean was thrust immediately into the debate over where the Society should reestablish its headquarters. Feelings about various locations were mixed, but the Boston Medical Library was the favorite of Charles Storey. At Number 8 The Fenway, part of the building was old and in need of much repair; its trustees, moreover, had decided to move to more spacious quarters. But Storey was so impressed with the location that he rashly pledged the support of the Council for its acquisition. The West Church north of Beacon Hill was also regarded as an attractive site, and an even more attractive location was the New England College of Pharmacy building on Mt. Vernon Street, not far from the old library and near government offices. A fourth location, favored eventually by most councilors, was the former office of the New England Trust Company on numbers 99-101 Newbury Street in the Back Bay. The building was only three stories high, but could easily be extended skyward by three or four stories. Built in 1928, it was pronounced a sound structure, and was offered at $175,000. Its massive entrance hall, where people had formerly awaited the service of tellers, was well proportioned, as were other rooms in the attractive building. A surprise vote on February 6, 1963 when Storey was absent showed seven councilors favored the site, with one "no" vote and one abstention; Montgomery left the meeting before the vote. Storey regarded the overwhelming vote in favor of the Newbury Street site an intolerable criticism of his leadership because he was known to favor the Boston Library on The Fenway. Within the month, he resigned as president. At the same time Vice President Montgomery also resigned—but for reasons of health.[57]

In this interim period Robert Churchill Vose, Jr., the talented councilor and Corresponding Secretary, presided over the Council and monthly meetings. He was elevated to the senior vice presidency, and on Dean's motion the Council elected Walter Muir Whitehill president. The famous director of the Boston Athenaeum Society was well acquainted with Society problems and agreed to serve if he had the help of Dean and the Council.[58]

Whitehill had been director and librarian of the Boston Athenaeum Society since 1946. He liked being regarded as a prodigious writer of Boston history, an author, scholar, and commentator known for the elegance of his language. He was also a brilliant speaker, whose urbane humor and insights pleased audiences. His *Boston: A Topographical History* (1959) was described as "a work of awesome erudition; meticulously researched, tightly and elegantly written, technically accomplished, and beautifully illustrated."[59]

What more might be said of such a figure? He was intensely egocentric, opinionated, and outspoken, but he was also extremely busy giving speeches, lectures, and seminars. He had really little time for the Society, but he accepted the obligation of presiding over the Council and rarely, if ever, missed a meeting. In associating his name with the Society's, he gave it much distinction as president.

With Dean at his side, now formally appointed director (and Pauline King librarian), Whitehill urged the Council to contract for the new headquarters on Newbury Street. The Turner Construction Company was chosen. Its bid of $546,000 covered essentially the construction of the additional floors. Fees for commission were not included, nor were provisions for heating, architectural fees, and book stacks. The date for completion of the building was set for August 1964.[60]

In the meantime, Whitehill presided over extensive discussions on the future of the Directory Library. In a hard, unemotional decision that pleased nobody, the Council decided to keep all pre-1860 and later New England directories. Non-New England volumes were to be given to the Boston Public Library and duplicates were offered to the American Antiquarian Society. Retained volumes became part of the main library collections (microfiching of post-1860 New England directories began in the early 1990s). Surplus books, in general, were sold or given away.[61]

The question of how to accommodate the allied patriotic societies which rented space in the old building was discussed at length. Organizations like the DAR and the Mayflower Society should be accommodated, it was felt, because they contributed to the patriotic atmosphere of the Society. But a preliminary examination of plans for the Newbury

Street building revealed that there would be less space than at Ashburton Place.[62] The Council, with much regret and embarrassment, was forced to notify its friends that they should look for other quarters, a decision that also meant the loss of rental payments.

Because patriotic societies provided additional respect for American tradition and heroes, the decision involved fundamental principles of the Society and raised other key questions. The Council liked the patriotic symbolism in its own entry hall and stairs immediately approaching the library reading room, where plaques, memorials, and statues lined the walls. This hall of heroes also had to be eliminated because of a lack of space at Newbury Street. The Council reluctantly ordered the storage and packing of the memorials, but refused to abandon the idea of a patriotic hall in the new building.[63]

Another decision, less emotional and dramatic, related to the Atkinson-Lancaster Museum. The collection of Indian art work and Atkinson family treasures was a wonderful, if curious, gift, but under Florence Conant Howes' imaginative direction they became an opportunity to involve the general public each year in a variety of programs at the museum. The collection's endowment was $41,895 in 1935 and $80,259 in 1964. The new building plainly did not have space for a museum. Art works—tables, the piano, and paintings—could decorate the offices and public spaces. In general Dean and the Council were opposed to the reestablishment of a museum at Newbury Street, but felt that the prominent display of important items of furniture and other art works in the halls would honor the Society's agreement.[64]

These decisions changed the character of the Society. When it moved in 1964, much of the past would be left on the hill. The president and council were well aware of what they were doing, but were probably not very sensitive to tradition. Few of them were genealogists, or practicing historians, or scholars from universities or academia. Their minds were set upon solving the difficult and expensive problem of moving the Society in the best manner possible. They did not stop also to ask what they could do about the memorial rooms. Should the John Foster Room be moved to Newbury Street? Should the Newbury Street building be named the William Prescott Greenlaw Building? Should the portraits of Society founders and leaders be rehung on the new walls? Would there be a Wilder auditorium?

Dean was an amazingly insensitive man, or he was too occupied with the move to Newbury Street, the negotiations with the state, and day-to-day dealings with the builder and suppliers to give thought to what was happening. He had little time to reflect upon issues of patriotism and history. But President Whitehill felt in midsummer 1963 that Dean should present a formal appraisal of the Society's condition as it planned to enter the new building. These observations were to be made available to officers and councilors in January 1964.[65]

A typed paper of ten pages was presented on schedule. It began with observations on leadership since 1940. The Society, Dean said, was primarily in the hands of the librarian, or the librarian-editor. The holders of these positions in the past did not exercise any sustained leadership. Since becoming director, he said, "I have tried to exercise intelligent, constructive, and positive leadership. It was, after all, one of the things I was hired to do." The problem, he continued, concerns changes of procedures and the modernization of the way the Society governs itself.[66] He plainly wanted the office of director to be powerful.

He would also change the direction of the *Register*. Its single-minded "pursuit of genealogy . . . to the almost total exclusion of local history" did not reflect the intentions of the founders. "I . . . have in mind things of significance. Vermont in the second half of the 18th century [for example] had a dramatic population boom. Although settlers came from New York, New Hampshire, and the Bay, the great majority came out of Connecticut. . . . Such a phenomenon, apart from the historical importance, has special significance for genealogy. It is local history that gives the bare bones of genealogy flesh and blood."

The second part of his paper concerned "money matters." New income for salaries, new activities, and the current construction, he said, were the "single most important issue[s] facing the Society!" "I propose . . . that the Society undertake to raise two million dollars over the next three or five years." The fundraising approach would be personal and individual, and timed to meet the demands of constructing the new building. The estimated cost of this last would be $670,000: $550,000 construction; $80,000 stacking; and $40,000 moving.

In the pending court case, Dean continued, the Society had challenged the condemnation award of $385,000 and asked for a jury trial.[67] It had hired appraisers in 1961, and Thomas F. Mc Sweeney Associates set $900,000 as a realistic award.[68] Dean, while writing this report, thought that even $700,000, although closer to reasonable expectations, was a speculative figure. The court case was yet to be docketed, but would be heard in 1964. The Society, in the meantime, had to borrow money to pay for the Newbury Street construction and other expenses.

The third section of Dean's report was entitled "Know Thyself." It consisted of four parts: the research library, the membership of 3,000, the *Register*, and the presence of the Society in the nation. The Society, he said, was "a library which makes available materials relating to genealogy and local history." It was not a museum, nor a patriotic organization. "We have a natural kinship . . . [with] the Boston Athenaeum, Massachusetts Historical Society, American Antiquarian Society, and the Essex Institute. I should like to see bimonthly luncheons of the staff heads of these institutions, to discuss common problems."

On the positive side he wanted the card catalogues improved; nonbooks or manuscript items should not be listed. He hoped that the catalogue, instead of the librarian, would be primarily consulted, and that it would list all research items in the library.

He commented favorably on the 3,000 members of the Society and urged, for them, a book loan service, a modest research service, genealogical seminars, and research help from the staff. He intended to give members, rather than the public, priority in using the library.

The Society finally was a publishing organization. The *Register* was primarily its voice. On *Register* pages should be "reading" articles, general book reviews, articles on local history, and compiled genealogy for a contemporary audience—"less space on the Merovingian kings." Dean eventually wanted a publications program which would include books, vital records, and genealogies.

Finally, he urged the Society to take a prominent role in national and state genealogical matters. Its voice should be raised to further research and encourage governments to make official records available.[69]

The Council received Dean's report warmly. His view of the future implied breathtaking changes, but study of the document was delayed until the most pressing problems of 1964—litigations with the state and preparations for moving—had been solved. The jury trial challenging the condemnation award began in Superior Court before Judge Frank J. Donahue, with Dean the major spokesman for the Society. His presence was impressive, but his answers to opposition lawyers were imprecise, often revealing less knowledge than one might expect from a director. He also had to defend an earlier maintenance policy for Society buildings that lacked proper attention. But his testimony surely left the jury puzzled. Since a verdict reflecting juror confusion could result in an unfavorable award for the Society, Dean had thousands of dollars to gain by giving clear answers. In the following extract from the court transcripts, the government attorney is asking the questions:[70]

> Q.: . . . the Society used one floor in No. 9A for storage. The rest of it has been allowed to remain idle. Is that also correct?
>
> A.: No, it has not remained idle from the time of its purchase down to 1961.
>
> Q.: How many years has it lain idle?
>
> A.: It was occupied by George Goodspeed and Company in the ten years from 1926 to '36.
>
> Q.: That is No. 9A also.
>
> A.: 9A, right.
>
> Q.: Goodspeed then occupied both 7 and 9A up until '36?
>
> A.: Correct.
>
> Q.: Now, from '36 onward what use was made of it, 9A?
>
> A.: I don't know what use the Society itself made of it because I wasn't associated with the Society in those years.
>
> Q.: Well, you weren't associated with the Society, yet you knew what use was being made of the main building and of others, but you don't know what use was being made of the upper five floors of No. 9A.
>
> A.: I would presume, though this is guesswork on my part, that after George Goodspeed moved out the whole area remained idle . . . [until] the Society began moving its own directories there . . .

Q.: Now, the directories in No. 9A are on the ground floor only, is that correct?

A.: Well, very technically, there are no directories in No. 9A. The directories are in 7.

Q.: All right. Now, No. 9A, what do you have on the ground floor?

A.: On the ground floor, inactive storage of books.

Q.: Of books. You don't have any inactive storage of books on the top five floors above that?

A.: Essentially, no.

Q.: Well, is it essential, or are there any up there? That's what I want to know.

A.: Because to be very . . .

Q.: Are there any up there, Mr. Dean, any books?

A.: I don't know. I mean this is purely a question of fact.

Q.: You don't know if there are any books stored today on the top floors of No. 9A?

A.: As to books . . . I don't know whether there might be a few books up there . . .

Q.: When you were up there a month ago, as you have told us, did you notice any of these stray books?

A.: I didn't notice any because I wasn't looking for that kind of thing at the time.

Q.: The answer is, you didn't notice any. . . . You noticed a great deal of deterioration up there, didn't you?

A.: Yes, and I noticed a great deal of basic strength there in the building.

Q.: What is the basic strength?

A.: I mean essentially sound walls . . .

Q.: Are you an engineer or builder, Mr. Dean?

A.: I am not an engineer.

Q.: Well, are you a builder?

A.: I am not a builder.

Q.: Have you ever been in the construction business?

So the questioning continued. Government attorneys were not always clear about the number of the building they were describing, but Dean was also unable to speak knowledgeably about the Society. In November 1964 the jury gave the Society $413,000. This sum was undoubtedly only equal to, or less than, the $385,000 offered by the state, with the added costs of litigation and interest charges for money borrowed from banks to pay contractors and suppliers.[71] The attorneys, however, petitioned the judge for a review of the jury award. Judge Donahue promptly granted the request, but wanted to inspect the buildings himself and then ordered several mediation sessions. Because Donahue was old and infirm, the discussions moved slowly. While this process was underway, the state agreed to release to the Society $300,000 as a partial *pro tanto* payment.[72]

In June 1965 Judge Donahue ruled that the state award should be increased to $830,540, plus interest. His ruling, understandably, brought cries of protest. No one seemed satisfied, but attorneys questioned the value of a second trial and noted the possibility of a younger judge if the litigation resumed. Finally the lawyers agreed that a fair price for the condemned buildings was $599,617.32, including interest.[73] The final award was admittedly much better than the jury award, but the Society nonetheless suffered a great loss. The new building eventually cost almost $800,000—some $200,000 more than the final award, but $100,000 less than what Mc Sweeney Associates originally estimated as a realistic expectation from the state. While the new headquarters were a substantial improvement over the library building on Ashburton Place, few members believed there was enough space to anticipate Society expansion into the twenty-first century. Many liked the new neighborhood on Newbury Street, but readily admitted that it changed the character of research and kind of patron. No longer would government bureaus be located within an arm's reach of the library, nor would officials from the hill regularly visit the library. Neighbors on Newbury Street were proprietors of specialty shops, clothing stores, restaurants, banks, and an insurance company.

By the time the final award was paid to Treasurer Frederick Kimball, the Society had moved into the Newbury Street headquarters. It missed the September 1 deadline for removal from Ashburton Place, however, and had to petition the state commission for extra time. The extension until December 31, 1964 permitted a clean-up of the new building, all inspections, and the shelving of most books. The D.W. Dunn Company managed the move for $22,900. Volunteers and staff helped put the books and pamphlets on steel shelving, and arranged furniture from the Ashburton building in logical places. Vice President Vose supervised the hanging of some paintings from the Society's collection and a few portraits of past leaders. The Council met for the first time in the New-bury Street building on November 4, 1964, more than a month before the library opened its doors to members on December 14. Pauline King, who had waited for years to be placed in charge of the library, cele-brated with much happiness. Frederick Kimball, the treasurer, an-nounced that the value of the Society's portfolio of stocks, bonds and other restricted funds, in spite of the pressure of debit finance, would soon reach a million dollars. The Society had debts, to be sure, but the bequest of Frederic Alonzo Turner was probated at $31,400 and 145 individuals had qualified in November for membership. Keys to the Ashburton Place properties were to be handed over to the Government Center Commission on December 29. Thus ended an era of anxiety for an institution restructured by changes of policy and location, but ready to assert its claim of being New England's premier society for family history research.[74]

1945-1965. Value of Bonds and Stocks

	Bonds	Stocks	Total
1945	$45,261.46	$193,579.78	$238,841.24
1946	$95,333.57	$160,738.66	$256,072.23
1947	$110,426.06	$156,134.77	$266,560.83
1948	$109,400.56	$153,100.31	$262,500.87
1949	$109,400.56	$141,303.11	$250,703.67
1950	$120,290.56	$119,012.72	$239,303.28
1951	$127,091.21	$136,763.85	$263,855.06
1952	$144,332.24	$149,140.72	$293,472.96
1953	$149,042.24	$151,181.69	$300,223.93
1954	$140,175.87	$166,186.41	$306,362.28
1955	$202,147.10	$168,949.67	$371,096.77
1956	$233,153.69	$161,591.58	$394,745.27
1957	$213,765.74	$184,240.24	$398,005.98
1958	$194,216.99	$216,322.55	$410,539.54
1959	$254,395.52	$282,628.44	$537,023.96
1960	$254,564.27	$306,923.93	$561,488.20
1961	$285,119.80	$304,705.33	$589,825.13
1962	$285,063.55	$351,471.24	$636,534.79
1963	$205,043.19	$341,859.74	$546,902.93
1964	$180,679.74	$441,982.08	$622,661.82
1965	$80,132.55	$431,127.40	$561,259.95

1945-1965

Funds	Unrestricted	Restricted	Nonparticipating
1945	$73,473.49	$461,733.90	$269,663.49
1946	$73,630.34	$465,433.90	$269,680.49
1947	$73,785.86	$466,803.90	$269,833.49
1948	$73,922.18	$467,965.15	$269,889.49
1949	$75,061.74	$469,255.15	$269,922.49
1950	$75,251.60	$474,222.52	$269,958.49
1951	$81,730.29	$475,732.52	$270,002.49
1952	$109,363.37	$477,093.15	$270,084.49
1953	$116,072.89	$478,818.15	$270,235.99
1954	$124,722.88	$480,558.15	$270,275.99
1955	$125,779.36	$490,264.40	$270,988.49
1956	$126,621.96	$502,458.40	$270,231.99
1957	$127,903.28	$516,529.49	$273,609.03
1958	$129,107.44	$524,447.90	$276,609.03
1959	$125,054.73	$566,417.90	$279,621.03
1960	$125,267.72	$571,922.90	$308,263.49
1961	$126,337.10	$574,091.90	$308,270.99
1962	$132,588.93	$577,141.90	$308,270.99
1963	$138,997.40	$579,546.90	$308,270.99
1964	$140,742.50	$581,665.90	$308,270.99
1965	$145,998.17	$584,515.90	$308,278.49

Notes

[1] William P. Greenlaw regularly agitated for additional space and a building fund. See Meeting of March 1, 1938, Council Records, 1934-1941, pp. 253-255, NEHGS.

[2] Arthur Adams, "James M. Hunnewell", *Register*, 108 (1954): 241-243; Gilbert H. Doane, "Frederic A. Turner," ibid., 118 (1964): 81-82.

[3] Mrs. Franklin E. Scotty, September 30, 1941, Council Papers.

[4] Gilbert H. Doane, "Frederic A. Turner," *Register*, 118 (1964): 81-82.

[5] Meetings of February 11, April 1, 1941, Council Records 1934-1941, pp. 375, 377. Since December 1940 the women had collected $3,344.27.

[6] James M. Hunnewell, in *Register*, 95 (1941): 99.

[7] Report to Council of December 26, 1940 by Alan T. Smith, Council Papers.

[8] Ibid., p. 11. Alan T. Smith undertook most interviews, with disappointing results.

[9] One amazing aspect of this campaign is the reporting in the Council Records. Almost nothing was reported in 1941. In 1947, at the meeting of April 1, the Tamblyn-Brown campaign was mentioned as a failure.

[10] Meetings of December 1, 1942, April 6, 1943, Council Records, 1942-1951, pp. 35, 56.

[11] Meeting of October 6, 1942, Council Records, 1942-1951, p. 30.

[12] James J. Healy to William P. Greenlaw, July 13, 1943, Council Papers. Contract work occurred regularly in the Society, but few records were kept to document the practice. President Chase had his famous genealogy prepared by George W. Chamberlain in 1928.

[13] Meeting of February 15, 1944, Council Records, 1942-1951, p. 83.

[14] Meetings of January 5, 1943, January 5, 1944, Council Records, 1942-1951, pp. 38, 76-77.

[15] Meetings of October 3, 31, 1944, Council Records, 1942-1951, pp. 100, 103-104.

[16] Florence Conant Howes, "Proceedings of the New England Historic Genealogical Society," January 3, 1945, *Register*, 99 (1945): 134-137.

[17] Ibid. In 1945 the Society still had bond holdings in five railroads and stocks in six others.

[18] Arthur Adams, "James Melville Hunnewell," *Register*, 108 (1954): 241-243. He would serve a few additional years on the Council.

[19] Ibid., *Register*, 108 (1955): 241-242.

[20] Florence Conant Howes, "Henry Edwards Scott," *Register*, 98 (1944): 211-214.

[21] G. Andrews Moriarty, "Harold Clarke Durrell," *Register*, 97 (1943): 303-306.

[22] Walter G. Davis to Walter M. Pratt, May 17, 1949, Council Papers. Davis, a constant critic of Hill's, preferred the editorial standards of Scott and Durrell .

[23] G. Andrews Moriarty, "Mary Lovering Holman," *Register*, 102 (1948): 3-5. Torrey would continue to work into the late 1950s. See Donald L. Jacobus, *Register*, 116 (1962): 158-159.

[24] Everett J. Beede Report, January 3, 1946, Council Records, 1942-1951, pp. 174-175.

[25] See Frederic A. Turner, "Report on the Committee on Finance," *Register*, 101 (1947): 117.

[26] Meetings of February 5, December 3, 1946, Council Records, 1942-1951, pp. 150, 153. Wages were admittedly low and the Council ordered a general increase.

[27] Meeting of March 6, 1947, Council Records, 1942-1951, p. 201.

[28] Meetings of December 2, 1947, January 4, 1948, Council Records, 1942-1951, pp. 211-213, 254-255.

[29] Meetings of June 30, 1950, February 6, 1951, Council Records, 1942-1951, pp. 313, 347.

[30] Walter G. Davis to Walter M. Pratt, May 17, 1949, Council Correspondence, NEHGS.

[31] Walter M. Whitehill to Walter M. Pratt, May 19, 1949, Director's Correspondence.

[32] *Who's Who In America*, 26 (1950-1951): 2211. Pratt served as president until 1954 and then retired to Brattleboro, Vermont, where he died in 1974. He attended Council Meetings until 1967.

[33] Meeting of January 6, 1953, Council Records, 1952-1963, p. 34.

[34] Walter M. Pratt, "*New England Historical and Genealogical Register*," in *Register*, 105 (1951): 121. "Last year the printing of this publication cost $9,033.32. As a means to help reduce this expense and so the deficit of the Society, it has been suggested that such members, if any, as may not care to receive *The Register* will be glad to direct the Treasurer to remove their names from *The Register* mailing list."

[35] Frederick M. Kimball, "Thomas Temple Pond," *Register*, 115 (1961): 161-162.

[36] Meeting of December 4, 1956, Council Records, 1952-1963, p. 160; Meeting of January 5, 1960, ibid., p. 266.

[37] Thomas T. Pond, "Report of the Committee on Finance," *Annual Meeting*, February 3, 1960, p. 3; Meeting of November 4, 1964, Council Records, 1963-1973, p. 56.

[38] Thomas T. Pond, "Report of the Committee on Finance," *Annual Meeting*, February 6, 1957, p. 3.

[39] Meetings of March 1, May 3, October 4, 1955, Council Records, 1952-1963, pp. 102, 107, 116.

[40] Meeting of February 4, 1958, Council Records, 1952-1963, p. 201.

[41] Meeting of March 4, 1958, Council Records, 1952-1963, pp. 212-213.

[42] Meeting of May 6, 1958, ibid., p. 219.

[43] Meeting of March 3, 1959, ibid., p. 238. Pond apparently forced Adams' retirement.

[44] Meetings of April 5, May 3, October 4, 1961, ibid., pp. 323, 328, 333.

[45] Meeting of November 1, 1960, ibid., pp. 299-300.

[46] Meeting of February 2, 1960, ibid., p. 271. Vice President Montgomery sponsored Doane's candidacy for the *Register*. Doane wanted the combined position of editor and librarian but the Council thought otherwise.

[47] Meeting of April 5, 1961, ibid., p. 325.

[48] Frederick M. Kimball, "Thomas Temple Pond," *Register*, 115 (1961): 163-165. Reprint of memorial resolution.

[49] Theodore Chase, "Charles Moorfield Storey," Massachusetts Historical Society, *Proceedings*, 92 (1980): 151-156.

[50] Meeting of November 1, 1961, Council Records, 1952-1963, p. 340.

[51] Charles M. Storey, "Report of the Committee on Finance," *Annual Meeting*, February 7, 1962, p. 3.

[52] Meetings of October 4, and December 6, 1961, Council Records, 1952-1963, pp. 337, 344.

[53] Pauline King, Report of the Acting Librarian, *Annual Meeting*, February 7, 1962, p. 5.

[54] Meeting of November 6, 1963, Council Records 1963-1973, p. 27; Walter M. Whitehill, Report of the Committee on Finance, *Annual Meeting*, February 5, 1964, p. 3.

[55] Elsie McCormack, Report of the Committee on Membership, *Annual Meeting*, February 6, 1963, p. 3; Pauline King, Report of the Acting Librarian, ibid., p. 5.

[56] Edgar Packard Dean, Résumé, 1962, Director's file. Stories of Dean's behavior are still repeated in 1994, especially his habit of taking an afternoon siesta. Dean was employed at a salary of $6,000 in 1963, but his services were recognized in 1965 with a raise to $9,600, and in 1967 to $10,560.

[57] Meeting of January 30, 1963, Council Records, 1952-1963, p. 394; meeting of February 6, 1963, ibid., p. 363. Seven councilors voted for the Newbury Street site, one was negative and one abstained. Storey lived until 1980, but his bitter experience separated him from NEHGS. See Theodore Chase, "Charles Moorfield Storey," Massachusetts Historical Society, *Proceedings*, 92 (1980): 151-156.

[58] Meeting of June 3, 1963, Council Records, 1963-1973, pp. 16-17.

[59] Wendell D. Garrett, "Walter Muir Whitehill," Massachusetts Historical Society, *Proceedings*, 90 (1978): 131-138.

[60] Meeting of November 6, 1963, Council Records, 1963-1973, p. 29.

[61] Meeting of December 4, 1963, ibid., p. 31.

[62] Meetings of March 4, and April 1, 1964, ibid., pp. 44, 48.

[63] Meeting of May 6, 1964, ibid., p. 51. The decision to store the tablets did not mean that they were not to be restored to some place of honor. Whitehill expected that there would be some space in the Newbury Street building.

[64] Pauline King to Walter M. Whitehill, March 28, 1963. Director's Correspondence. Dean was utterly opposed to reestablishing the Atkinson-Lancaster Museum at Newbury Street.

[65] Walter M. Whitehill to the Council, January 13, 1964, Director's Correspondence.

[66] Edgar P. Dean to Walter M. Whitehill, January 2, 1964, Director's Correspondence.

[67] Dean's Report, ibid., p. 4.

[68] Thomas F. McSweeney Associates, January 10, 1964, Director's Correspondence. Other appraisers had judged the value to be nearly $900,000.00. See Louis A. Donovan, March 21, 1961, Director's Correspondence.

[69] Dean's Report, ibid., p. 7.

[70] A copy of the transcript of Dean's testimony is in the Director's file.

[71] Meeting of November 4, 1964, Council Records, 1963-1973, p. 57; Meeting of March 4, 1964, ibid., p. 44.

[72] Meetings of March 3, and May 5, 1965, Council Records, 1963-1973, pp. 74, 81.

[73] Meetings of May 5, and June 8, 1965, Council Records, 1963-1973, pp. 81, 85.

[74] Howard Moore Turner, Report to the Council, Annual Meeting, February 2, 1966, p. 6; Meeting of January 6, 1965, Council Records, 1963-1973, p. 62.

CHAPTER 7

On Newbury Street

The Back Bay of Boston, where the Society reluctantly moved its headquarters in 1964, is an amazingly varied part of the city, with residences, colleges, and seats of national institutions like the Christian Science Church, Northeastern University, and the Boston Public Library. Copley Square in the middle of the area is the meeting place for thousands of youths almost any weekday and is bordered by the massive Hancock Tower, beautiful Trinity Church, a large assortment of banks, hotels, and restaurants, and the impressive Prudential Center. A few yards north of the square is Newbury Street which extends from the Public Garden to Massachusetts Avenue, and is lined for about a mile with specialty shops and restaurants on both sides of the street. Only across the street from the six-story Society building is a massive business structure, the New England Mutual Life Insurance Company, which had then no retail shops. The crowded sidewalks of Newbury Street reflect the variety of life in the Back Bay. Well-dressed young adults carry in their arms pretty packages from the book and clothing shops as they walk past the entrance of the Society.[1]

Its Council felt uneasy about selecting this location on Newbury Street when it moved off the hill, and its leaders continued to feel uncomfortable for years about this new site. Memories of old Ashburton Place, amid the government offices, haunted the staff, but crowds of professional visitors who gathered to inspect the new headquarters gave warm praise for the facilities and cheered the incredulous officers. Walter M. Whitehill found the commuting distance from the Boston Athenaeum a bit tedious, but Edgar P. Dean promised to schedule meetings of the Council and membership on the same afternoons. A similar agreement had been made a half century earlier for James Phinney Baxter, who limited his railroad trips from Portland, Maine, to Boston and presided over meetings for nearly twenty years.[2]

Edgar P. Dean, as the Society's methodical director, had been primarily responsible for arranging the move to Newbury Street. He had negotiated contracts, tramped with workmen into the hard-hat construction areas, and assigned the building's future space. He shared the excitement of being in charge of the move with Whitehill, whom he took to the site of the new building, and with the staff of librarians and secretaries. As a guide he had no warm personality, nor the ability to tell stories, nor the wit to seize a moment of levity for humor, but he spoke warmly about his future plans for the Society. He was bent on turning the Society toward historical research as a discipline and even mentioned his intention of writing a book himself on the Pilgrim founders of New England. His major accomplishments, however, were administrative, especially the move to Newbury Street. He also sought health care for the staff, better salaries, pensions, and additional personnel.[3] His speeches and reports in the mid 1960s were well presented; sometimes he seemed to pause unnecessarily in choosing his words, but he regularly showed deference for the opinions of Whitehill and Frederick M. Kimball, the treasurer, and dressed as they did, conservatively and properly. Observers thought these men spent an inordinate amount of time keeping their shoes polished, or in the words of a critic were aloof and stiff-necked gentlemen of Beacon Hill. Through his association with them, Dean exercised much influence as he completed the move to Newbury Street and furnished an office for himself on the first floor of the new building, within sight of the people walking on the street.

The Newbury Street location, Dean discovered, brought increased maintenance costs, and the move generally was expensive. Worried continuously about finances, he spoke regularly with Kimball, who managed the portfolio, about the increasing expenditures. Dean wanted a drive to raise additional endowment once the move of the library was completed. His wishes were shared by Kimball who also strove through

1965 to terminate litigation with the state over the seizure of Ashburton Place. The Boston law firm of Ropes and Gray consulted regularly for him with John E. Sullivan, chief of eminent domain for the Commonwealth, and concluded that only a second trial might win a favorable award. In the meantime, the First National Bank of Boston held the mortgage of $280,000, with over $11,000 annual interest, and operating expenses for the Society in 1965 were producing a deficit of more than $25,000. Bequests of nearly $10,000, new memberships, and sales of surplus books and pamphlets reduced this sum slightly, but the potential deficit was still serious. Dean wanted a ten-year budget projection to guide the Society out of its financial morass, but he was also struggling with rising wage and price inflation and a reluctance by the membership to make donations. His idea for a plan was complicated by unpredictable financial conditions.[4]

Everything seemed to move unnecessarily slowly. The Commonwealth of Massachusetts placed the litigation in the hands of a succession of tough-minded negotiators. Donald R. Grant for the Society described a new Assistant District Attorney as "not unduly belligerent," when explaining to Kimball and Dean the legal attitude of the Commonwealth; he would be a hard bargainer. Both Society and Commonwealth had dug in their heels, and the Society's attorneys prepared for another court case. The Commonwealth was unwilling to allow the award of Judge Frank J. Donahue to be taken seriously because it had provided for resettlement costs. In 1963 the Society Building Committee had estimated that the total cost of resettlement would be approximately $851,000, which included the price of land, architect's fees, and the purchase of book stacks.[5] Judge Donahue had later recognized these larger costs by awarding $830,000 and accumulated interest. Other charges, however, like moving and the storage of books and portraits in preparation for the move, he had not figured into the total cost of resettlement.[6]

When the lawyers on both sides finally sat down to compromise, the state threatened the Society officers with the reality of a costly trial and another judge. At first they were undecided, but then gave way to most

demands. The final award in June 1966 was $580,000 plus interest—
about $200,000 less than expected. It included the *pro tanto* award of
$300,000, for which the Society had to wait nearly a year before it could
pay its debt with the First National Bank of Boston, but appraiser's fees
and storage were not included.[7] On the credit side the Society secured
an attractive modern edifice for its headquarters. The building was
constructed on its higher floors with steel and brick, like an office
building, but it had not sufficient bracing if the need ever arose to use
other floors for stack space. It had the advantage of concrete construction on floors one to three, and two elevator shafts. The installed elevator was then, and it remains, undoubtedly the slowest elevator in New
England. A second elevator was never installed. The new headquarters
was not so large as the Ashburton Place buildings, but it was modern
and spacious, with available book shelving for several decades.[8]

Dean was now urged to integrate the Arthur Adams gift of books
into the general collection. This gift from the revered librarian had been
presented to the Society in 1951, but there was not at the time sufficient
shelf space to incorporate it. Scarce funds and the uncertainties of the
early 1960s forced the Council to store most of the 7300 volumes, which
were primarily genealogical. For some reason Dean refused to mix this
rich collection with the larger general holdings of the Society. Though
he reported it catalogued in 1968, he left it separated on the fifth floor of
the stacks, and not until 1976 was it integrated into the main collection.[9]
Likewise stored in the 1960s were some of the Society's portraits of past
leaders, and almost all of its monuments and tributes to heroes. Pressure from Whitehill forced Dean to have them returned to the Society.
Robert C. Vose of the Council was asked to place suitable paintings on
the walls, and he sent assistants from his gallery to make judgments on
possible locations. Paintings on loan to neighboring institutions were
now returned to the Society so they could be enjoyed by members. Dean
cooperated with Whitehill and Vose in these measures to exhibit the
treasures of the Society, but he plainly was not sympathetic to creating
another hall of heroes by hanging the plaques.[10] The walls were too
thin, he declared; and further there was not enough space for them. His

excuses did not please the romantic Whitehill and members of the Council, but they had no solution for the problems of exhibiting these mementos of an earlier day and let Dean's judgment prevail.

Council members had other things, however, to worry them. The mid-1960s were troubled years of urban crime, violence, and threats. The jewelry shop next to the Society was robbed, and elsewhere in Boston thieves were breaking into stores. Strangers had entered the rear door of the building and were seen in the library. Even walking on Newbury Street at night was unsafe. Much discussion occurred, but a meeting of the Council rejected Dean's idea of putting rare paintings in the vault.[11] Violence in Los Angeles, Chicago, and Detroit frightened the Council, nonetheless, and security measures, including the registration of readers, were adopted. Somewhat later, briefcases and purses were inspected and an iron grating was placed at the entrance of the rare book stacks. Happily, Boston did not suffer the violence of other cities, nor did the Society experience much more than apprehension about a raid on its quarters. For a time, evening meetings were canceled and patrons of the library hurried down Newbury Street in the late afternoon on their way to the safety of a hotel lobby or waiting automobile.[12]

In spite of their worry about safety, Dean and his staff planned a large genealogical conference for August 16-20, 1965 and announced that if their experiment were successful, there would be more such conferences in the future. Dean was careful to limit enrollment to approximately 46 people and the program to a week. Mornings were to be devoted to lectures and study; afternoons to exploration in the library. The fee was $15. The popularity of the conference was unusual, and pressure was applied to admit more participants, but Dean continuously held his ground. His report on the conference, however, was enthusiastic. Both he and President Whitehill had addressed the participants. His lecture on the "Great Migration and Expansion of New England," had opened the conference, which featured Catherine Fenelley of the Old Sturbridge Village, Claude W. Barlow of Clark University, and genealogists of such stature as Jean Stephenson, Lucy

Mary Kellogg, Anne Borden Harding, and Laura K. Pettingell. As for the seminarians, according to Dean,

> One could hardly hope for a better group. They were consistently punctual, they were attentive, they asked intelligent questions and they were hard-working. In age they ranged from 30 to 78; geographically they came from the "four corners" of the United States and many "parts in between." Approximately one-third were men and two-thirds women, a proportion representative of the membership of the Society. The Class of 1965—the first class—set a high standard. Will there be another class? We believe so.[13]

In 1966 he promised more places and a solicitation of enrollees on a "nation-wide basis." Fees were raised, but fifty seminarians applied. Actually five over the maximum qualified and attended. Everyone who came to the conference sessions was enthusiastic. Dean complained, however, that the conferences were too exhausting for him and the staff, and their planning interfered with more important activities.[14]

Actually Dean was thinking of holding a large conference for professional genealogists in 1968, possibly an invitational event of one hundred leading experts. Friends thought it was an excellent substitute for the seminars, but the Council immediately criticized the idea of limiting participation as undemocratic. It gave its support instead to a plan of the Genealogical Society of the Church of Jesus Christ of Latter-day Saints in Salt Lake City, which in 1969 was holding the 75th anniversary of the founding of its library. Dean's announcement of this event in the *Register* is most interesting in light of his desire for a professional conference in Boston:

> Since Utah is rapidly becoming a Mecca for genealogists, many of our members and readers may want to consider attending the conference and taking advantage of the opportunity which it will present to inspect the great wealth of records which have been amassed and stored in vast underground vaults.

Both Pauline King and Gilbert H. Doane were asked to attend the conference and present papers. In the meantime, the Council promised to help Dean organize a seminar for 1968 and invited some of the leading genealogists in the United States to Boston, including John I.

Coddington, Meredith B. Colket, Jr., and Gilbert H. Doane, but none of Dean's fellow historians. The seminar drew 72 participants, at least seven more than the capacity of the room, but happily a few dropped out before the sessions began. It was reportedly as successful as those held in 1966 and 1967.

Dean felt his first priority was reform of the Society's governance. Since he first became director, he had wanted some changes, but delays caused by the resettlement on Newbury Street and litigation with the Commonwealth postponed his plans. By mid-1966, he was ready to proceed. Deliberating for weeks with councilors, he encountered some opposition from Pierre Belliveau, who did not appreciate Dean's ideas but left no record of what he disliked. Their disagreement spread into such issues as staff morale. As the dispute intensified, Whitehill moved to protect Dean from the attack and gained approval to remove any harsh criticism from the minutes. The bylaws were sent to the membership in March 1967 and adopted in June.[15]

The new bylaws made significant changes in the way the Society was governed. While power ultimately resided in the Council, which included most officers, the number of vice-presidents was reduced to one—who would preside during the absence of the president and would succeed the latter in the event of the president's death. The president became primarily a ceremonial figure. The most dramatic change was the creation of the position of Director, who served at the pleasure of the Council but held executive power. The Treasurer, however, still was in charge of the financial operations of the Society and passed on expenditures. Most officers were elected annually, while Councilors had a three-year tenure that rotated by thirds.[16]

By placing power directly in the hands of Edgar Dean, the Society had a responsible official who could be praised or blamed for its operations. Dean's highest objective now became the search for donations. He convinced Whitehill that a committee of the Council should study the needs of the future and make some recommendations. The Committee, Whitehill, and Dean quickly agreed upon the appointment of Arthur

Alexander Dunn of Shrewsbury, an insurance executive, as chair of a capital campaign. Dunn, a man of great energy, readily accepted the burden of leadership and set two and a half million dollars as the targeted sum. Their enthusiasm, however, disturbed Vice President Vose, who insisted that Dunn, Dean, and all others concerned in the drive must find a "structure" for money-raising activities. He praised their spirit, objectives, and good will, but he believed failure would certainly threaten their efforts without a well-conceived plan.[17]

During the spring and summer of 1968 the staff and officers worked assiduously on address lists from many sources, and mailed letters by the hundreds, possibly the thousands. Much was apparently undertaken, but amazingly little remains in the Society's archives to document their exertion. At one point Arthur Dunn notified the leadership that he might have to resign because of business responsibilities in New York City. The possible loss of his dynamic presence seemed almost too much for Dean to face and he urged Whitehill, Kimball, and Vose to persuade Dunn to remain at the head of the Capital Drive.[18] The summer and fall of 1968 passed, but Dunn eventually had to resign. His departure brought the chaos Dean sought to avoid, and the drive was reluctantly dropped in 1969 by the Council. Happily in 1970 the Society received at least $150,000 from the Florence S. Dustin Trust and the promise of a share of the undistributed remainder—which might amount to fifty thousand dollars.[19]

Notwithstanding this wonderful gift, the Society had operated in the red consistently almost every year since the early 1960s. The deficit in 1968 was nearly $30,000 and in 1970, $27,000. Kimball adopted strategies for shifting stocks of high price and low dividends to stocks of equal quality but better dividends. He would announce in 1971 that the portfolio had reached one million dollars, but the deficit that year was $8,000. Another gift later in the year, of $35,112.01 from the estate of Edna Smith, seemed a godsend to Kimball, who may have toasted a glass of brandy in her memory.[20]

This concentration on Society leadership obscures other significant

trends. Membership continued to grow without any long-lasting de-
clines.[21] Study of the membership statistics in 1974 and 1977 revealed
major gains in the past decade and a half:

1962	2,955	1972	3,733
1964	3,093	1973	3,873
1966	3,083	1974	4,082
1968	3,372	1975	4,097
1970	3,277	1976	4,324

But yearly losses were always present. The most disturbing drop—
251 members—occurred in 1969. Conferences and seminars, however,
attracted many participants and may have produced new members.
The book loan service remained popular and even the numbers of
readers in the library may have slightly increased. The staff was devoted, but elderly, and signs of youthful enthusiasm were rare. Pauline
King, the librarian, always generous with her time, celebrated her fiftieth year with the Society in 1969. Critics of the Society, but not of Miss
King, felt the reading room was musty. A broken arm in 1971 slowed
her activity, and in January 1972 she decided to accept a yearly pension
of $2300 from the Society and retire. Other staff assistants like Mildred
E. Leavitt and Edith (Hazel) Hazelton, both assistant librarians, also
took advantage of the pensions.[22] Miss Hazelton was age 75 at retirement.

These years also brought the retirement of Gilbert H. Doane, the
illustrious editor of the *Register*. This tall, impressive man had always
served part-time, living for most of the 1960s in Madison, Wisconsin
and later in nearby Rhode Island. He depended first upon Elsie McCormack and later on Anne Borden Harding for day-to-day decisions. In
Boston, however, Doane was almost revered by the Council and officers. His retirement engendered a letter of appreciation from the Council, a scroll of formal remembrance, and a pension. His successor was
not the vivacious Anne Harding, who was his right arm, but John
DeLong Austin, Jr. of Glens Falls, New York, a lawyer and genealogist.
Most of the work of the *Register* fell upon Anne Harding, however, who
often had a difficult time finding material. She included her own ar-

ticles, often ghost-edited pieces for other genealogists, and serialized some longer genealogies—especially the large corpus of articles on Sandwich, Massachusetts families by Maclean W. McLean.[23] The *Register* continued to have much good material, but there was general dissatisfaction with its direction. Dean wanted more local history and fewer source records.

The size of the *Register* reflected the tastes of the editors and their assistants as well as the cost-cutting measures of the Council. In 1971, the four issues covered about three hundred fifty pages of content and index. In 1972, an impressive index brought the page total to 361, but the *Register* articles spread over only 308 pages. While Gilbert Doane was editor, he regularly added a few pages of comment on new books and genealogical happenings, newsworthy and informative. But the *Register* never became a journal of opinion on genealogy or local history. It had, notwithstanding some dullness, loyal supporters who treasured each issue. Members of the Council considered a new design for its cover and typeset for the pages, to replace the traditional format, but then let the matter ride probably because of costs. The Council worried instead about overruns of the *Register* and the accumulation of back issues that were filling storage space in the Society's basement. Given this huge surplus, Whitehill wondered about such costs as paper, printing, and storage and urged caution in the management of the *Register*. He pressed Dean, who now moved slowly, to find answers to these problems.[24]

Elsewhere in the Society new technological developments were appearing almost every year. A new catalogue was developed by Edith Hazelton who contributed even to the cost of the cabinets. Some councilors wanted to name the catalogue after her, but her modesty brushed aside such thoughts. A donor gave the Society its first electric typewriter in 1969, and leases were negotiated later for a duplicating machine which would be operated at cost, at twenty-five cents a page.[25]

Library additions were primarily books, but some microfilms of Federal censuses and *The Boston Transcript* were acquired. Almost every year new microfilms were ordered. A collection of town records was eventually purchased, but most readers preferred to consult the written word. Many new books were both purchased and received as gifts, and readers urged a special bookcase for the display of these newly acquired items in a permanent location in the library.[26]

Few people argued about the kinds of books and films in the library, but when the staff wanted a room set aside for luncheons, opposition from Dean was vigorous and sustained, perhaps explosive. He did not like the possible damage which the resulting garbage might do to the books and spoke of contamination in the air. His opposition delayed permission from the Council, but the common-sense notion of a room for staff conversation and lunches was not to be denied. Support for the staff position now came from an unexpected source.[27]

About this time the Massachusetts Society of Mayflower Descendants petitioned the Council to be admitted as a tenant, to enjoy again the friendly relationship that its members had experienced at Ashburton Place. The Council quickly surveyed space needs and decided that three offices on its third floor were available. It settled on an office rental of $4,600, which eased some budget pressures, but then took several months to negotiate the use of other space on the first floor where Mayflower members from time to time wanted to gather for tea and cake. Permission for them obviously meant a weakening of resistance by Dean and others to a recreation room for the staff.[28]

The additional income was undoubtedly the lubricant, because Dean was unable to reduce general operating expenses. The building was costly to heat in winter or cool in summer. Staff salaries, though miserably low, were raised yearly because of the inflation caused by the Vietnam War and unsettled conditions in society. The building needed to be further secured when robbers broke in and took some money. Miss Edith Hazelton was a victim of assault and robbery in the hallways of her apartment. Her experience there inspired study of controls in the Society to prevent uninvited people walking into the library building. Bars were placed on some windows and book use by non-members was restricted.[29]

The genealogical community obviously changed as did the Society.

One unmistakable fact of life is the aging of everyone. President White-hill was attending in the late 1960s to less Society business and de-pended upon Robert C. Vose to preside at more and more meetings. Dean was preoccupied with plans for his own retirement. Some influen-tial genealogists, including George Andrews Moriarty, Walter Goodwin Davis, and Harold Bowditch, died in the 1960s. Moriarty was ever-present in the library until a few years before his death at eighty-five in July 1968. His genealogical articles appeared in many journals for nearly sixty years, but he was also an historian who contributed to Albert Bushnell Hart's *The Commonwealth History of Massachusetts* and George Francis Dow's *Two Centuries of Travel in Essex County, Massachusetts*. As well known in England as at home, he was widely considered the greatest antiquarian of his generation. Moriarty had been a councilor, a longtime member of the Committee on Publications, and a member of the Committee on Heraldry for twenty-six years. A correspondent of many scholars, he exchanged gossip and information on the Society and was always ready to promote its activities.[30]

Davis died in 1966 at age eighty-two. A native of Maine, he lived most of his life in Portland and devoted much of his time when not serving as president of banks in the city to genealogical research. The author eventually of sixteen volumes tracing the entire American (and much English) ancestry of each of his great-great grandparents, he was also a major contributor to the *Genealogical Dictionary of Maine and New Hampshire*. He served on societal committees and contributed gener-ously to its operating funds. A close friend of Bowditch and Moriarty, he was an avid promoter of genealogical activities. In 1959 and 1960 Moriarty and Davis tried unsuccessfully to win for John Coddington, their younger colleague, the post of librarian-editor in the Society. They blamed Thomas Temple Pond, the president, for turning to Gilbert Doane instead of Coddington. Pond was denounced as ignorant, preju-diced, and inflexible, but Pond spoke for the majority of the Council.[31]

Bowditch surely heard their complaints against Pond. But he then lived in Peterborough, New Hampshire, too far from the politics of Boston. Bowditch was occupied with heraldry, his own family genealogy, and bird-watching in addition to a small medical practice. Bowditch at his death gave his large collection of heraldic books to the Society and its Committee on Heraldry.

These men represented a powerful part of the genealogical community. They drew also into their fellowship former president Storey, Winifred Holman Dodge, and others who offered advice to the Society leadership. Since most Society presidents and Director Dean were not major genealogical scholars, there was some tension concerning the direction of the Society. President Whitehill, although not a genealogist, was an antiquary, local historian, and published scholar. His vice president, Robert Churchill Vose, was an art dealer who was an expert in eighteenth-century American paintings. Like his distinguished father before him, he was deeply interested in the Society. In April 1971 when Vose succeeded Whitehill, members of the Council urged him to take some strong measures to invigorate the Society. Aged sixty and a businessman, Vose possessed considerable wisdom and vitality. He felt that he had no alternative but to retire most of the older employees and hire some youthful, energetic people to replace them.[32]

He began with the director, who was sixty-six—not an old age for Society leaders. But Dean had begun to retire in the late 1960s when he failed to increase the endowment. He lost his temper from time to time, was described as "a mean man," and may have contributed to much pettiness among members of the staff. Dean was seen by many people passing by Newbury Street with his feet on his desk, appearing to be sound asleep. Perhaps he was in deep thought, rather than asleep, but too many people critical of him rejected his explanation and reported their hostile impressions to Vose, Kimball, and others. Dean was permitted to retire as of December 31, 1972, and was refused an extension to train his successor.[33]

Vose was a busy man like Whitehill, but he was determined to reinvigorate the Society, which he considered lethargic and in bad condition as a research institution. He made every aspect of the Society's management a matter for his personal attention. With Dean's forced retirement Vose assumed the powers of director and appointed an administrative committee on governance to advise him.

Under the chairmanship of Henry Vincent Strout, an expert in personnel management and a man of energy and conviction, the committee held many conferences and presented in a year four major reports to President Vose and the Council. Strout was a graduate of Boston College, with training in the law and business, and lived in Marblehead with his wife and ten children. Like Vose he was methodical in his work habits and wanted himself to succeed Dean as director. His committee concluded in its first report that the director need not be a librarian, historian, or genealogist, but a person with "strong executive direction" and a "comprehensive and executive background."[34] Another report quickly followed with emphasis upon management principles, with recommendations that offices be defined and duties delineated.[35] In the meantime, the Council and Vose sought a successor for Dean, and early in 1973 found Richard Donald Pierce, Unitarian minister, librarian, teacher, and formerly dean (and for a while acting president) of Emerson College in Boston. At fifty-eight, he appeared to have many of the personal qualities of a successful director. He had, additionally, knowledge of local history, having written his Ph.D. dissertation on the "History of Temple, Maine: Its Rise and Decline." He edited a three-volume set of *The Records of First Church of Boston* and was then working on the records of the First Church of Salem.[36]

Most people who met Richard Pierce immediately liked him. A short, quiet man who seemed more a scholar than an administrator, he was easily approached. One friendly critic who met him in 1962 at his apartment on Beacon Hill described his home and person thus:

> I recall the high ceilings of his airy apartment, its walls hung with portraits of ancestors who, from their gold frames, looked out disapprovingly at an unfamiliar world. The richly variegated colors of orientals and the sheen of carefully polished woods made an indelible impression on me. But, it was Dr. Pierce who stood out most significantly. He seemed almost to have stepped from another gold frame, for a pair of pince-nez, a Pierce trademark, rested on the bridge of his nose and he greeted me with a

restrained but polite welcome. No effusion, merely a few simple words to put me at my ease. He was short and round and his hair tufted in curls. . . . he was clad in a short-sleeve shirt. . . . he enriched our conversation with a variety of references, wit and great understanding. . . . he loved people and once wrote 'I am not a loner—I like clubs, I like organizations, I like to be with people'. . . . He was forever attending meetings. . . . he attended meetings the way a monk attends divine worship, endlessly, with delight and conscientiously.[37]

President Vose was greatly pleased at the appointment of Dr. Pierce—maybe even more for finding a replacement for Dean, whom he thoroughly disliked. Dean was now fully retired, presented with the *New Oxford Dictionary* as a parting gift, and offered a reception which he had the good sense to refuse. In the meantime, the Committee on Governance continued its deliberations and turned its attention to art objects owned by the Society.[38] Strout angered staff members because he criticized some routines of publishing the *Register*, managing the library, and maintaining the building, but his committee arranged for the return of paintings on loan and ordered dirty and damaged ones repaired. It issued a manifesto to the Council and officers regarding the plaques that had customarily graced the entrance hallway in the Ashburton building: "In the committee's opinion [the Society] has a moral obligation to the donors of such plaques to display them as intended at the time of their presentation."[39] The Committee's abrasive words, however, did little more than irritate the Council, which was still perplexed by the problem of what to do with the plaques.

Other important work took precedence. The Associate Editor of the *Register*, Anne B. Harding, developed a style sheet for contributors and reported on personal problems over the years with Dean and other staff members. Later in 1973 she wanted to retire because of overwork and the backbiting of contentious staff members. She called her rewards as associate editor a "financial disaster."[40] Harding was an excitable, talkative person of medium height who knew her way around genealogy and felt rightly, or wrongly, that she was not given full credit for editorial work she had performed while Doane was the part-time editor. As a skilled professional she would be difficult to replace.

Miss Harding agreed not to retire immediately, which gave Vose ample time to canvass the genealogical community for a competent person who would succeed her and John DeLong Austin, Jr., the editor, who also wanted to retire. Austin still lived in Glen Falls, New York, was then a public official and a practicing lawyer, and had little time for editing. The Publications Committee thought that a younger, full-time editor might replace both Austin and Harding, but it was the Council which pondered these drastic changes.

The Council thus called Miss Harding to its December 5, 1973 meeting shortly before she planned to retire, in order to report on the *Register*. Addressing the Council on the journal's importance, she stressed that it was the "face of the Society" and that past issues were in great demand by genealogists. The *Register* was, in her opinion, "a teaching organ of the Society for beginning members." It was financially of even greater value: "we get 58 journals in exchange, saving us $750 in subscriptions annually; . . . we solicit books in exchange for listings (332 last year) saving us some $3,500; . . . one half the regular $25 membership fee goes toward paying for the *Register*; and . . . we have about 516 paid subscriptions to the *Register* at $12.50."[41]

Miss Harding did not speak about the content of the *Register*, except to say that the longer articles she was publishing might easily have been printed as books by the Society. Her observations were well received by the Council, but some members renewed sentiment to change the format of the *Register*, design a new cover, use a new typeface, and diversify its content, possibly emphasizing local history. The Council soon appointed Susan L. Patterson as an assistant editor of publications. With experience on the *William and Mary Quarterly*, she had degrees from the University of Illinois and William and Mary College. However, she was an historian, youthful and talented, with good technical training, but without connections in the field of genealogy. Another appointment of a more mature person was obviously intended.[42]

Before Miss Harding could retire as associate editor, she was shocked, like most of the Council, at the sudden collapse and death of Richard Pierce on August 1. She had not anticipated, moreover, that her distant relative Richard B. Johnson, the longtime Recording Secretary, would succeed Vose as president in April 1974. This handsome, witty lawyer had nearly died of cancer in 1971, but then seemed to recover almost miraculously and resumed his law practice and tasks at the Society.[43]

Vose had planned to leave the presidency as soon as he could, but put the well-being of the Society above his own personal comfort. The death of Pierce only six months after entering office delayed indefinitely Vose's plans to retire. Pierce was actually not the kind of director that the Society should have appointed. He had the prominence, age, and distinction of a potential president. He was apparently an interim candidate to fill the vacancy of director, with possible later promotion to the presidency if Johnson again became ill. Pierce had saved nearby Emerson College from financial disaster and his talents might be similarly used to help the Society. His sudden death, however, forced Vose to conduct a search for a successor, and he decided to reach out across the nation for talent. Vose looked primarily for a good administrator, young and healthy, who might raise money and invigorate the Society, and he found quickly at least fifteen men with fine qualifications. He liked Henry Vincent Strout personally, and also liked the papers of James Brugler Bell, who was recommended by the Rev. Eugene Van Ness Goetchius of the Episcopal School of Theology at Cambridge. Goetchius, a longtime member of the Committee on Heraldry, was Bell's teacher, and had admired his former student in the classroom. Personal contact with Bell later convinced him and the Council that Bell was the leading candidate.[44] Vose also found him charming, youthful, energetic, and available, and favored him over Strout who was ten years older than Bell and not so ebullient. Bell had graduated from the University of Minnesota in 1955, at age 23, and obtained a master's degree in theology in 1961. He also obtained an advanced degree in history (D.Phil.) from Balliol College, Oxford in 1964, but had no doctorate from an American university. He had lectured at Ohio State University, the College of Wooster, and Princeton and had run for the U.S. Congress. To these attractive educational attainments he could add a graceful wife and family of four. He was looking for a permanent position which would permit him to send his sons to college and showed unusual eagerness for the appointment when he heard of Pierce's death. His only weakness, the Council sensed, was a lack of appreciation of genealogy as a scholarly pursuit—and no historical publications of real merit. But the Council brushed aside these limitations for a person of his charm, talent, and education and expressed its joy in having him direct the Society.[45] Bell's lack of administrative or business experience was apparently unnoticed.

The later announcement of his appointment in the *Register* reveals the pleasure of the president and council in attracting such talent to the directorship:

> We were indeed fortunate that Dr. Bell was able to assume the duties of his new position immediately after his appointment. Since that day there has been an apparent new atmosphere of confidence and interest at the Society's house. We have complete faith in Dr. Bell's leadership to initiate a new era of progress in the activities of the Society.[46]

With Bell's appointment Strout resigned in anger as chairman of the Committee on Governance, and Vose hastened to appoint Rodney Armstrong, Whitehill's successor at the Boston Athenaeum, to that committee, with the hope that Armstrong's personality and new position at the Athenaeum would give additional support to Bell's appointment. Just a few months later Frederick M. Kimball resigned as treasurer—for health reasons primarily. His nearly eighteen years of service were valuable as well as colorful, but he could not prevent the deficits plaguing the Society. Kimball had already relinquished day-to-day duties to bookkeeper Dorothy M. Daybre, and at the 1974 annual election Zane Albion Thompson was chosen treasurer. This delightful man shared many personal qualities with Kimball, but suffered ill health and was not always present at the Society to advise Bell concerning its financial affairs.[47]

Kimball's departure in many ways was a distinctive loss—some of his talents were not so obvious at first. Long known for his consumption of liquor, he kept a supply in his Society office and celebrated the end of council meetings with favorite trustees by toasting the Society with a glass of brandy. At the Union Club he presided over a table of kindred spirits who broke the fast each noon with a martini or two. Witty and sociable, he was a portfolio manager for wealthy people like himself. NEHGS was ever in his thoughts as he moved about Boston society. His brother-in-law, Walter Whitehill, died of a stroke in 1978, but Kimball enjoyed fair health into the 1980s. His retirement soon after Dr. Bell's appointment was a significant event because Kimball was a careful financial manager and knew many potential donors. An equally experienced successor was necessary if his policies were to be maintained. In presenting the annual report on the budget in 1972, Kimball had these comments on the Society's finances: "We are operating on an entirely different basis from that of the olden days of Ashburton Place. As the saying goes, this [budget] is now an entirely different ball game."[48]

The mixed metaphor may confuse his point, but Kimball was dealing with nagging budget deficits, often threatening to enlarge, which were absorbing most available funds. The first duty of the new director and treasurer, he believed, would be to address this financial condition of the Society by increasing the endowment and attracting gifts to meet operating expenses.

James Bell began in the fall of 1973 his curious tenure of nine years as director. His service over those years was both applauded and criticized, but almost everyone, while he served as director, remarked favorably on his personal qualities. An actor at heart, he was tall and slender in appearance and engaging in conversation. He was warm in meeting the trustees and cold in handling the staff. Appearing to have much on his mind, he never seemed particularly happy as he went about his daily chores, but was visibly concerned first about the Society's welfare and secondarily about his family's.

The Society was clearly riding heavy waves when he took the helm. The years of Dean and Kimball left the Society with an accumulation of problems which seemed to defy solutions. Vose had used his power when he became president to hire younger staff, but expected Bell to provide direction and discipline. Bell was determined, as he told the Council, to change the course of the Society, which he felt was drifting toward a mostly arid genealogy, and was irritated by the *Register* emphasis on vital data and documentation. He looked for a blend of history and genealogy which would be attractive to professionals in both fields and contribute to renewed interest in the *Register*.[49]

Anne Harding probably told him, as she had others, that there was a shortage of material to publish in the *Register*. She had used Bible entries, census data, and McLean's long articles on Sandwich families to fill the empty pages. But the shortage prevailed. Her resignation as associate editor in 1974 gave Bell an opportunity to search for new leadership. His task was quickly solved, however, by Miss Harding, who introduced Ralph J. Crandall, from the University of Southern California, then working in the library, whom she had assisted recently in the research on his doctoral dissertation. Crandall's blend of history and biography in his study of Charlestown as a "haven port" seemed to be what the *Register* urgently needed—a kind of multi-biographical approach to genealogical phenomena—and he was immediately hired as associate editor. Bell urged Crandall to solicit similar materials from historians specializing in social history. The idea was attractive to the young editor, who quickly contacted distinguished historians and was rewarded with a good collection of papers. John J. Waters of the University of Rochester offered his study of "the New England Peasants . . . of Seventeenth Century Barnstable," William M. Fowler, Jr., of Northeastern University, his "John Hancock: the Paradoxical President [of the Continental Congress]," and John A. Schutz of the University of Southern California, his "Those who Became Tories." To inaugurate the new era, Bell ordered a bright new format for the *Register* and dedicated its April 1975 and July 1976 issues to the bicentennial of American independence.[50]

Even so, Crandall was wise enough to include traditional genealogical material in each issue. McLean's continuing study of the Gifford family of Sandwich, edited by Anne Harding, appeared in installments for several years. Peter Walne authored a valuable appraisal of new genealogical evidence of George Washington's ancestry, and Richard B. Johnson, the Society's new president, edited the diary of Israel Litchfield, which appeared in several installments. Other scholars who answered Crandall's call for papers were Byron Fairchild, John Eldridge Frost, William Pencak, James M. O'Toole, and G. B. Warden, a most talented group. None of them, however, was as supportive of the new policy as was President Johnson. In a letter to Rodney Armstrong, a friend and confidant, Johnson used forceful words:

> The object of the change in subject matter is just that: to attract new members by putting out a magazine that is readable for people who are not yet genealogists and yet contains bait to lure them into genealogy. . . . I would hope that even a 100% genealogist would appreciate learning a little more about his ancestors than simply whom they begot and who their sires and dams were. . . . I suspect that 90% of the members have been as disappointed as I usually have been on reading to the back cover in two minutes and finding nothing but someone else's begots or tombstones.[51]

Many other officers liked this change in the *Register*'s traditional offering and sent Bell glowing letters of approval. But many genealogists admired the old format and feared that the *Register* would be transformed into just another historical journal. The most unresponsive group were the social historians who had founded their own magazine and supported its publication. Crandall continued to look for good papers, however, from both disciplines and gradually built up a two-year backlog of prospective articles which had the quality that was traditionally part of the *Register*. He used outside readers and experts to appraise each submission and leaned toward genealogical materials whenever he could justify their publication to the director. Crandall depended for a few years on Susan Patterson, who had a master's degree from William and Mary College, for technical services, and later upon Edward Hanson, who had a local bachelor's degree but was anxious to study for a doctorate in history at a Boston university.[52]

Bell never seriously appreciated the importance of the *Register* as a depository for genealogical research. He was willing to sacrifice its long successful history for another type of journal. The reaction from some members eventually was a loss of interest in the Society. Bell interpreted this decline in membership differently by proposing instead a single, larger issue of the *Register* each year and other uses for the publication money. His suggestion, however, was cautiously received by the Council, which tabled it for future consideration.[53]

In justice to Bell, the *Register* had drastically changed over the years. It no longer published memoirs, obituaries, or antiquarian history. Even less appeared on Society proceedings. Bell's idea of turning toward collective history was new, but the journal carried history in its title through all of its existence. Some very good historical research had appeared in the *Register*.

Bell was much more successful in making the library usable and modern. He was distressed with the filing of all sorts of handwritten materials alongside published genealogies and histories. Problems of size, housing, and cataloguing disturbed him. His conversations with Stuart Myers, the young librarian and cataloguer, troubled him even more. He turned to outside, professional advice. Rodney Armstrong suggested consulting Maurice Taubler of the Columbia University School of Library Science. Correspondence with Taubler continued for some months, but Bell became convinced himself that a complete re-cataloguing of the book collection according to Library of Congress standards was his objective. It would be costly, but if done over a decade or two, would modernize the way the books were housed and processed. In evolving his policy, Bell fired Stuart Myers, who was argumentative, and found more congenial cataloguers. James C. Agnew, a professional librarian, was immediately hired to begin the task.[54] Sometime later Michael Gorn, an historian, became manuscripts librarian.

The manuscript collection was likewise in serious need of care. Many boxes of papers had no report of contents or proper storage. There was no archives as such and rare books, not yet designated as all pre-1840 imprints, were poorly catalogued. Bell raised questions about retaining such manuscripts as the Hancock Papers which contained almost entirely historical documents. But he curiously worked to return them to the Society from their loan to the Harvard Business School. He wanted rare books not identified as genealogy or history removed from the collection and sold to booksellers. The practice of putting manuscripts on the "floor of the safe"—at least as the designation of their location—Bell ordered discontinued. Manuscripts should have call numbers and regular places on shelves in the fifth floor depository.[55]

By its nature cataloguing was then a slow and costly process. Bell attracted some foundation support and interested one or two of the councilors in pledging additional help. The basic problem facing him, however, was an acute shortage of undedicated funds. Almost every budget of the last fifteen years had a deficit. But routine daily operations were only slightly affected because the Society had many small endowments, called permanent funds, which paid for certain kinds of services like purchases of books, office expenses for the *Register*, care of furniture, and preservation of manuscripts, and these funds could not be used for any other purpose except those provided by the donor. Otherwise, most expenses were funded by the endowment and an annual request for donations. Here the devices of Bell and Thompson in finding money were creative. They applied yearly gifts (institutionalized in 1975 and much cultivated as the Annual Appeal) to operating expenses, and searched the general endowment to locate necessary money, sometimes by buying and selling stocks. In this way, salaries could be raised, books purchased, and the building maintained, but these were not lush times. Sometimes the general endowment had to be raided. Likewise, staff replacements were hired at the lowest prevailing wage. They were often too young, on their first assignment, recently married, and taking a job to supplement family income, or they were older, re-entering employees drawing from family annuities to supplement low salaries.[56] When Bell needed an experienced maintenance man in 1977, he changed his policy and hired Chris (Christopher Patrick) O'Sullivan, who painted, sealed damaged window frames, and attacked the accumulations of dust and grime. Sometimes Chris had to await money to purchase the paint.

Willing as Bell was to conduct a capital campaign by mail, which would advise members of the financial exigencies of the Society, he was aware of past failures of this form of solicitation. Members plainly did not respond generously to financial drives without some personal contact—and Bell hated to ask for money. He decided, therefore, to consult endowment advisers and employed an assistant to uncover specific opportunities. His selection of John Shugart, who became "a marvelous personal friend and congenial staff member," was the first step.[57] Shugart, in his late twenties or early thirties, was immediately instructed to study the member files and identify likely people whom Bell should meet and befriend. Shugart and Bell would then develop together a list of likely donors.

These plans were barely matured when treasurer Zane Thompson became critically ill, and Johnson, Bell, and Armstrong urged him to resign in favor of Ralph L. Pope, who enjoyed good health and had experience with campaigning for funds.[58] Rather than depending entirely on Shugart, Pope advised Bell to use a firm of solicitors. But he deferred to Bell's opinions and decisions. Bell had not fully charted his course when Richard B. Johnson died suddenly of cancer, though his tall, thin figure indicated for years the presence of a serious physical ailment. The presidency now seemed naturally to be destined for the lively director of the Boston Athenaeum, Rodney Armstrong, who had a long acquaintance with the Society—longer than any of the current leaders.[59]

A fast friend of Bell and a fellow member of the Somerset Club, Armstrong had great confidence in Bell and had grown to admire him. They began now a formal correspondence, even though their offices were about one mile apart, and met regularly for lunch at the club. But despite Armstrong's superior qualifications for the presidency, his own position was competitive with Bell's, many of their institutional friends were the same people, and certainly they drew from the same pool of donors.[60] Both men, nonetheless, liked the new relationship.

These changes in Society leadership brought new people around Bell, but they did not provide the consultative role of institutional checks and balances, and Bell took advantage of the latitude. President Armstrong, however, realizing that the control of expenditures was sloppy, advised Bell through a letter to the new treasurer in 1977—"we never seem to get an accurate idea of what our income [is] . . . at any given point and [have] very little control over expenditures." Armstrong, a skillful administrator himself, hoped for better accounting procedures in the Society—perhaps from Pope—and less reliance upon the expedient of using bequests to balance the budget.[61]

Bell's advisors had already suggested that he conduct a series of seminars all over the United States, as preliminary to the announcement of a capital campaign. He asked John Shugart to accompany him, and employed David W. Dumas, an expert in legal history, as one of the speakers. Staff librarian David Dearborn often accompanied them. These seminars were frequently held at libraries, on college campuses, at homes of Society members, and at almost any suitable hall which would accommodate an audience. This outward reach of the Society continued for the next four years. Participants paid a nominal fee for a day's session and frequently talked with the speakers. Most left the seminar in the late afternoons fully satisfied that they had met a wonderful leader of the Society and his knowledgeable staff.[62]

In Los Angeles, Bell and his staff held day-long seminars for three years in succession at the University of Southern California as guests of the dean of the social sciences. They attracted seventy to eighty participants each year. Bell knew the participants by first names and genealogical projects, and brought some genealogical information to aid them in continuing their research. There were handouts for the audience, membership applications, and copies of the *Register*. Bell usually spoke at the end of the day's seminar, often with humor, folksy illustrations, and genuine guidance.[63] His tall thin figure in the midst of a crowd of admirers was that of a successful, experienced performer.

Bell and his staff appeared always well dressed, in black suits, and drove in expensive rental automobiles. The tours were intended to be first-class affairs, sometimes ending with a reception at the home of a prominent member. Bell was always hesitant to make any pitch for funds, but depended on the fees of participants. Eventually, of course, he expected them to give to the endowment and remember the Society in their wills. For any year these seminars were costly, using Bell's time and the scarce resources of the Society. In 1981-82 seminar expense was $69,012 and income $50,773.[64] Councilors (later trustees) thus questioned whether Bell should continue holding almost monthly seminars. He was understandably sensitive about these expenditures and spoke generally of their cost in reports to the trustees and President Armstrong. The tours were a gamble, which could pay great dividends, but a gamble just the same.[65]

If the seminars were to be justified, they had to produce commensurate increases in gifts and bequests and new members. But any evidence of success was negative. The seminars had to be measured instead by the friendly greetings of many warm-natured members who were charmed by their acquaintance with Bell. Most sent only small contributions to the Society and regarded genealogy as a hobby. Some may have given larger sums to well-known charities and universities.

Bell was not openly discouraged by this lack of response. He was building the goodwill of members and expressed an upbeat attitude toward the future. A letter of February 14, 1978 reveals his public mood and intentions:

> I leave on Sunday for a two and a half week lecture tour, which will take me to Stanford, the University of Southern California, the University of San Diego, and various other universities through the sun-belt to Florida. We will be meeting and chatting with friends and members of the Society along the way, and it is gratifying to know, for example, that at Stanford we have more than one hundred and fifty people registered for our day-long lecture program. Hopefully, it will breathe new and stronger life into this splendid old New England institution.[66]

His view of these seminars was given sharper focus for Ralph L. Pope, the treasurer, when Bell said that these tours were preliminary to a capital fund drive. "I think we ought to continue to build our fences and establish our friendships with people who can help the Society."[67] Bell hesitated to say that the Society was threatened with bankruptcy if he did not commence his long-awaited campaign. But he delayed that campaign repeatedly. His letters were hopeful, however, full of plans to attract money, and praise for the reception that he and the staff were receiving everywhere.

In Boston Director Bell was confronted with harsh realities. Society bills were regularly delinquent, sometimes by one to four months, and even the printer of the *Register* held the 1980 October issue for nearly three months while he pressed for payment.[68] Payroll was difficult to make, but with the help of Pope and Mrs. Daybre he found money. Bell searched for rare library books which could be marketed and pressed Robert Vose for a good appraisal of portraits which might then be sold. Actually his greatest problem was the delinquency (or delay) of membership dues. In September 1980 Bell wrote in anguish to Armstrong that the Society had an operating deficit of $137,000, which included $78,000 in delinquent dues:

> I want to chat with you about the procedures we should put in place during the coming . . . twelve months in hopes of offsetting the constant scramble to meet our payroll and pay our bills. We have eliminated all expenses except those which are absolutely essential or which generate additional revenue. I fear the runaway assaults of inflation and the curious economy are having their bruising affects on the Society.[69]

Personally Bell was encountering opposition from his staff, who wanted a voice in the management of the Society. Bell insisted upon being addressed as "Dr." and had developed some personal idiosyncrasies. He discontinued holding staff conferences and met individuals face-to-face in the privacy of his office. His words there were often sharp. Only vague reasons were given for firing Reference Librarian Gary Boyd Roberts in 1977. Roberts, hired in 1974, had come immediately from the graduate school of the University of Chicago and earlier from undergraduate work at Yale University. He was a native-born Texan interested in royal descent and the ancestry of notable historical figures. Outspoken in his opinions, which were frequently given in unguarded conversation, Roberts had perhaps outraged a trustee, possibly also Bell himself.[70] The reaction of some members to his release was instantaneous. A few canceled their memberships and complained to Bell who would years later (1981) restore Roberts to the staff. The

treatment of Roberts had larger implications because genealogists regarded him as one of their own.[71] He was a competent young scholar in
an organization that had only David C. Dearborn as the other resident
genealogist.

Probably sensing this feeling toward him, Bell kept his home life
separate from the office. He rarely entertained at home, but relied upon
Rodney Armstrong to host the trustees and staff, or used memberships
in clubs and the availability of restaurants in the Back Bay.[72] Armstrong
had a beautifully furnished home at the foot of Beacon Hill near the
Charles River, spacious and suitable for modest-size groups. A conversationalist, he and his wife provided much luster at trustee dinners.

Bell had two sons whom he was readying for college. These sons
were added occasionally to the Society staff when they were at home,
and Scott Bell in 1982 was receiving a salary at the rate of $12,000 a
year.[73] Bell's own compensation in 1982 was $39,930, about $15,000
more than he was paid in 1976.[74]

In administering the Society, Bell abandoned the traditional use of
committees. Thus the usual affairs of the Society were often unknown to
the Council which concluded, nonetheless, that Bell was doing a competent job under distressing circumstances. They were aware of the
red-ink budgets. Some councilors from time to time reacted to the lack
of information and pressured for an internal audit, but the director was
able to keep the Council's respect overall.[75] In 1979-80 Bell successfully
urged changes in the governance of the Society. Control of the Council,
he felt, was unduly concentrated in New England; a larger number of
councilors would enable the western United States to be represented.
He also wanted the governing body to be called a Board of Trustees,
reflecting their responsibility as leaders of the organization. His authority was slightly increased as director, but the changes, except for the size
of the board, were not significant.[76]

These changes did not materially modify Bell's major problem: the
acute financial condition of the Society. The threat of bankruptcy was
facing the Society in 1980 because of declining revenues and rising
costs, and drastic action was necessary. The trustees reacted not as one

might have expected by ordering an audit of expenditures, nor did they challenge Bell's policy of holding costly seminars across the nation. Curiously, with them he remained popular. While Rodney Armstrong had become uneasy in 1979 and spoke of resigning, he remained in office and continued his support.[77] He knew that Bell was dipping into the endowment for operating expenses and that the financial crisis was deepening. He was likewise aware of the failure of annual giving to provide sufficient income.[78] His concern was apparently not communicated to the Trustees.

The practice of dipping into reserves had so reduced the endowment by 1980 that it was worth about $572,000, or nearly half its value in 1972.[79] Two years later, the endowment fell to $536,000. By that time Bell arranged with the Vose Art Gallery to sell a small collection of paintings worth $500,000. These funds were then placed in money market accounts which could be drawn upon to pay daily bills.[80]

The sale of the paintings provoked the trustees to question the advisability of selling Society treasures. The heat of their reaction was evident to Bell. Several trustees wanted part of the money invested in stocks and placed in the endowment. But Bell explained to them that the Society would close its doors without the availability of this money. A majority of the trustees with advice from President Armstrong reluctantly decided that this most drastic measure was better than alternatives of selling the library building or joining another Boston organization—if these were truly alternatives. But the sale of the paintings, though serious, was no more than a temporary solution. The trustees, notwithstanding their new awareness of severe economic problems, did not appoint a business manager nor take into their own hands the management of the Society.[81]

The operating deficit was nearly $235,000 in 1980-81 and over $200,000 in 1981-82. Armstrong, from his experience at the Athenaeum, told Bell that he was "greatly concerned."[82] John Shugart, who was advising Bell on the coming capital campaign, abruptly resigned to take a position on the staff of the Harvard Medical School. Apparently Bell had decided to cut office expenses and helped Shugart secure a job elsewhere.[83] Bell continued, nonetheless, his hectic schedule of trips around the United States. In 1981, he spent $95,635 on these seminars and in 1982 almost $69,000.[84] The weak response to the seminars began to disturb even Bell, who had expected to collect some sizeable gifts to offset the deficits, and he surveyed, privately at first, possible job opportunities for himself. At seminars in California, New York, and elsewhere he inquired cautiously about vacancies in libraries and spoke off-the-record with hosts about giving him recommendations.[85]

Not all members of the Society were ready to back Bell in his hectic race with bankruptcy. Mrs. Robert G. Fuller, the vice president in 1980, had doubts about Bell's policies, as did President Armstrong who resigned his post in 1982 in favor of Arthur A. Dunn. Armstrong was uneasy about the extent of expenditures, accounting practices, and his own ability to give the help that Bell apparently needed. Dunn was then retired as an executive of the U.S. Life Credit Corporation, living in nearby Shrewsbury, but willing to give his advice on the administration of the Society. He was knowledgeable about the running of large corporations and possessed a commanding personality that tolerated no sloppiness in the management of a business.[86]

Bell realized immediately that Dunn would make demands upon his time, question his policies, and look into expenditures.[87] In July 1982, when he received an attractive offer from the prestigious New-York Historical Society, an older and wealthier institution than the New England Historic Genealogical Society, he resigned his directorship as of July 31. The offer gave him an opportunity to sharpen his administrative skills at a well endowed, strategically located historical institution that had grown old and needed energetic leadership. Delighted as he must have been to escape the problems of pulling the Society out of its difficulties, he regained his self-confidence, thought of taking to New York members of his Boston staff, and bought five round-trip tickets for his family to visit New York—flights charged on his Society credit card.

The reaction on Newbury Street to his sudden departure was one of disbelief. His secret was well kept from nearly everyone. The Society's *News-Letter* featured the announcement as the cover story of its summer issue, with a page-and-a-quarter tribute to his nine years of service. A photograph, almost Lincoln-like in its impression, was included. Only a few words were quoted directly from Bell's resignation remarks, but they were most revealing: "People, like plants, sometimes need to be re-potted to continue to grow and develop." Bell expressed his appreciation to the staff and trustees whom he said gave the Society the "revitalization" it was then experiencing. Former president Rodney Armstrong and several officers or trustees expressed florid tributes. None was more extensive than that of Professor John A. Schutz:

> In the life of any institution there are steps to progress and when Jim Bell took over the directorship of the Society in 1973, he decided that there should be a modern library standard of operations and the publication of genealogies. And he succeeded marvelously in bringing new technology to the Society. Further, he extended the reach of the Society's scholarship to every city in the United States and eastern Canada . . . . Jim has brought warmth and energy to the Society's relations with its members. We will miss his leadership.[88]

The Board of Trustees were genuinely sorry to lose Dr. Bell. His abrupt resignation bewildered them, but President Dunn was not one to hesitate. Appointing forthwith a special committee of three trustees, he held a full discussion of the crisis as they understood it. Some trustees asked for a national search for a new director; others felt the crisis was too overwhelming to waste time in hunting for a director when they had a young man on the staff who could work with them and President Dunn and take immediate measures to relieve the emergency. The trustees interviewed Ralph J. Crandall, historian, editor of the *Register*, and a native New Englander, and offered him the position of acting director, even though a few trustees protested that he had not the experience of James B. Bell.

Bell left for New York with the warm regards of most trustees.[89] They continued to hold their favorable opinion of him and his service into 1982-1983. They did not blame him for the crisis in the Society's fortunes, but they had second thoughts about his travels around the United States. They wondered why he never launched the promised capital fund campaign, why he spent money for experts like Shugart and a New York fund-raiser and never used them, and why there were no sizable gifts received as a result of his seminars. They believed Bell to be a hardworking, honest, and efficient director, and thus they never asked for an accounting of his personal expenditures, nor challenged his judgment and policies, nor interrogated the staff, especially the bookkeeper, about the welfare of the Society. They knew very little about the operations of an organization they loved and served.

Permanent Funds and Income, 1974-1982

	Funds	Income
1974	$902,727.00	$42,126.00 [*]
1975	$924,120.00	$41,022.00 [*]
1976	$954,692.00	$36,949.00
1977	$955,614.00	$23,746.00
1978	$964,473.00	$37,808.00
1979	$970,798.00	$35,840.00
1980	$954,044.00	$35,944.00
1981	$1,006,366.00	$45,490.00
1982	$1,049,904.00	$50,000.00 [†]

The Bell Years 1974-1982
Market Value of Bonds and Stocks

	Stocks	Bonds	Budget-Closure
1974	$632,435.00	$153,769.00	-$99,637.00
1975	$809,795.00	$164,677.00	-$132,883.00
1976	$809,795.00	$229,875.00	-$97,121.00
1977	$667,111.00	$190,254.00	-$40,005.00
1978	$615,150.00	$119,517.00	-$141,843.00
1979	$479,940.00	$145,192.00	-$169,464.00
1980	$496,600.00	$76,050.00	-$206,219.00
1981	$379,648.00	$68,630.00	-$234,585.00
1982	$389,460.00	$156,810.00	-$209,595.00

[*] Includes receipts also from Special Funds.
[†] Estimated income.

Notes

[1] Newbury Street was depicted by Susan Berk and Jill Bloom in their *Uncommon Boston: A Guide to Hidden Spaces & Special Places* (Reading, 1987), p.124. "Newbury Street, with its authentic nineteenth-century charm, has been home to the finest merchants and art dealers for over a century. When Beacon Hill residents moved into this area after its creation in the mid-1800s, the shops that were serving Beacon Hill residents moved here along with them. Everything from imported rugs to groceries was sold here, and the street today displays the same broad selection of goods . . . .As you browse along, don't forget to look up at the eccentric rooftops at the bay and bowfront windows, down at the tiny patios with their surprising little gardens and occasional sculpture. No space is wasted on this street. You'll notice that many shops occupy either the second story or basement levels and that the buildings have been put to both commercial and residential use."

[2] Edgar Dean to Walter M. Whitehill, January 16, 1968, Director's file, NEHGS, MSS. "I have long thought it is asking a lot of the president to come here two consecutive afternoons in the same week."

[3] Edgar Dean's Report to President, January 2, 1964, Director's file; Dean to Roger B. Tyler, April 18, 1967, Director's file.

[4] Frederick M. Kimball's reports in Council meetings, October 5 and November 30, 1965. Council Records, 1963-1973, pp. 89-90, 98-99, NEHGS.

[5] Building Committee Report, September 9, 1963, and Donald R. Grant to John E. Sullivan, December 30, 1965, Director's file.

[6] See Council Records, 1963-1973, January 6 and March 3, 1965, pp. 62-66, 74-75; May 6, 1964, pp. 49-51.

[7] Edward B. Hanify to Frederick M. Kimball, August 19, 1966, Director's File.

[8] Space was not adequate in the opinion of the Council for rentals to other societies. See Council Records, 1963-1973, March 4 and April 1, 1964, pp. 44, 49-51.

[9] When a water pipe broke in the basement in 1966, part of the Adams library was damaged. It was dried out and saved, but Whitehill wanted the collection removed to the stacks and catalogued. Delays occurred for years and the collection had a special limited-access section on the lower sixth floor. See Council Records, 1963-1973, October 3, 1965, pp. 164-165. Interview with David Dearborn, October 27, 1993, who joined Gary Roberts in moving the collection in 1976 before it was integrated into the main library.

[10] The disposal of the plaques was a recurring problem. Robert Vose wanted the problem settled in 1968. See Council Records, 1963-1973, November 6, 1968, pp. 196-197.

[11] Council Records, 1963-1973, October 3, 1967, pp. 164-165; October 7, 1970,

pp. 239-240. The only serious report of a theft of a Society owned portrait occurred in early 1982, when James Bell discovered on a regular inspection of the library that the Ephraim Turner portrait by John Greenwood (1727-1792) was missing. Bell was reportedly aroused, but he did little to locate the painting. In August 1982 Ralph Crandall, his successor, reported its loss to the Art Dealers Association of America. The painting then was valued at well over $50,000. Some years later it was discovered almost accidentally at a flea market sale and returned to the Society. See file 43-55, Turner Portraits, NEHGS archives.

[12] Council Records, 1963-1973, October 7, November 4, December 2, 1970, pp. 239-251. Miss Edith E. Hazelton was the victim of the violence. Already nearly blind, she was frightened and resigned her connection with the Society after 46 years of service. She was given a pension of about $2,500 in 1971. See Council Records, 1963-1973, October 6, 1971. See also her obituary notice in NEXUS 2 (1985): 134.

[13] Dean reported on the seminar in the *Register* 119 (1965): 241-243. The only disagreeable part of the meeting was Boston's summer heat.

[14] Council Records, 1963-1973, April 5, 1966, p. 117. The fee was set at $20.00. Dean canceled the 1967 seminar in February but the Council objected and delayed the decision. Ibid., April 4, 1967, p. 155.

[15] Council Records, 1963-1973, January 31 and February 14, 1967, pp. 143-148.

[16] Robert C. Vose was selected as the new sole vice president, but the former holders of that office were asked to be honorary vice presidents and continue in office to 1970. See Council Records, 1963-1973, June 6, 1967, p. 161.

[17] Council Records, 1963-1973, February 6, 1968, pp. 176-177.

[18] Dunn changed his residency several times, but the new responsibilities took him eventually to Illinois with corporate offices in Chicago. He would return to his Shrewsbury residence when he resigned as president of the U.S. Life Insurance Credit Corporation in 1979. Renewal of activity on the Society's behalf brought him to the presidency in April 1982.

[19] The Society experienced deficits in the late 1960s, but had a rising membership and a few substantial gifts. The Florence S. Dustin Trust gave the Society nearly $200,000 over these years. See Council Records, 1963-1973, November 4, 1970, pp. 248. The only explanation for abandonment of the 1968 fund-raising campaign appeared in 1971 when Kimball was surveying Society finances. He said the drive was suspended because of the "reluctance of individuals to make substantial gifts at this time."

[20] Council Records, 1963-1973, October 6, 1971, no page numbers. Kimball emphasized that his objective was a million-dollar endowment. See ibid., March 3, 1971, p. 261.

[21] Memberships tended to rise and fall without much reason, although the Council thought an increase in annual dues was the major explanation. In February 1971, members numbered 3700; in April 3790; in November 4029; and in January 1972, 4020.

[22] Council Records, 1963-1973, October 6, 1971 and February 2, 1972.

[23] Interview of Anne B. Harding with author, Killeen, Texas, September 1993.

[24] In December 1968, Doane wanted the cover of the *Register* redesigned. Nothing was done for some months, but Whitehill led a discussion of the costs of the *Register* on April 2, 1969. He thought the overruns, mailing, and manufacturing costs needed careful attention and urged Doane and Dean to investigate. Apparently little was accomplished until the May 1970 meeting when the rag content of the *Register*'s paper was changed. The number of *Register* pages was set at 80 or within budget limitations.

[25] Council Records, 1963-1973, May 6, 1970, pp. 237-238. The new electric typewriter was received formally by the Council at the December 3, 1969 meeting. Ibid., p. 220. By 1976, the cost of duplicating materials had been reduced to fifteen cents.

[26] Council Records, 1963-1973, January 7, 1970, p. 223.

[27] Council Records, 1963-1973, January 6, 1971, p. 252.

[28] Council Records, 1963-1973, February 2 and April 5, 1972, no page numbers.

[29] Council Records, 1963-1973, November 1, 1971, no page numbers. The library was robbed of $155 in cash.

[30] A tribute was paid George A. Moriarty (1883-1968) in the *Register*, 123 (1969): 3-5. The memoir recognized Moriarty's major contribution to the Society as a committeeman (Publications) and councilor 1912-1919, 1949-1954, 1954-1957. He was vice president for Rhode Island from 1920-1949. A man of strong, authoritarian views, he sometimes used harsh language. For an assessment of his contribution to genealogical scholarship see Gary Boyd Roberts' introduction to *English Origins of New England Families From The New England Historical and Genealogical Register*, 1st series (Baltimore, 1984), 1: viii-xi.

[31] John I. Coddington and George A. Moriarty exchanged some views in the 1960s when Coddington was seriously considered for the position of librarian-editor and Doane selected as editor. See Moriarty to Coddington, February 19, 1960, Coddington Papers, NEHGS.

[32] Robert C. Vose to author, July 1993. The records do not indicate that Vose planned further dismissals; King, Hazelton, Doane and Harding all asked for retirement.

[33] Council Records, 1963-1973, May 3, September 7, and December 6, 1972 on Dean's retirement.

[34] Reports of Committee on Governance, H. Vincent Strout, Chairman, August 17, 1972, Director's file.

[35] Ibid., October 30, 1972.

[36] George R. Ursul, "Richard D. Pierce: A Personal Reminiscence," *Register*, 128 (1974): 3-9.

[37] Ibid., pp. 3-4.

[38] Committee on Governance, H. Vincent Strout, Chairman, Second Report, October, 1972, Director's File.

[39] Ibid.

[40] Anne B. Harding to Robert C. Vose, April 30, 1973, Director's File.

[41] Council Records, 1963-1973, December 5, 1993, NEHGS.

[42] Her vita is in the Director's file. Susan L. Patterson attended St. Olaf College, 1966-69 before enrolling at the University of Illinois.

[43] Richard Brigham Johnson lived in Swampscott, practiced law, and enjoyed genealogy. A kindly man, tall and thin, he held strong opinions about politics and was intolerant of fools.

[44] James Brugler Bell was born in St. Paul, Minnesota, in 1932. He called himself a "country boy." He was introduced to the Council by Eugene V. Goetchius who gave him a fine recommendation. Bell and Goetchius lived near each other for a year in England when Bell was preparing for his D. Phil. at Balliol College.

[45] Vose was likewise impressed with Bell's qualifications. In January 1974 he told the Council that "Dr. Bell immediately proved himself a gentleman not only qualified for the position, but possessed of considerable courage." See Council Report for 1973, Vose's Correspondence, NEHGS.

[46] Robert C. Vose, "Dr. James Brugler Bell," *Register*, 129 (1974): 81-82. This announcement is an amazing tribute by the president to the director.

[47] Both Vose and Kimball retired at the same time. Johnson, Bell, and Thompson became their successors as the new leaders of the Society. Bell was elected a member of the Union Club in May 1974. He began his correspondence with Rodney Armstrong about the time he was hired as director, but Armstrong as a member of the finance committee gave Bell advice on the problems of running the Society beginning in 1974. Their close association made Armstrong another of these leaders.

[48] Kimball's report at the Annual Meeting, April 5, 1972. He had announced two deficits of about $23,000 each for budget years 1970-1972. Council Records, April 5, 1972, Correspondence file, NEHGS.

[49] Bell told Richard B. Johnson on November 28, 1973 that he was looking for a younger replacement for Anne Harding. In July 1974 he admitted to Winifred Dodge that Ralph Crandall was the type of person and specialist he desired. See their correspondence beginning July 3, 1974, in Director's file. Armstrong to Bell, July 29, 1975, praised Bell and Crandall for the new direction in which they had taken the *Register* .

[50] This new format and focus for the *Register* brought a letter from William Bentinck-Smith to Richard B. Johnson, November 3, 1975, in which he praised the blend of local history and genealogy, Director's file.

[51] Richard B. Johnson to Rodney Armstrong, June 5, 1975, Director's file.

[52] Interview with Ralph J. Crandall, October 29, 1993. Genealogists like Winifred Dodge were insistent that genealogical content was the mission of the

Register. See Dodge to James B. Bell, August 8, 1975, Director's file. She complained that there was "too much would-be history and not enough genealogical history." Armstrong told Bell just three weeks earlier that he thought "this issue [of the *Register*], represents a real step forward into the right direction." Armstrong particularly liked the article by John A. Schutz. See Armstrong to Bell, April 30, 1975, ibid.

[53] Opposition to these experimental measures with the *Register* was mounting. See Rodney Armstrong to Stephen Millett, October 11, 1978, Director's file. Armstrong blames Robert C. Anderson, a young genealogist, for some of the opposition. The Council rejected Anderson's written complaints in the summer of 1978. See Armstrong to Millett, October 11, 1978. Director's file.

[54] Bell added Gary Boyd Roberts to the staff in October 1974, and David Curtis Dearborn in January 1976. Both gave lectures for the Society and received praise for their efforts. See Stuart G. Waite to Richard B. Johnson, April 9, 1976. Director's file.

[55] The Society received a grant of $35,000 for the care of the manuscript collection in 1979. Bell hired Michael Gorn, a young historian, and later Nathaniel N Shipton to work on the collections. See Bell to Armstrong, April 27 and July 13, 1979, Director's file.

[56] Personnel costs were obviously a major part of the expense of operating the Society. Armstrong raised the possibility of reducing staff. See May 4, 1979, Director's file.

[57] Bell to Armstrong, August 11, 1980, Director's file. Shugart was hired in 1977. His salary was $15,000.

[58] Rodney Armstrong to Ralph L. Pope, March 7, 1977, Director's file.

[59] Richard Brigham Johnson died in June 1977. Bell began his nationwide tours soon afterward. He accepted a speaking engagement with John I. Coddington and others in Phoenix for February 30, 1978. See Bell to Robert Young, December 15, 1977, Director's file. Coddington later cancelled.

[60] Bell listed for Armstrong nearly $61,000 in gifts for 1978, but felt a systematic giving program was necessary. See Bell to Armstrong, July 5 and July 6, 1978, Director's file.

[61] Rodney Armstrong to Ralph L. Pope, March 7, 1977, Director's file. Apparently neither man wanted to monitor Mrs. Daybre's accounting.

[62] Bell told Armstrong on March 6, 1979 that his latest speaking tour was a major financial success. Expenses were $4,790 and receipts $16,375. But the general Society deficit was $72,000.

[63] Observations of John A. Schutz at the University of Southern California, 1978.

[64] Auditor's Report for August 31, 1982, Director's file.

[65] The tours were admittedly costly, but they do not reflect all expenses—telephone, postage, staff time, etc. would need to be added. Bell himself was

giving time when he should have been planning a capital campaign. While annual giving increased in 1981-82, few bequests were received.

[66] Bell to John Wells Davidson, February 14, 1978, Director's file.

[67] Bell to Ralph L. Pope, March 22, 1978, Director's file.

[68] Bell to Arthur Dunn, November 23, 1981, Director's file. Bell estimated "an accumulated backlog of current bills amounting to $136,000."

[69] Bell to Rodney Armstrong, September 3, 1980, Director's file.

[70] Interview with Gary Boyd Roberts on October 28, 1993.

[71] See Elizabeth Booth to James B. Bell, December 15, 1979, Director's file.

[72] Tradition among the staff describes only one reception at the Bell home during the entire time he was director. Bell used a variety of fine restaurants in the Back Bay for the annual dinners. He reserved the Harvard Club in downtown Boston at least once.

[73] Executive Committee Report, August 24, 1982, Director's file.

[74] Executive Committee Report, August 24, 1982, Director's file; Council Records, December 8, 1976, lists the salary of $25,000. Pierce's salary in 1973 was $17,000.

[75] Mrs. Anne McCarthy asked at the trustees meeting "if an annual audit is undertaken of the Society's books." Trustees Meeting of October 14, 1981, Trustees Papers, NEHGS. At the July 14, 1981 meeting James Bell gave the figure for annual giving and admitted that solicitation costs were 20%.

[76] Most of these explanations of enhanced responsibility for the new Board of Trustees should be treated as hyperbole. In a letter of Rodney Armstrong to James B. Bell and Arthur Dunn, June 19, 1981, Armstrong notes that: "There is, in my experience, little point in trying to get good advice from trustees who only had a half hour or so to glance over detailed financial reports." Quarterly department reports, and their receipt by all trustees well before meetings, began in 1988. Longer trustee meetings, with much expanded discussion, began with the presidency of Theodore Chase.

[77] Rodney Armstrong to James B. Bell, July 1, 1980, Director's file.

[78] Ibid. Armstrong expressed his deep concern about financial conditions at the Society.

[79] The market value of bonds and stocks in 1973 was $1,043,930. In 1980, it was $572,650; in 1981, $448,278.

[80] The Society paintings sold in 1980 were Hathaway's "Ruth (Thomas) Winsor;" Hathaway's "Seth Winsor;" Hathaway's "A View of Mr. Joshua Winsor's House and Docks;" and Corne's "Landing of the Pilgrims, December 22, 1620."

[81] Armstrong suggested to Dunn and Bell that a business manager might be a solution. See his letter of June 19, 1981, Director's file.

[82] See budget reports for 1980-82, Director's file.

[83] Shugart left the Society in August 1980. See Bell to Armstrong, August 11, 1980, Director's file.

[84] Bell's autumn schedule of seminars for 1980:

> 27 Sept.: Rochester, NY, University of Rochester
> 29 Sept.: Seattle, WA, University of Washington
> 30 Sept.: Portland, OR, Portland State University
> 4 Oct.: Arlington, TX, University of Texas
> 6 Oct.: Asheville, NC, University of N.C., Asheville
> 27 Oct.: Denver, CO, Colorado Women's College
> 29 Oct.: Kansas City, MO, Kansas City Public Library
> 31 Oct.: Indianapolis, IN, Indiana University and Purdue University
> 18 Nov.: Lexington, MA, Museum of Our National Heritage
> 20 Nov.: Greenwich, CT, Greenwich Public Library
> 22 Nov.: West Barnstable, MA, Cape Cod Comm. College

[85] Income and costs of seminar program in 1981-1982, by month:

		Income	Expense
Sept. 1981	Salt Lake City	$10,401.84	$ 4,322.76
Oct.	"	3,664.00	5,579.34
Nov.	"	4.16	17,545.79
Dec.	"	——	8,633.83
Jan. 1982	Misc. Seminars	2,218.00	292.85
Feb.	"	4,410.00	3,484.69
March	"	4,686.00	7,429.56
April	"	3,269.95	12,322.84
June	"	1,828.00	2,054.39
July	"	1,950.00	8,353.38
August	Salt Lake City	16,579.82	2,684.96
		$50,772.77	$71,868.13

Bell resigned on July 26, 1982. He left at the end of August.

[86] Armstrong advised Bell and Dunn, who were studying the finances of the Society, that a business advisor service might help trustees and officers understand the financial conditions and chart a course of action. See Armstrong letter of June 19, 1981, Director's file.

[87] Dunn presented to the trustees a wise and informative analysis of Society problems on January 19, 1982. He noted that the Society needed at least $300,000 additional income which could be met by increased dues, a capital drive, sale of paintings, and a rise in book loan fees. His report was a major part of the trustees meeting of January 19, 1982.

[88] *News-Letter of the New England Historic Genealogical Society,* Summer, 1982. Almost everyone who commented on Bell's contributions emphasized the quality of his leadership, his personality, and his energy. Mrs. Joan Ferris Curran said that his leadership "these nine years has been truly outstanding." Mrs. Shirley Goodwin Bennett mentioned his "intelligence, professionalism, and a gracious

personality." Rodney Armstrong, the former president, was a bit restrained, but cited progress in the library and the publications program.

[89] Bell's experiences at the New-York Historical Society were most unfortunate from the day he took charge as director until his resignation about six years later. "Administrative expenses . . . went from $46,000 in 1981 to $534,000 six years later. 'Professional services' . . . multiplied eightfold, to $639,000." Bell's own salary rose to $90,000, with provisions for overtime. The result was a drastic use of endowment, sale of Society treasures, neglect of preservation of paintings, and a release of staff, and still the budget continued in the red. The market value of the endowment dropped from $13.6 million in 1986 to $7.6 in 1988. See articles by Douglas C. McGill in the *New York Times*, June 28, July 10, July 13, July 19, July 25, and July 28, 1988, and a *New York* magazine feature of July 25, 1988 by Kay Larson.

Five major twentieth-century genealogists much assoicated with the Society (above and on the following page): Mrs. Mary Campbell Lovering Holman (1868-1947, above left) and Clarence Almon Torrey (1869-1962, bottom right), from the *Register* 102(1948):opposite p. 3, and F.C. Torrey, *The Torrey Families and their Children in America*, vol. 2 (Lakehurst, N.J., 1929), p. 276.

George Andrews Moriarty, Jr. (1883-1968, top); Walter Goodwin Davis, Jr. (1885-1966, bottom left); and John Insley Coddington (1902-1991, bottom right), from *Harvard Class of 1906 Twenty-Fifth Anniversary Report* (Cambridge, Mass., 1931) (Moriarty) and the *Register* 120(1966):opposite p. 241; 145(1991):196. The manuscript collections of Mrs. Holman (and her daughter, Mrs. Winifred Lovering Holman Dodge), Torrey, Moriarty and Coddington were given to the Society.

Anne Borden Harding (born 1907, picture above ca. 1946), assistant or associate editor of the *Register*, 1969-1974. Misses Harding and Elsie McCormack undertook the day-to-day work of the *Register* during the editor-ships of Gilbert Harry Doane and John D. Austin, Jr.

Walter Muir Whitehill (1905-1978), 19th President of the Society,
1963-1971, Director of the Boston Athenaeum, 1946-1973 (courtesy
of the Boston Athenaeum).

Rodney Armstrong (born 1923), 22nd President of the Society, 1977-1982, Director of the Boston Athenaeum since 1973 (courtesy of the Boston Athenaeum).

NEHGS staff in December, 1974, in the sixth-floor Reading Room at 101 New-
bury St. Seated (from left): Director James Brugler Bell, Diane MacLachlan,
Comptroller Dorothy M. Daybre, Cynthia D. Fleming, assistant *Register* editor
Susan L. Patterson, Anne Pulling, Mary Haskell. Standing (from left): George

DeMetz, associate *Register* editor Ralph J. Crandall, Margaret Hazen, Stuart F. Myers, David Hall, Henry P. Blakeslee, reference librarian Gary Boyd Roberts, Burgess E. Nichols.

NEHGS staff in 1983, in the old third-floor trustees room at 101 Newbury St. From front left: Gary Boyd Roberts, volunteer Steven Burns, David Curtis Dearborn, Alice I. Ledogar, *Register* assistant editor Donald M. Nielsen, Elizabeth Hersey, Comptroller Dorothy M. Daybre, Director Ralph J. Crandall (center), Christopher P. O'Sullivan, *Register* editor Edward W. Hanson, Linda Naylor, Nathaniel N. Shipton, James C. Agnew, Danny Williams, and Valentine ("Val") Bean.

Longtime member and Fernald genealogist Mrs. Harold G. Bruce, nee
Katharine Fernald (1908-1986), then of Milton, Mass., beneath a 1793 portrait
of Mrs. Joshua Winsor, nee Ruth Thomas (1755-1793), by Duxbury artist Rufus
Hathaway (1770-1822). This photograph by Ted Dully appeared on p. 1 of the
Boston *Globe* of Thursday, 17 February 1977. The Winsor portrait was sold in
1980 (courtesy of the Boston *Globe*).

Ralph J. Crandall (born 1945), fourth Director of the Society (1982-1987, since 1988, left) and Arthur A. Dunn (born 1914), 23rd Society President (1982-1987, right) in the old third-floor trustees room at 101 Newbury St., beneath a portrait, ca. 1840, by Bass Otis (1784-1861) of the family of founder Lemuel Shattuck (1793-1859). This Shattuck family portrait is also featured in the 1983 staff photograph.

Theodore Chase (born 1912), 24th President of the Society (1987-1991, left), benefactor and later trustee Ruth Chauncey Bishop (center), and Director Ralph J. Crandall (left), at the dedication, on September 28, 1990, of the Ruth C. Bishop reading room at 101 Newbury St. Miss Bishop's gift of $1,000,000 was the largest in Society history. This photograph appeared on the cover of the October-November 1990 NEXUS (7:133).

William M. Fowler, Jr. (born 1944), 25th President of
the Society (since 1991).

President Fowler and Director Crandall in the old third-floor committee room outside the Director's office. Among the surrounding objects are a walnut Queen Anne high chest (ca. 1725, left) and a cherrywood Federal tall case clock (ca. 1790, center) from the Atkinson-Lancaster collection.

CHAPTER 8

Opening the Door to Boston and the World

In the 1980s the Society dramatically changed its entrance to the library building by cutting a path through the small park in front and adding a new walkway and garden. It then needed to repair the massive bronze doors of the old entrance, closed since the departure of the bank years ago, and provide a reception desk immediately inside the great doors. The impressive entrance put readers into a large, hardwood-paneled room, lined with portraits of Society leaders, historic paintings, and objects of art. Since 1982, Sotheby Parke Bernet, the well known antiquarian dealer and auctioneer, had leased most of the first floor, except for this great room which it shared with the Society. In the room were soft chairs, small and large tables, some display cases filled with rare books, and a few carpets which invited one to relax from the walk on Newbury Street and prepare for research in the library on the sixth floor. Behind the left wall of the entrance hall were the elevator and packages of books waiting for the postmen. The elevator, hidden by the paneled wall and approached through a hallway with doors at either end, was a reliable contraption, which took no notice of readers or time as it moved slowly to the floors above.[1]

Ever since Alex Haley published *Roots: The Saga of an American Family* in 1977, the elevator had been taking crowds of people to the library—readers eager to trace their own families. Society members increased, book loan services expanded, and researchers tripled. Though *Roots* was a gentle mix of fact and fancy, the narrative attracted the largest television audience in viewing history, and the series of eight episodes left a fantastic impression upon the nation. It earned Haley a Pulitzer Prize and a special citation from judges of the National Book Award.[2]

Haley was understandably in constant demand as a speaker, and the Society, through the efforts of James B. Bell and Mrs. Robert G. Fuller, invited him to give a major lecture, which was performed graciously before a large crowd. The warmth of the audience toward him personally and his subject directly was exceptional. Bell later estimated that memberships in the Society doubled in the coming years as genealogical research became increasingly popular. Additional chairs and tables were placed in the library to accommodate the overflow of readers, and the Society reacted promptly to the urgent calls for instruction on genealogical techniques.[3] Summer classes were held at Harvard and Brandeis universities, yearly treks taken to the Mormon Library at Salt Lake City, and study tours conducted to archives in England. Bell's speaking tours around the United States were motivated in part by this awakening interest in genealogy; whether the phenomenon should be attributed entirely to Alex Haley or to other causes one need only speculate.

This growing awareness of genealogy as one of the most popular hobbies in America was almost obscured at the Society by financial crisis. The trustees and officers, led by Bell, had pondered whether the Society would survive the downward plunge in contributions by members. Bell had repeatedly tested Society opinions and found little encouragement when he asked friends or members about the likelihood of an upswing. His successor, Ralph J. Crandall, faced in 1982 a heavy operating deficit as well as this attitude of bewilderment and desperation, but he was fortunate to have the assistance of Arthur A. Dunn, the new president, and Lowell A. Warren, Jr., the new treasurer. Both of these key officers were mature business executives who were willing to face the adventure of lifting the Society from the abyss.[4]

Their major problem was not fundamentally membership dues nor annual contributions, but operating income. Although contributions from the Annual Appeal were off slightly, the endowment was shrinking yearly. The Society had not received a substantial donation for nearly a decade, and bequests were equally scarce. Gifts of books and manuscripts were received regularly and generally enriched the library, but generous help from the membership was missing.[5] Another kind of support, however, was reported in the *News-Letter* for Autumn 1980. School children in the fifth grade of the Lotspeich School District in Cincinnati, Ohio, answered the Society's appeal for funds to preserve the John Hancock papers. They organized a craft sale, featuring their own handmade items, and collected twenty-five dollars which they contributed to the Hancock fund. James Bell responded to this noble spirit in these words:

> As you have learned in your American History class, John Hancock was a famous patriot. . . . The Society is fortunate to have many of his account books, ledgers, letters and other papers under its roof. With generous contributions such as yours, we will be able to restore and preserve these important documents so that people like yourselves can enjoy and learn from them.[6]

Across the page from the children's story was the beginning of a list of 1863 names which covered a few additional pages. These members of the Society partially answered the Annual Appeal for 1979-1980 when they gave $98,580. In the 1981-1982 Annual Appeal gifts of $118,840 were received from 1583 members. Both appeals were generous expressions of goodwill, but totally inadequate to meet the larger financial needs confronting the Society. Deficits each year were draining the endowment and forcing the sale of treasured portraits. The deficit in 1981-1982 reached $209,000. One year later, in 1983, however, the deficit changed into a surplus of $6,644.[7]

This remarkable change in Society fortunes requires some explanation. In August 1982 Ralph J. Crandall and his advisors began a cost-cutting campaign which they hoped would bring the budget into balance. The gap of $209,000 in income required careful monitoring of daily expenditures, and Crandall in addition had to release five junior employees and apply to the deficit almost all of Bell's former salary. Bell's costly seminars were also abandoned for a less expensive program.

Emphasis was now placed on the Annual Appeal and months of hard work followed. In 1983 the amazing sum of $164,747 was collected from many of the sixty-five hundred members. This generosity revealed an extraordinary desire to cooperate.[8] Crandall and the trustees were obviously cheered by this response, but other sources of money also had to be found. They decided eventually to lease part of the first floor to Sotheby Parke Bernet and most of the second floor to the Massachusetts Society of Mayflower Descendants and the Society of Colonial Wars. The chart below reveals broadly Crandall's strategy:

	1982	1983	change
Wages	$340,043	$284,543	$55,500
Rents	0	26,552	26,552
Annual Appeal	105, 536	164,747	59,211
Memberships	228,555	234,945	6,360
Director's Expense	4,123	2,419	1,705
Maintenance	18,884	12,593	6,291
Budget deficit (or profit)	- 209,595	6,644	

Economies appeared almost everywhere in the 1982-1983 budget. These savings could be tolerated for a year or two, but over time they would harm staff morale and library efficiency. Since these were years of emergency, belt-tightening measures were justified. Despite the crisis Crandall appointed two new people to his staff. Linda Naylor and Alice I. Ledogar received administrative appointments, that of executive assistant in charge of the office and development officer, respectively.[9] Both brightened the central office with their personalities and their ability to undertake many tasks at the same time. In the library George Freeman Sanborn, recruited from New Hampshire where he was a teacher and language translator, soon became director of library operations, and his staff worked tirelessly to catalogue books and manuscripts, fill book loan orders, and update that department's catalog.[10] These appointments were justified in this period of crisis because these persons were expected to bring greater efficiency to the Society's operations—and they did.

Through 1982 and 1983 Crandall and his staff investigated the nine years of Bell's tenure as director to determine how best to redirect the Society's leadership. They unearthed some ethical issues, but both President Dunn and Crandall wanted to concentrate on debt reduction and better administration. Dunn instructed Crandall to find good library personnel, interested trustees, and generous donors—a nearly insurmountable task which Crandall accepted as a challenge.[11] The old committee system that formerly involved councilors in Society administration was slowly restored for the trustees. Their talents from business, the professions, and academia, Crandall hoped, would give him expert advice on running the Society.

Members of the staff were invited to meet again on a regular schedule with the director, who then reviewed week-to-week operations, sometimes in painful detail, but with good long-term results. The staff recommended a counting of library holdings, the first ever in the Society's recent history. It had the effect of determining the condition of books, locating many missing books, and replacing some that were lost.[12] Sanborn expanded the reference section and established guidelines for collection development. The staff and Crandall also analyzed the publications program. No one advocated any significant reform of the *Register*, except to let its contents slowly return to the successful blend of genealogy and history that existed in the 1950s, and regain the ground lost by the doubtful experimentations of the 1970s. Crandall decided, however, to relinquish his own personal involvement with the *Register* in favor of Edward W. Hanson, who had served as his assistant and associate editor. A young man of much energy, Hanson promised that he would concentrate his efforts "on publishing more methodological articles, family genealogies, and primary source materials."[13]

Undoubtedly, some of the staff, perhaps Crandall himself, realized that the *Register* had preempted more and more space used formerly for current-interest materials in order to include historical and genealogical articles of enduring quality, and he recommended a new type of publication, in no way a substitute for the *Register*, which would serve as an additional resource for members. As Crandall described their idea:

The Society is instituting a new newsletter to supplement our services. We all hope that this [publication] will be a more informal way for members to communicate with one another through the query column, notices of family reunions, research in progress, interesting articles and other letters and communications. This will be an added benefit of membership, and we hope it will soon reflect your interests as much as possible.[14]

A contest was held for the title of the newsletter, which was finally determined by the third issue. Professor Peter R. Knights of Ontario, Canada, suggested NEXUS (for "New England across the U.S."), and the editorial board after some deliberation accepted the name. William Bradford Towne, Sr., was named first editor of NEXUS. An avid genealogist from Asheville, North Carolina, Towne was an enthusiastic supporter of newsletters as a form of communication and gave great energy to the task of getting the project underway. Since its first issue Towne and his successors have let the flow of letters and submissions into the editorial office determine the content of the newsletter. They tried to be efficient in maintaining a schedule of the publication, but like the *Register*, the NEXUS was often late getting into the mail.[15]

To his amazement Crandall discovered that more members read the NEXUS, particularly the "events," "news," and "queries" sections, than read the *Register*. Members kept the NEXUS for immediate reference and then discarded it, while they put the *Register*, often lightly read, in a bookcase for future reference. Libraries showed the same doubt about the permanence of the NEXUS as a reference journal.[16] By 1985 it was published six times yearly and had approximately 24 pages in each issue. Enthusiastic readers frequently sent gifts to defray the costs. Their requests for professional information drew staff and noted genealogists to the magazine, and Nathaniel Shipton, Gary Boyd Roberts, and Robert C. Anderson were listed as contributing editors. Marian White soon became general editor; she was often of fixed opinions, but the style of the journal was set by its materials.[17] She continued as editor until 1989 when Julie Helen Otto and Robert Shaw were named associate editors under the general supervision of Gary Roberts. Even more important to its survival, advertisers were attracted to the NEXUS and the director used it as a major source of public announcements.

In the meantime, Crandall was attempting to define his own role as director. The stark necessity of endowment was ever present, and he began a nationwide search for funds by asking businesses and foundations for help. Their response at first was most disappointing. But in December 1984 the National Endowment for the Humanities heard his pleas and awarded the Society a $500,000 Challenge Grant, to be matched in three years by three dollars for every one from NEH. The magnificence of the grant was described by Crandall to a select group of trustees, members, and friends who gathered in the great hall of the Society to hear these optimistic words:

> If we succeed . . . , our grandchildren in the year 2045 will find the Society as vibrant and creative at its 200th Anniversary as it was at its founding in 1845.[18]

Before he sat down, he introduced John W. Sears as the honorary chairman of this Challenge Fund. Sears was an unusually distinguished person to undertake this responsibility. Boston-born and Massachusetts- and English-educated, he held a law degree from Harvard University and a M. Litt. from Balliol College, Oxford, before he entered politics as a state legislator, candidate for mayor and governor, and city councilor.[19] He served later as sheriff of Suffolk County and campaign manager in Massachusetts for President Gerald R. Ford. A man of diversions and hobbies, he became interested in genealogy and the Society, and was often seen in the library tracing not only his ancestry but also that of friends and associates.

With John Sears at the head of the fund drive, Crandall could pass news of the Challenge Grant across the United States. The task seemed to some members a near impossibility, certainly daring and adventurous, because the Society had rarely raised more than $150,000 annually in its entire history. To obtain ten times that amount from members unaccustomed to giving substantial donations was Crandall's challenge.[20]

Crandall had many infectious qualities which would attract members to share the challenge with him. A New Englander by birth and a Californian by education, the best of two worlds, he joined the Society immediately upon the conferring of his doctorate in history by the University of Southern California. Crandall had some exposure to genealogy at the university and through a family that traced its roots to the immigrant John Crandall of Rhode Island. He lived with his wife, Linda Morse Crandall, and their three daughters first at Maynard and then at Harvard, where he enjoyed tennis and gardening as hobbies and the experiences of raising a family. What probably most attracted members was his devotion to the Society, a transparent honesty and dedication to the ideals of family life, and his tall, clean-cut appearance. Crandall appreciated this attention, but he also appreciated the businessmen he was meeting daily who were creative in establishing their enterprises and seemed to be immersed in delivering their products. He was likewise inspired by foreign travel and living, which were especially appealing to him and his wife when they spoke of their relatives in the Orient.[21]

With the capital drive pressing him, Crandall began to use background information on members collected during James Bell's tenure as director; he realized that to succeed he had to travel from Newbury Street to meet these members. His staff had already mailed several informational documents, a case book, and pledge forms. The best approach, Crandall now decided, was to persuade the trustees and other supporters of the Society to hold receptions in their homes. Their personal support was most important. He arranged to stay in the homes of trustees, to speak at local church halls, and to greet important people. His presence, occasionally accompanied by a well-acquainted member, won listeners. His message dwelled upon the traditions of the Society, its great library, and the importance of family history, and had an instantaneous effect. Donations, at first, were meager, and he was compelled to follow these introductions with other kinds of contacts.

Donors were impressed, however, by the organization which Crandall represented. Its capacity to offer them help in their research was important. They appreciated the book loan department which was attempting to provide orders in less time than in the past. They liked the research service, which put their problems in the hands of experts. They welcomed the advice of Gary Boyd Roberts, David C. Dearborn, and George F. Sanborn whenever they visited Newbury Street. The expert staff of resident genealogists, also including Jerome E. Anderson, was giving luster to the Society. For others the reference collection, which expanded steadily, proved invaluable because it put within a few yards most finding aids to research. Conversations with Nathaniel Shipton often yielded valuable manuscripts. Crandall also joined these experts with two new books of his own. His *Shaking Your Family Tree* told how to research, prepare, and publish a genealogy. His press, Yankee Publishing, Inc., put the book in stores and libraries across the nation.[22] It had the effect of introducing Crandall to members before he ever appeared in the libraries, auditoriums, and church halls where he came to explain the Challenge Grant. His second book, *Generations and Change*, with Robert M. Taylor of the Indiana Historical Society, was a scholarly collection of sixteen essays published by Mercer University Press. Nineteen scholars of national reputation presented studies of various aspects of genealogy through family history.[23] Crandall was likewise already visible in the issues of the NEXUS.

By 1986 the NEXUS had won wide popularity among genealogists everywhere. An advertisement in the Queries section often brought thirty to forty responses from readers. The section was frequently torn from the booklet and saved for future reference. In addition many members were finding more and more of the columns so worthwhile that they saved the entire magazine. Roberts' "Notable Kin" was unusually popular, especially his references to royal descents. Lee Kugler's column on the "Book of Corrections" likewise drew the attention of members anxious for accurate information on their families.[24]

The NEXUS listed, in addition, lectures, tours, genealogical conferences, notices of the Society and staff publications, and reports of month-to-month Society activities. In the October-November issue for 1986, it announced a conference on family history at the University of Leeds, with optional tours to London and Stratford-upon-Avon. The major lecturer was Dr. George Redmonds of Huddersfield, Yorkshire, an experienced speaker, traveler, and historian who had a fascinating knowledge of the geographic origins of English family names.[25] The Society also offered recordings of its lectures. Since most members could not attend Boston meetings, these addresses of speakers were put on audio cassettes and made available through the Book Loan Department. Sixty-eight tapes were eventually offered on nearly every conceivable topic relating to the family and genealogy.[26] Lecturers included the Society staff as well as national genealogists like George E. McCracken, John B. Threlfall, Roger D. Joslyn, and Anne B. Harding. These tapes, however, proved to be disappointing; nothing substitutes for a lecturer in person.

The NEXUS provided many announcements in each issue. The most promising news were major publications of the Society and staff. Roberts edited fifteen volumes of *Register* excerpts—all compiled genealogies of Connecticut, Rhode Island, and *Mayflower* (and related) families, all articles on the English origins of New England families, and all source records for Plymouth, Bristol, Barnstable, Dukes, and Nantucket counties. The *Register* was being indexed through the effort of Jane F. Fiske, who would later succeed Donald Nielsen as editor. The records of Sandwich, one of the important towns on the Cape, were being gathered for future publication, and Roger D. Joslyn, the editor of volume one of the Charlestown vital records, agreed to complete a second volume. Other announcements included many of the family reunions which have traditionally been part of the pageantry of genealogy.[27]

Crandall continued to use the NEXUS for his own announcements because he was eager to keep readers informed of the money-raising activities of the Society. Nearly every issue featured a graph showing the progress of the Challenge Fund. By the October-November 1986 issue the fund had risen to the astonishing level of $780,000, over half the necessary sum. Crandall was jubilant. He also offered members a variety of other ways to serve both their interests and the Society's. A pooled income fund, he wrote, assured members income for life, a tax write-off, and the benefits of a bequest. With a gift of only $5,000, a pooled income fund could be established by any individual. It had the advantage of permitting future increases in the amount of investment and a means for helping the Society. Crandall also encouraged members to establish life memberships. These worthy people were then honored in the NEXUS as special friends of the Society.[28]

Crandall was most successful in his fundraising efforts. His attraction of important donors to the Board of Trustees especially assured the Society of experienced, thoughtful, and energetic leaders. Expanding the geographic area of the Board brought the trusteeship of Lloyd Welch Pogue of Washington, D.C. A chairman of the Civil Aeronautics Board during World War II, Pogue was a well known corporate lawyer who later published a genealogy of his family. Another new trustee was Robert Croll Stevens of Pittsford, New York, a businessman of unusually wide experience in management, the use of the computer, and corporate investments. A man of humor and energy, he offered to help the Society reorganize itself, create management charts, and study the work load of the staff. Likewise, Dean C. Smith and Elysabeth C. B. Higgins, both vitally interested in the success of the Challenge Grant, and Ethel Farrington Smith of Hull, Massachusetts and Boynton Beach, Florida brought special insights to the Board. Ethel Smith gave the Society $100,000 for the study of New Hampshire families and institutions. These trustees, including a good many other dedicated people, brought a new spirit of activity into the management of the Society.

Almost everyone, understandably, was astonished when Ralph Crandall announced in January 1987 that he would be leaving Boston for a business opportunity in Bangkok, Thailand. His wife's sister and brother-in-law, he said, were owners of a transportation business there and he was invited to join the company. The trustees, surprised also by his resignation, decided to appoint John W. Sears, the chairman of the Challenge Fund, whom everyone knew, as interim director while they searched the nation for a suitable replacement for their well-liked director.[29] Sears was a few years older than Crandall, a lawyer and officeholder. During his brief tenure there were several staff departures, changes or reassignments of note. Marie Daly, former business manager for several units of Mount Auburn Hospital, succeeded Mrs. Daybre who retired. Daly's experience as a manager won much approbation

205

from the trustees. Alice Ledogar completed her good work for the Challenge Grant (she was particularly successful with the two auctions on its behalf, in 1986 and 1987), but left the Society in early 1988. Edward W. Hanson had resigned as Director of Publications and editor of the *Register* in the summer of 1986; Donald M. Nielsen, his associate editor and successor, left for law school the next year. Jane Fletcher Fiske, a noted Rhode Island genealogist and author of that state's chapter in *Genealogical Research in New England*, was appointed editor of the *Register*. Gary Boyd Roberts, former reference librarian and director of research and special projects, was named Director of Publications. William H. Schoeffler, who had worked part-time in the publications department, was named Director of Education.

These shifts of personnel, except for Mrs. Daybre's, were speedily accomplished. Sears then turned promptly to other matters of importance. He opened the library for evening research on Wednesdays and Thursdays, installed a water cooler for readers on the sixth floor, and surveyed salary levels of the staff. He answered letters from members with personal, handwritten messages, and revealed an intense curiosity about every aspect of Society operations.[30] His good and generous instincts were sometimes hidden, however, by a formal manner. Conferences with the staff were businesslike, often more lecture than give-and-take discussion. He experimented with methods to improve procedures, determine workloads, and find ways to use the diversified talents of the staff, but the reaction was mixed, and Sears resigned in early December. The trustees asked Nathaniel Shipton, the manuscripts archivist, to serve until another director was selected.[31] Shipton graciously agreed.

Happily, news had recently come from Thailand that Ralph Crandall was willing to return as director in the spring of 1988; the trustees warmly accepted Crandall's offer.[32] The Challenge Fund was approaching its matching goal of the one and a half million dollars. Alice Ledogar agreed to write the preliminary report for the NEH before leaving the Society; Crandall, after reviewing the pledges and donations, had the responsibility of filing the final report in August. Everyone was jubilant as this great moment approached; the Society would add two million dollars to its endowment.

Under the affable Nat Shipton the 1988 elections were held for five new trustees, a treasurer, a vice president, and the reelection of the acting president, Theodore Chase, who had succeeded Arthur A. Dunn in late 1987. W. Robert Mill, the new treasurer, had been senior vice president of United Investment Counsel for many years, and also widely acquainted locally in New England as a churchman and horticulturist. The first vice president was William M. Fowler, Jr., a professor of history at Northeastern University, and the second vice president was Nicholas Benton, a former editor of Time-Life publications. Trustees included Morton (Terry) Baker of Houghton Mifflin Company, Elysabeth (Lys) Higgins, John A. Schutz, Robert D. Stueart, and Lorraine N. Tyler. Theodore Chase, a trustee since 1983 and vice president since 1986, was a partner of Palmer and Dodge (a Boston law firm), an overseer of Harvard University, and active in the town government of Dover, Massachusetts, where he lived. He was also past president of the Association of Gravestone Studies and editor of *Markers*, its journal. Chase was an exceptional selection to serve as president in this year of transition. Elderly, cautious and wise in offering his opinions, and willing to hear the advice of his fellow trustees, he set the stage for an appropriately warm reception for Ralph Crandall.[33]

Crandall was scheduled to attend a "gala dinner . . . [in the Society's great entrance hall] on April 26." Twenty pounds lighter than when he left for Bangkok, he was visibly happy to be re-appointed director. The NEXUS published this response to the near universal applause of welcome:

> After a wonderful but brief encounter with the Land of Smiles, my family [and I are] . . . delighted to return to New England. . . . 1987 will always remain an unforgettable year for us. We developed a deep appreciation of the Kingdom of Thailand, its intelligent, enterprising, and warmhearted people, the magnificent natural beauty of the countryside outside of Bangkok, the world-famous beaches of Pattaya, Hua Hin, and farther south at Phuket, the beautiful city of Chiangmai, Thailand's "Rose of the North". . . .

> The year I was away was one of positive change and growth of the Society. John Sears and Nathaniel Shipton, the trustees, the volunteers, and especially the staff all made enormous contributions of thought, time, and energy, as did our wonderful, responsive and devoted membership, now 11,000 strong.
>
> I am proud to be back as director. The Society was founded in 1845. . . . It is among the first historical institutions in the United States, and it is certainly the oldest genealogical society in the western world. It is a very special organization. . . . The Society has been the one great repository in the nation that has been devoted exclusively to the remembrance of families and whence they came. It is now a very big organization endeavoring to maintain an open door to anyone who seeks to know about his or her family origin. The challenge [of being home] is great, but so is the [future of the] Society.[34]

So spoke Crandall to his large, appreciative audience.

Crandall added some personal remarks about his life in Bangkok in a letter to Helen J. Sanford that congratulated her on her work as a trustee, then noted:

> Bangkok was everything we expected, and a lot more! I think it was the "lot more" aspect that convinced us to return to New England. Linda really did not like raising our children in the expatriate community, and we both found the extremely hot and humid weather debilitating. I am very happy to be back at 101 Newbury.[35]

Although Crandall was happy to be home, he returned in poor health and had to combat for some years a variety of illnesses. But he rarely missed a day in Boston. He promoted Natalie Marko, who had worked with Alice Ledogar, to head the development office and urged her to write proposals for corporate support and expand the Pooled Income Program. A kindly person who took a personal interest in many members, she became amazingly successful in her new position. Crandall placed Linda Naylor in charge of the administrative offices whenever he was away on Society business. Linda performed her duties so well that she seemed almost to be an assistant director. She and her talented husband were soon installing a computer communication system in the Society. Her health was precarious, however, and she was frequently forced to be away from the Society.

Other signs of change were everywhere. Julie Otto and Robert Shaw became editors of the NEXUS. The energetic trustees themselves formed a study group to look into the Society's future, and Crandall continued his efforts to attract large donations. The most impressive was a gift of $1,000,000 from Ruth Bishop of Portland, Oregon. The trustees, moreover, were equally ready to create new programs. Robert C. Stevens, in particular, was interested in modernizing the bylaws, introducing business management policies, and extending the use of the computer to library and administrative functions. While Sears was still acting director Stevens had written multiple-page letters to Sears and Chase on Society problems and then sent these letters to Crandall when he heard of the latter's re-appointment.[36] "I do not need to tell you how delighted I am (and the rest of the Trustees are) that you are returning to lead the Society to bigger and better things! Some good news for today is that Dean Smith [a fellow trustee] just delivered a check of $80,000 for furthering the computerization of the library, book loan, and desktop publishing."[37]

James Naylor, Linda's husband, was developing programs to input data on members (names and addresses primarily), but also designing programs to record payments of dues, geographical location, etc. He aided Marie Daly in 1987 and 1988 in transforming the functions of the business and accounting department to computer use. Daly was well acquainted with some computer languages, but needed software to establish accounting procedures. They were successful in putting the general ledger of the Society on line in 1988, accounts payable in 1989, and accounts receivable in 1990. The process was slower, however, than she and James Naylor had anticipated and required various kinds of software. She worried about protecting the privacy of these records, but a system of passwords was eventually installed which confined computer use to selected individuals in each department of the Society.[38]

The computer was becoming a modern tool for nearly every staff member. Jane Fiske, the editor of the *Register*, had long realized that the much delayed *Register* index of volumes 51-148 could be inputted and stored on diskettes. With help from her husband, John, and several assistants, the index was all but computerized by the summer of 1994, and its publication in four volumes was scheduled for later that year.[39] Several trustees, especially Stevens, were eager to see the entire *Register* on CD-ROM, which would provide extraordinary access to this most valuable collection of genealogical volumes. Automated Archives of Orem, Utah, producers of these laser disks, described the revolutionary process to Stevens, Robert C. Anderson (the chairman of the CD-ROM committee), and others, who were enthusiastic:

> Imagine having the power to search 500 volumes of research material, page by page, for every occurrence of your ancestors' names in just a matter of SECONDS!!! Think of the benefits. Not only could you uncover large amounts of valuable information, but you would also save time and money. Would such a power be helpful to you in doing your genealogical research?
>
> As incredible as it may seem, that is exactly what the technology developed by AUTOMATED ARCHIVES has made possible. By using computer-aided indexing and retrieval, the GENEALOGICAL RESEARCH SYSTEM (GRS) enables you to have this fantastic power. Now you can do in MINUTES what before would have taken days, even months, to accomplish.
>
> How is this possible? Books and documents are entered into a computer and every single word indexed. The information is then stored on a CD-ROM disk (a laser storage disk similar to the music compact discs). Each disk can hold hundreds of thousands of pages of text. Using the GRS software on a computer, desired text can be quickly located and displayed on the computer screen.[40]

Incredible as seemed this description of the CD-ROM process, in 1993 the Society had acquired the Family Search program of the Church of Jesus Christ of Latter-day Saints, which seemed equally amazing. The Ancestral File contains family group genealogies for many millions of people. The International Genealogical Index (IGI) now includes over 200 million vital records. Social Security death records to 1988 and a Military Death Index for the Korean and Vietnam wars gave additional information on thousands of people. Lending fees for these records were only $3600 per year.[41]

The computerization of the Society library had only begun by 1992. The catalog had been nearly reclassified to the Library of Congress system, but most new books and a percentage of already catalogued books were being rapidly computerized, with the expectation in a few years that members would be able to access the catalog from their homes. Some dreamers at trustee meetings had predicted a library of books on CD-ROM which could be read at home, with library time reserved for reading manuscripts and consulting the research staff. More realistic members were urging the Society to create its own "bulletin board," or to join an organization that already had one, so that members with computers could communicate with each other about genealogical problems. Instead of waiting months for help on a research problem, bulletin board access could reduce the waiting time to hours. The genealogical community then could speed up its research and mountains of new books might appear, or data could be put on CD-ROM diskettes and read by machine.[42]

Notwithstanding the computer, the Society has already procured thousands of microforms, both films and fiches. Its massive collection had been developed within the last decade, but a few films can be dated to purchases near the beginning of the Second World War. The great collection of film supplemented printed vital records of Massachusetts and added major probate and town records for New Hampshire, Vermont, and Maine. Canadian census records were complete through 1901, as were New England federal censuses through 1880. Canadian Maritime records were also extensive. Much of this buying of records was the responsibility of George F. Sanborn, the director of technical services, who had taken great pride in ordering these films as they came on the market. The Society lacked, however, a large area in which to consult them.[43] A letter from Theodore M. Atkinson of Great Barrington, Massachusetts, described in June 1990 his two experiences on floor 5A of the library.

> In August of last year I left my mountain fastness on two consecutive Saturdays, drove three hours to Boston, found adequate parking outside of the city, came to town by public transport, but had much trouble using the library facilities. . . . A small handful of the same people dominated the tiny, downstairs scene for the whole day; and as luck would have it, bad luck, one of the viewers had a burnt out bulb. . . . I forgot to mention that the reading room . . . had only one or two users the entire day.

Everyone seemed to be jammed into the fiche area. It was as if books were suddenly out of style, which may be right on.

On the second Sat., the reading room was jammed to the gills with "Back to N.E." people—and the viewers, too, although many that day seemed to be . . . going with books not films.[44]

The computer, microfilms, fiche, and the Family Search program have drastically changed research in genealogy not only in the Society, but elsewhere in the United States. More and more members come to the library with laptop computers and notes already entered at home on computer diskettes and printouts. Three of the Society's most ambitious research projects reflecting this new process are those being prepared by Ernest Flagg Henderson III, Robert C. Anderson, and Judith A. Norton. Henderson has developed upwards of 1900 ancestral charts which trace his entire known ancestry from the beginning of recorded memory. He is presently overseeing the computerization of these charts, which will make this vast information available both as a book and database. Anderson is identifying approximately 20,000 English people who crossed the Atlantic to New England in the Great Migration of 1620 to 1643. His findings, though aided by computer technology, will appear in essay form, in several volumes, and distill present knowledge or extend it whenever possible by new research. Norton has computer entries for nearly 2400 Planter households of Nova Scotia for the migration beginning in the 1740s. "The database is a stand-alone system, written for the Clarion Professional Developer . . . , with fields for personal, genealogical, and social information."[45]

With genealogical research demanding a variety of documentation, researchers like these scholars are consulting many sources. Manuscripts of family, town, and church are no longer sufficient when graveyard, court, land, and census records would insure more insightful identifications. Comprehensive documentation would seem to be the rule for any modern researcher. Such major genealogical journals as the *National Genealogical Society Quarterly* regularly publish commentaries on research techniques. The Millses, Gary B. and Elizabeth Shown, use their "Editors' Corner" to advise the profession on methodology:

Reaching reliable conclusions may require us (Nay, compel us) to corre-
late birth data in vital records with the metes and bounds of legal surveys—searching for, and comparing, the not-so-obvious elements that
such disparate documents have in common . . . because the minutiae of
such records identify people as surely as modern fingerprints and DNA.[46]

Crandall, the trustees, and officers of the Society were well aware of
these evolving standards, and in April 1988 they appointed a Long
Range Planning Committee to steer the Society through the rocky paths
toward progress. Chaired by Robert C. Stevens, for a time, it included
Theodore Chase, Benjamin H. Gaylord, W. Robert Mill, Elysabeth
Higgins, Dean C. Smith, and Robert C. Anderson. Each year with new
elections of trustees, its membership changed slightly. In 1991 William
M. Fowler, Jr., the new president, and John G. L. Cabot, a new trustee,
joined the committee. Following several years of recommendations the
committee evolved into a forum for planning modernization of the
Society's facilities and the sesquicentennial anniversary in 1995.[47]

Probably no one had thought in April 1988 that the committee's
deliberations would be as fruitful as they became. But many subcom-
mittees were methodically formed by the chairman to collect information on Society operations—good points as well as the bad. Plans were
then developed by each department of the Society and the recommendations were passed to the large trustees' committee. Regularly the
subcommittee included Crandall, Dean C. Smith, and the director of
that part of the Society whose basic needs were being examined.[48]

Fairly clear assumptions were deduced from these deliberations.
The trustees wanted to keep the Society at 101 Newbury Street because
of proximity to commonwealth, county, and Boston city records, hotels,
and transportation. Although Crandall raised possibilities of moving
outside Boston, to Cambridge or Waltham, because of less expensive
real estate, the trustees were not ready for such a drastic resettlement.
The 1964 move to Newbury Street had been costly and disruptive. The
present building, they thought, could be redesigned and enlarged by
acquiring additional space; and the lending library and other operations
could be shifted to another site. Almost every subcommittee, however,

recommended additions of space, personnel, and computers, so endowment became an immediate consideration. Computers were costly, but to Robert C. Stevens they were essential if current technology was to contribute to the modernization of the catalogue, process books for the circulating library, and keep current the ever-increasing membership rolls of the Society.[49] Three hundred thousand dollars was thought a minimal sum for installation of computers. The individual reports from Society departments took much time to develop. That for the library was the most expansive.

As then director of library operations, George F. Sanborn presented a statement of nearly fifteen pages covering essential needs of the library in the near future. His report was in response to the subcommittee interrogation of his department. His comments on the Reference Division reveals the overall tone of his report:

> At the present time our Reference Division is inadequately staffed and very cramped for space. . . . I regret that this division is also the weakest part of the whole library department, but I have not been given much to work with. We need . . . increased staff; we need new library furniture; we need a photocopy center; we need expanded areas for the reading room, for stacks and for microtext.[50]

He recommended that the entire sixth floor be expanded into a reading room and copy center—from approximately 1600 square feet to 3500 square feet. He would find the room "by taking out walls and stacks, [then] carpeting the floor and installing stripped mahogany paneling and bookcases throughout." New staff would cost approximately $55,000; new furniture for the library about $25,000; and the construction an additional $30,000. Cost of reshelving the library on another floor he estimated at $45,000.

The report described floor-by-floor needs, adding costs of personnel, shelving, construction, and budget allocations. The entire sum was approximately $500,000. It had the effect of emphasizing to the trustees that under ideal circumstances the Society faced enormous expenditures if it wished a state-of-the-art library. The report was indeed sobering, but the package it outlined was beyond the reach of the Society, possibly never realizable. The Board of Trustees, meeting quarterly, decided finally that some renovation was absolutely essential and instructed Crandall to develop a space plan for the whole building, seek professional advice, and engage an architectural firm. In the months which followed he was advised that city codes mandated a modern fire prevention and alarm system and that the Commonwealth had passed new legislation to benefit the handicapped or physically challenged. They must be given access to entry ways, restrooms, and research facilities. The entire building, he was told, needed to be inspected for asbestos, and for the safety of property and individuals if threatened by fire. Other problems would follow; in each case Crandall found possible solutions, which sometimes required great expenditures.[51]

Happily the Society engaged Powers and Company to provide architectural advice and manage the entire project of modernization. Its president, the knowledgeable Darleen Powers, gave herself wholeheartedly and supervised personally the entire project. Working with Crandall, she drew architectural plans and cost estimates for the work, secured licenses from a variety of zoning commissions, including the Back Bay Architectural Commission, and was able to adjust regulations (or have them interpreted) so that the Society could proceed with its plans.[52]

For months Powers and Crandall met weekly as plans and contracts for the renovation were drawn. They met with the president, officers, trustees and staff to explain decisions and gain consent, often in half-day sessions during which trustees or staff pored over plans and asked nearly impossible questions. The trustees, for their part, entrusted general care of the Society's interests to a facility committee, chaired by John G. L. Cabot of Waltham. Born in Rio de Janeiro, he graduated from Harvard College and Harvard Business School and is vice president of the Cabot Corporation. His prestige, along with the support of President William Fowler and the trustees, much aided Crandall and Powers in doing their job. The project was eventually divided into several phases because of cost and disruption of ordinary library business. The first phase of renovation included removal of fire hazards and dangerous asbestos and the installation of fire doors and alarm boxes. The entire third floor was then redesigned for offices, work spaces, conference meeting places, and computer use. Much was done in the renovation to provide color, advanced design, lighting, and convenience. The magnificent conference room was dedicated on Monday afternoon, October 25, 1993, to Ethel Farrington Smith. Long a member of the Society, Mrs. Smith was honored that afternoon with a full-color portrait by Melvin Robbins. Placed in a prominent location, it was intended as a reminder of her constant and generous efforts to assist the New England Historic Genealogical Society in its mission of service and scholarship.[53]

To accomplish various goals, including book preservation and the much needed renovation of the building, Crandall began an extensive fundraising campaign that took him to most parts of the United States. He wanted to raise five million dollars, with two million for renovation and three million for endowment. At the very beginning of the campaign Ruth C. Bishop of Portland, Oregon, pledged a unique gift of one million dollars. Her generous spirit was shared through 1994 by almost two thousand other genealogists and some corporations, who together gave another $4,000,000. In January 1993 Crandall made the first formal announcement of the campaign and called his effort the "the New England Historic Genealogical Society Sesquicentennial Celebration and Campaign." His announcement begins:

> 1995, the 150th anniversary of our founding, will be a momentous year for the Society. . . . The centerpiece of our celebration . . . is a Sesquicentennial Campaign to raise $5,000,000, a goal established by the Society's trustees in 1990. . . . $2,000,000 will be used to renovate the Society's "house" in Boston. $3,000,000 will be added to the permanent endowment, and its income used for book preservation, to enlarge the Circulating Library, to expand the microtext area, and to complete the library re-cataloging program.[54]

Ruth Bishop and Ethel F. Smith were publicly thanked and acknowledged by naming the Reading and Conference rooms, respectively, in their honor. Both magnificent gifts, almost unthinkable decades ago, were tributes to the growth of genealogy as a part of American culture and of the Society's role as the largest private depository of family histories and manuscripts in the United States. Continuance of the Sesquicentennial Campaign to completion would be the great preoccupation of Ralph Crandall and his staff in 1994 and 1995.[55]

Notes

[1] Almost nothing appears in the records on the opening of the great front doors. No ribbon-cutting was staged. The rental of the first-floor rooms appears in formal agreements. The *Register* [138 (1984): 312] lists rental fees. Ralph J. Crandall remembered some details of rentals and the door-opening. Interview of January 25, 1994.

In this entrance hall are hung a few portraits. The collection of Society historic portraits and landscapes is modest but includes many portraits of past officers of the Society and some charming paintings by J.S. Copley, Joseph Greenleaf Cole, and Rufus Hathaway, among others, and a few unknown artists. E.D. Marchant was the artist who painted some early Society leaders.

[2] *1978 Britannica Book of the Year* (Chicago, 1978), 78, which includes a picture of Alex Haley.

[3] *News-Letter of the New England Historic Genealogical Society*, 4 (1977): Nos. 1 and 3; ibid., 5 (1978): No. 2, hereafter cited as *News-Letter*. Haley spoke on May 12, 1977; the occasion was described as "timely, topical, and significant."

[4] Both Dunn and Warren gave hopeful accounts of their first year in office. See Annual Report for 1982-1983, in *Register*, 137 (1983): 260, 264. See *News-Letter*, 11 (1984): No. 1. The profile of Arthur C. Dunn is the featured article in this issue.

[5] Only a gift of $25,000 from the estate of Frank Miller Hutchins is mentioned in Annual Report for 1982-1983, *Register*, 137 (1983): 264.

[6] "A Special Contribution to the Hancock Collection," *News-Letter*, 7 (1980): No. 3.

[7] *Register*, 137 (1983): 266; 138 (1984): 310. Treasurer Lowell A. Warren described the financial change as a "notable achievement."

[8] See *Register*, 138 (1984): 312-313. Note that "Donations and Fund Drive" had generated $103,543 and the Annual Appeal $164,747. Two systems of accounting gifts were obviously in use.

[9] The announcement of their promotions is made in Director's Report, *Register*, 138 (1984): 313.

[10] See *News-Letter*, 11 (1984): No. 1, under staff news.

[11] Some of the trustees elected 1982-1988 included Benjamin H. Gaylord of Bar Harbor, Maine; C. Frederick Kaufholz of Lakeville, Connecticut; Theodore Chase of Dover, Massachusetts; William M. Fowler, Jr. of Reading, Massa-

chusetts; David A. Nichols of Lincolnville, Maine; Wayne C. Hart of Farmington, Connecticut; Mrs. Robert C. Nordblom of Harwich Port, Massachusetts; and Mrs. Eugene C. Fowle of Kennebunkport, Maine.

[12] *News-Letter*, 10 (1983): No. 1; NEHGS-NEXUS, 1 (1984): 58-59. Hereafter NEHGS-NEXUS will be cited as NEXUS.

[13] "The appointment of Edward William Hanson as Editor," *Register*, 138 (1984): 3. Hanson continued as editor until 1986.

[14] "Preliminary Issue," December, 1983, of future NEXUS.

[15] "Preliminary Issue," No. 2, February 1984, of future NEXUS.

[16] Most of the issues of the NEXUS could be regarded as experimental. Important announcements often were featured on the covers. The size varied sharply from one issue to another. The February 1986 NEXUS was 60 pages, while the April issue was 41. By 1986 attractive illustrations were brightening its pages.

[17] Marian White Blackwell succeeded William Bradford Towne, Sr. as editor of NEXUS with the fourth number in 1984. She had been query editor for issues two and three. She left the position of editor in 1989.

[18] NEXUS, 2 (1985): 1-2. Crandall gave a schedule for the necessary solicitations and payments of the NEH matching grant.

[19] NEXUS, 2 (1985): 149-151.

[20] NEXUS, 2 (1985): 152; ibid., 3 (1986): 66. These up-to-date reports of the fund became a regular part of NEXUS.

[21] NEXUS, 4 (1987): 3. Crandall gave a parting interview to the NEXUS.

[22] Ralph J. Crandall, *Shaking Your Family Tree: A Basic Guide to Tracing Your Family's Genealogy* (Dublin, N.H., 1986).

[23] Robert M. Taylor, Jr. and Ralph J. Crandall, eds., *Generations and Change: Genealogical Perspectives in Social History* (Athens, Georgia, 1986).

[24] Gary Boyd Roberts began his series "Notable Kin" in February 1986 [NEXUS, 3 (1986): 26-27.] By 1994 over forty essays had appeared.

[25] NEXUS, 3 (1986): 240 (his picture is on 211).

[26] Tapes were likewise produced for "New England in Your Blood," August 24-27, 1988, but were available through National Conference Record Services, NEXUS, 5 (1988): 150-151. The earlier listing of speakers on tape is in NEXUS, 3 (1986): 243-244.

[27] NEXUS, 5, No. 2 had an attractive cover advertising family associations. A publication announcement for the Sandwich vital records appeared in NEXUS, 5 (1988): 151.

[28] See NEXUS, 3 (1986): 163.

[29] The search did not fully get underway because of Sears' visit to Ralph Crandall in April, Linda Crandall's visit to New England in the summer, and much correspondence which suggested that the former director might be willing to return to Boston.

[30] Many of Sears' letters are in the Director's Correspondence. Sears felt

comfortable writing letters and left most formal correspondence to his secretary. He obviously devoted many hours of each day to personal messages.

[31] Linda Naylor to Ralph J. Crandall, November 30, 1987 and February 5, 1988; John W. Sears to Ralph Crandall, November 1987; Alice Ledogar to Ralph Crandall, March 16, 1988, in Crandall's personal correspondence.

[32] Robert C. Stevens to Ralph J. Crandall, November 19, 1987, Director's Correspondence, 1986-1987.

[33] For pictures and biographies of the new trustees see NEXUS, 5 (1988): 117-118.

[34] NEXUS, 5 (1988): 76-77.

[35] Ralph J. Crandall to Helen J. Sanford, April 21, 1988, Director's Correspondence, 1988-1990.

[36] Robert C. Stevens to Ralph J. Crandall, November 19, 1987, Director's Correspondence, 1986-1987.

[37] Ibid. Stevens' letter was full of information and observations. He highly approved of Marie Daly's appointment: "Marie Daly is a gem! Things are getting whipped into shape in that office."

[38] John A. Schutz, interview with Marie Daly, January 25, 1994.

[39] Minutes of the Trustees Publications Committee, January 23, 1994, the Committee Records.

[40] Insert, entitled "Automated Archives," in Greg MacKett to Scott A. Bartley, September 18, 1990, Director's Correspondence, 1986-1990.

[41] *Family Search: Administrative Guide* (Salt Lake City, 1992). Enclosed with the instructional booklet is an informative document, entitled "Tips on Using Family Search."

[42] Minutes of Trustee Computer Committee meeting, October 26, 1993, January 23, 1994, Trustee Computer Committee Records.

[43] Long Range Plan, July 28, 1988, presented by Dean C. Smith, in Director's Correspondence, "Long-Range Plans." See also Long-Range Planning and the Library Department, December 1, 1989, Director's Correspondence.

[44] Theodore M. Atkinson to Ralph J. Crandall, June 7, 1990, Director's Correspondence, 1989-1990. Crandall replied with a sympathetic letter on June 12, 1990.

[45] Judith A. Norton to Ralph J. Crandall, January 3, 1994, Director's Correspondence; see *Great Migration Newsletter* (1990-   ) published by the Great Migration Study Project, for Anderson's study.

[46] Editors' Corner, March 1993, *National Genealogical Society* 81 (1993): 3, signed by the Millses.

[47] In the Director's Correspondence and Papers there are a considerable number of planning documents, including a statement on fundraising. Dean C. Smith succeeded Robert C. Stevens as head of the Long-Range Planning Committee in 1990.

[48] At the beginning of deliberations, the Long-Range Plan was named the "Three-Year Plan." But in the Preliminary Report of 1989 the sesquicentennial celebrations were mentioned. See Three-Year Plan, Draft, December 28, 1989, Director's Correspondence, 1988-1989.

[49] Robert C. Stevens to Ralph J. Crandall, November 19, 1987, Director's Correspondence, 1986-1987; Stevens to Crandall, August 23, 1989, Director's Correspondence, 1988-1990.

[50] George F. Sanborn, Jr., "Long Range Planning and the Library Department." Director's Correspondence, 1988-1990. The total requested for the library in the Three-Year Plan of 1989 was $355,000, which did not include construction, furniture, and other expenditures.

[51] Most of these later problems and costs were not mentioned in the Three-Year Plan of 1989. They were obviously a surprise to the Trustees.

[52] Darleen D. Powers to Ralph J. Crandall and the Board of Trustees, January 24, 1994, minutes of Board of Trustees, NEHGS.

[53] See "New Trustee Room Dedicated; Ethel Farrington Smith Honored," in NEXUS, 10 (1993): 136-137. The article includes a photograph of Mrs. Smith's portrait.

[54] NEXUS, 10 (1993): 4-5.

[55] NEXUS, 10 (1993): 173-174. A list of early sesquicentennial donors is printed.

The new Ethel F. Smith trustees room on the third floor of 101 Newbury St., dedicated October 25, 1993. Mrs. Ethel Farrington Hawes Smith, whose portrait by Cambridge, Mass. artist Melvin Robbins is at left, is a former trustee, contributor to the *Register*, author, and patron of New Hampshire genealogy.

NEHGS trustees in April 1994, in the sixth-floor Ruth C. Bishop Reading Room beneath an 1853 porthole portrait of George Washington by Rembrandt Peale (1778-1860) (center) and anonymous portraits of Edward Rawson (1615-1693), Secretary of the Massachusetts Bay Colony (right) and his daughter, Mrs. Rebecca Rawson Ramsey (1656-1692) (left). First row, left to right: Ruth C. Bishop, Dorothy B. Erikson, Margaret P. Speckman, Eleanor D. Grant, Dr. William R. Marsh, Dr. Harrison Black. Back row, left to right:

Director Ralph J. Crandall, President William M. Fowler, Jr., Robert C.
Stevens, Dr. Oglesby Paul, Prof. John A. Schutz, Joan F. Curran, Kenneth E.
Haughton, Meriwether C. Schmid, Elysabeth C.B. Higgins, Helen S. Ullmann,
Sandra M. Hewlett, Nicholas Benton, Judith Avery Newkirk, Lewis Bunker
Rohrbach, William S. Olney, and Dean C. Smith. The terms of trustees Bishop,
Rohrbach, and Ullmann expired after this meeting.

NEHGS staff in August 1994, also in the sixth-floor Ruth C. Bishop Reading Room beneath the Washington and Rawson portraits. First row, left to right: Jackie Kamlot, W. Denis Hanley, Julie Helen Otto, Marshall K. Kirk, Gary Boyd Roberts, Virginia B. Augerson, Robert Shaw, Shirley L. Bartlett. Middle row, left to right: Phlo (John) Phlay, Allison Dyson Johnson, Ann L. Dzindolet, Marie E. Daly, Dennis P. Dahill, Eleanor Yee, Janet Mullen,

Susan W. Gillespie, Jane Fletcher Fiske, Lynne Burke, Scott A. Bartley, Barbara J. Robinson. Back row, left to right: David A. Lambert, Mary S. Erlewine, Gomer U. Sanchez, Kenneth S. Paulsen, D. Brenton Simons, Jerome E. Anderson, Nathaniel N. Shipton. Some staff members were not available for the picture.

Volumes of *The New England Historical and Genealogical Register*, together with some smaller early American genealogies, as displayed in 1935 at 9 Ashburton Place. An index to volumes 1-50 was first published in 1906-1911. An index to volumes 51-148, edited by Jane Fletcher Fiske, appears as the Society celebrates its sesquicentennial anniversary in 1995. A CD-ROM version of the *Register* will also be available.

CHAPTER 9

At the Sesquicentennial

For the past three decades membership in the Society has increased each year until it reaches in 1995 about 16,000, or nearly 12,000 more members than in the 1960s. Those angry, turbulent years, along with the book by Alex Haley in the 1970s, had aroused people throughout the nation to think about family origins. Their interests broadly reflected changes not only in the ethnic and sexual mix of society, but in its economic life as well. Many people had more leisure time and more had college and professional degrees. Often the first members of their families to receive a university education, they were curious about their origins, and sought help. Some enrolled in special classes at 101 Newbury Street in order to penetrate genealogical lore and rushed to buy ancestral charts to list what they knew of past generations of their families. The new information they sought was not always immediately available, but any delay was annoying. They entered the Society's library for the first time asking questions, taking tours of the collections, and learning about reference and guide books, the catalog system, and the book stacks—an experience that reminded them of freshman days at college.[1]

These demands for additional information are often satisfied by the Society's reference service or staff of resident genealogists. Both groups work directly with members to obtain ordinary and elusive information. The inquiries service under Dr. Neil Todd, who heads an impressive staff of experts, provides assistance by mail, with a nominal per hour contract fee which usually secures the desired assistance within days.[2] It does not produce the excitement of a personal search, but help is provided efficiently and quickly. The Society's staff of genealogists, known as the tutorial service, guides members who can travel to Boston and want to search the records themselves. Genealogical research, they discover, is intricate, sometimes tedious, but the guidance of these tutors taking them through the labyrinth of sources makes the search spellbinding—like putting pieces into a gigantic jigsaw puzzle. Their success at the moment of discovery often echoes through the library.

In the past thirty years the expectations of members for assistance have met with a variety of fascinating programs. Annual seminars, like those entitled "Come Home to New England," provide a week of concentrated instruction by experts on the technical problems of tracing families—the use of such items as land records, court files, and church documents. Similar but shorter seminars are frequently held outside Boston in Florida, California, and Arizona, for example, where staff experts of the Society offer advice to members who cannot leave home for distant Boston. Bus service is frequently arranged also from neighboring New England states to Boston, enabling members to spend a day of research in the Society's library. They soon find that one day is hardly enough time, but become acquainted with books in the reference library and the services of the circulating library. They discover that its books can be borrowed for nominal postage and service charges and can bring a little of the Boston library into their own homes.[3]

Members who have the resources and time find that another exciting service of the Society is its British and Irish tour program. Tours of Wales, East Anglia, Yorkshire, the highlands of Scotland, or Ireland, accompanied by expert genealogists, give members guidance in visiting libraries, graveyards, and genealogical societies where they may locate data on their ancestors. They learn through lectures the origins of family and place names; they visit farms and villages, tour castles and cathedrals, and exchange observations with fellow participants.[4] Also gaining in popularity is the Society's research tour to Washington D.C., where NEHGS staff guide members in using the National Archives, the DAR Library, and the Library of Congress. No yearly conference, however, is more satisfying than the annual week in Salt Lake City at the Mormon library. Members of the tutorial staff, joined by other genealogists, often experts like C. Frederick Kaufholz for German research, regularly provide a heart-warming experience of lectures and research for nearly one hundred participants.[5]

The Society, moreover, offers genealogical information to members in many other forms. Its rich variety of publications in 1993 included the *Genealogist's Handbook for New England Research* by Marcia Wiswall Lindberg. This work's third edition, enlarged and updated, incorporates the advice of nearly 200 professional librarians and town officials and gives the reader basic data on local history, county government, and state depositories, as well as names, addresses, phone numbers, and fees for many public and private libraries.[6] Other publications of the Society include the recent multi-volume index of the *Register*, which puts that great repository of family history into the hands of most researchers. Publication of such vital records as those of Swansea, Townsend, Sandwich, Charlestown, and Pepperell extends an older series begun in the early decades of the century. The publications division, through Roberts' supervision, is ever alert to offer new books on genealogical topics; Roberts is himself an expert on royal and presidential descent. His most recent book, 700 pages in length, traces the royal descents of 500 immigrants to the American colonies and the later United States. His *Ancestors of American Presidents*, published in 1989, is now being updated.[7] Other authors associated with the Society who are publishing immigration studies include Robert C. Anderson, Ruth-Ann M. Harris and B. Emer O'Keeffe, and Judith A. Norton. The Harris-O'Keeffe series of volumes on Irish immigration now totals three, with two more in preparation.[8]

Most Society publications may be described as reference, or source books, or genealogies. Such works are intended to further research and enable members to trace their families. Some members collect a small library of these publications for the convenience of home reference. Since the search for ancestors seems nearly endless, most members also choose to renew their dues each year, and continue their research as they find the time; some even enroll as "life members." Many annual renewals continue for decades, revealing an attachment to the Society beyond their own research. Many members too enjoy the fellowship of annual trips to Salt Lake City, Washington, D.C., England, Wales, Scotland, and Ireland—even Boston itself. At least twenty members have enrolled in over half of the annual trips to Salt Lake City since 1979. Others want to encourage the study of family history in a patriotic effort to support democratic ideals.

Since its origin in 1845 the Society has attracted people who want to strengthen the ideals of the nation through family history. Their contributions to the Society library, publications, portrait gallery, and manuscripts are only one part of their benefactions. They promote education through seminars, lectures, and travel, give their family records, objects of art, and libraries, and have also endowed the Society with monetary gifts and bequests.

Since Ralph Crandall became director in 1982, the Society has operated within its budgets, which is a welcome change from the deficit financing of the years between 1928 and 1982. This amazing success results as much from the Society's Annual Fund Campaign as it does from its interesting programs of research, travel, and lectures, which attract membership. Undoubtedly, it reflects the kinds of people who join the Society as well as the personality and drive of the director and his staff.

Between 1992 and 1995 these gifts to the Society have enabled it to renovate its building. A first phase, costing nearly one million dollars, modernized several facility services and reallocated space on the second and third floors. A second phase of work, scheduled for 1996 and 1997, will include book stacks, microtext reading areas, cubicles for private work, and expanded computer services. A long-term lease of the fourth floor of the neighboring commercial building may give the Society the potential for much workspace. The completion of these changes will place the Society near the cutting edge of technology and give members the advantage of ultramodern research tools for tracing their ancestors. Most of these innovations are possible only through the continued generosity of members.

In the past three decades the Society's staff has grown almost yearly with the ever-increasing membership. From less than twenty employees it now approaches forty. If contract researchers, authors, and editors are counted, the number of employees may reach well over fifty. Many of the regular staff have been employed more than ten years; most were hired within the last fifteen. They enjoy health benefits, Social Security, additional pension benefits through the Teachers' Insurance Annuity Association, standard vacations, and a written code of procedural rights which are guaranteed by the government and the trustees. Staff members were drawn from colleges or previous positions with the expectation of promotion and long service. Only a few are over fifty-five and more are under forty. Since 1992 the staff has lost in death two of its popular and senior members—Linda Naylor, the executive administrative assistant, and Natalie Marko, the director of development. Both were relatively young in years of service and death denied them prematurely the contribution that they might have given the Society.[9]

Three members of the research staff hold honors from the American Society of Genealogists. That prestigious organization, which defines the art of genealogy, limits its fellows to fifty distinguished practioners and elects individuals only when vacancies occur. Staff members named fellows (F.A.S.G.) are David Curtis Dearborn, Jane Fletcher Fiske, and George Freeman Sanborn, Jr. Other current fellows who have undertaken projects with the Society include Melinde Lutz Sanborn, Roger D. Joslyn, and Robert C. Anderson. Past fellows most allied to the Society include G. Andrews Moriarty, Jr., Mary Lovering Holman and Winifred Holman Dodge, Arthur Adams, William Prescott Greenlaw, Walter Goodwin Davis, Clarence Almon Torrey, and Gilbert Harry Doane, plus former trustees C. Frederick Kaufholz, Nils William Olsson, and Elizabeth Pearson White. While this recognition should not be compared with a university degree, it is a professional honor for genealogists and is well regarded by this institution. More staff members, however, have college degrees. Roberts graduated from Yale University and undertook graduate work at the University of Chicago (M.A.) and the University of California, Berkeley. Fiske took her Bachelor's degree at Swarthmore College and did graduate work at Columbia. Sanborn graduated from

Boston University and undertook graduate work at the Universities of Illinois, Urbana-Champaign (A.M.), New Hampshire (M.Ed.), and California, Los Angeles. Dearborn graduated from the University of Massachusetts, Boston, and holds master's degrees from Northeastern University and Simmons College. Jerome Anderson has degrees from the University of Wisconsin, Madison, and Harvard, and Marshall Kirk has a bachelor's degree from Harvard. The Director of the Society, Ralph J. Crandall, received all of his degrees from the University of Southern California, with the doctorate awarded in 1974.[10]

With the encouragement of the Trustees the staff has been offered time and financial assistance in securing degrees in library science (five members of the staff have or will soon receive library degrees). Research time is not only available for staff members with book projects, but is also regularly granted to attend professional meetings. Sabbatical leaves after ten years of full-time service are available to any employee who has an approved project. Employees receive full salary and benefits during their three-month sabbatical. The object of the Society in extending these leaves is the development of a knowledgeable staff who can advise members and who are themselves recognized experts in their chosen specialities.[11]

Under the presidency of William M. Fowler, Jr., since 1991, Society administration is divided into eleven trustee committees.[12] All of its major policies come before one or more of these committees and are given full and complete analysis. Obviously, many chairs of the committees are also members of the Executive Committee which reviews sensitive issues and passes recommendations to the full Board of Trustees. Except for the Executive Committee, staff members are named to committees which review problems in their areas. The Publications Committee, for example, includes editors Jane F. Fiske, Julie Helen Otto, Gary Boyd Roberts, and Robert Shaw from the staff, and ten trustees. The committee in 1994-1995 is chaired by Dr. John A. Schutz. An *ex officio* member on all committees is Executive Director Crandall. He is responsible for the day-to-day administration of the Society, which includes personnel, expenditures, and fundraising. He reports every three months to appropriate trustee committees and to the entire Board of Trustees. Weekly meetings with President Fowler allow immediate judgments on any pressing issue. The president, of course, speaks for the Society, chairs the Board of Trustees, and is responsible to them. He is an *ex officio* member of all committees as is the director.

Dr. Fowler became president in 1991, succeeding the venerable Theodore Chase, and gives to the Society youthful leadership, reflecting his distinguished academic and administrative career at Northeastern University, where he is presently the history department chairman. An author of many books, lecturer on American history and naval lore, and member of the Massachusetts Historical Society, the Colonial Society, and the Pilgrim Society, he is well known for his interest in New England families whose sons ventured out to sea.

Internal administration of the Society involves all or most of the full-time staff. Assembling almost every month, they have an agenda and minutes, and make recommendations to the director. The functions of the Society are also divided among thirteen managers who confer more or less frequently with the director. They have an agenda and minutes for their deliberations. Each individual manager may then speak with his colleagues in order to determine what may formally need to be discussed at divisional conferences. In the course of a month or two the executive director will also have spoken at length with almost every employee, and when issues are budgetary or require authority, the matter may go to the appropriate committee of the Board of Trustees. Some staff members meet privately as a group to discuss issues that may concern themselves and the Society. Their recommendations may then be given to the director. Finally, one must realize that the Society, though a deliberative body, is not organized like a collegiate institution, which shares authority with tenured staff, is bound by professional regulations and traditions, and, most of all, faces accreditation by a regional or national association.

Every April the Society holds its Annual Meeting, which all members are invited to attend. They hear reports from the current officers, vote on new officers and trustees, and listen to a lecture of importance to genealogists. In an earlier day when the Society was smaller and regional, presidents frequently gave addresses intended for a national audience. In 1993 President Fowler returned to that tradition when he announced the Sesquicentennial Campaign and spoke on the importance of its success to the Society's, and nation's, future.

The last 150 years have dramatically changed the Society. While no one should be surprised by these changes, they show the ability of leaders to adjust to the constantly evolving needs of members. The Society was founded in 1845 to satisfy the desires of a generally elderly business and professional community of men who wanted to discuss and record the history of their day. They were amateur, well-meaning men who saw in the deeds of families the threads of patriotism that made the nation strong and prosperous. They believed in family history most of all because it revealed important facts about the nation. Many of these men admired John Farmer (1789-1838), the first American to assemble comparative data on families, with inter-relationships, through a few generations.[13] Other founders were traditional historians who read George Bancroft, Francis Parkman, and William H. Prescott and wanted more such scholars. Still others liked the symbols of the past handed down through family crests, coats-of-arms, and shields and wanted to promote the study of heraldry.[14]

Their Society, founded in the center of Boston, was near members' businesses and homes, close also to state and county offices, bookstores, and churches. Until the Society acquired its own building in 1870, the members used rented quarters mostly to house what they regarded as significant materials of family history. This evidence of the past they saw everywhere—primarily in books, manuscripts, Bibles, newspapers, and keepsakes. Old walking canes, coins, flags, diaries, and even pipes found their way into the archives.

Members were unable to decide what kind of history, or genealogy, or heraldry, they preferred. Memory of the past, they felt, was most important, and anything that contributed to its enrichment should be treasured. They founded *The New England Historical and Genealogical Register* in 1847, and made it a reflection of their antiquarian and historical interests. It played a wholesome role in bringing together these varied interests. The *Register* had a little bit of everything in it—antiquarian, historical, genealogical, and heraldic materials—and bore the tone of a gentleman's magazine.[15] Not everyone was pleased with it, but a hard core of antiquarians subscribed, contributed, and formed a club to provide subventions. For them the quarterly issues were far more important in disseminating information than any gathering of members until the 1860s when the Society found larger meeting rooms at No. 13 Bromfield Street. Winslow Lewis, president from 1861 to 1866, liked to address members and urged them in his 1866 resignation oration to acquire an even larger home for the Society, where treasures could be displayed and members could gather.

Samuel Gardner Drake, the president in 1858, believed that nothing should be ever refused by the library, even if the Society's rooms were packed to the doorways.[16] Dr. Lewis was ready to follow Drake's advice, but he wanted space also for portraits, an autograph collection of American and European statesmen, and assembled biographies of deceased members. He encouraged memorials for prominent former members and the *Register* made such tributes one part of its contribution to genealogy. Lewis likewise desired sketches, portraits, and photographs of past Society presidents, and also welcomed likenesses of national personages such as Ulysses Grant and George and Martha Washington.

Since space was scarce, Lewis and his two successors, Governor John Albion Andrew and Marshall P. Wilder, solicited funds for a permanent home for the Society. At No. 18 Somerset Street in 1871 they found modest space for display cabinets, portraits, books, manuscripts, and newspapers. Soon afterwards John Ward Dean became the first full-time librarian. An unusually energetic man, he presided until 1901 over the reading room, accessioned books, advised researchers, and supervised maintenance of the building. Volunteers for specific jobs were plentiful, but Dean had little professional day-to-day help. Boys were occasionally hired to help cart book collections to the basement. Dean accepted nearly everything that was given to the library. For all of that time he was also editor of the *Register*.

While Dean undertook most of the nearly backbreaking duties of librarian and editor, Marshall P. Wilder served as president. His major contribution was his presence in the community as spokesman, promoter of Society activities, and fundraiser. With a host of friends gathered around him he celebrated the patriotic events that marked the nation's first century. He shared his joy by holding special lectures, joining parades, attending dinners, and lining the walls of the Society building with paintings and portraits. He also welcomed gifts of historic letters and diaries, and regarded the acquisition of the Henry Knox and John Hancock papers as particularly significant. His friend, John Tyler Hassam, who was much intrigued by English origins of American founders, excited him in this topic as well. Wilder joined Hassam in raising money to send Henry F. Waters to London, where Waters worked for most of two decades collecting data at Somerset House. Together Wilder, Hassam, and Waters turned the Society's attention toward research and used the *Register* for the publication of valuable articles on the family origins of John Harvard, founder of that Cambridge college, George Washington, and Roger Williams.[17]

The name of John Hassam appears often in the records as a knight going into battle—not the man he actually was, surrounded by law books and copies of the *Register*. More important than any other person in backing the publication of the fifty-year index, he called attention also to the need for vital records of Massachusetts towns and transcriptions of New England gravestones. At the turn of the twentieth century Hassam, then an old man, had the firm support of James Phinney Baxter, the distinguished historian, and Henry Ernest Woods, editor of the *Register*, who designed the vital records series subsidized by the Commonwealth. As chief editor for a few years, Woods turned the publication of these records into a major activity of the Society, and gave attention also to the preservation of manuscripts. With Baxter, the president from 1901 to 1921, and William Prescott Greenlaw, the librarian from 1902 to 1929, the attention of members was focused on facilities and resources. Neither man raised an extraordinary amount of endowment. The Society operated into the 1920s with balanced budgets, but losses began to threaten programs even before the Great Depression set in. Officers depended upon various kinds of memberships, a few bequests, and stock and bond manipulations to raise necessary money.

No change was greater, however, than the admission of women in 1898. They transformed the Society from a club of elderly men to a less formal organization where tea and coffee was served after monthly meetings. In time, they influenced programs, with travel, music, and costume displays as lecture topics. Flowers frequently decorated Wilder Auditorium, and female members may have chosen colors for the rooms of the new library building at No. 9 Ashburton Place. Surviving photographs of the reading rooms at Ashburton often show more women than men consulting genealogies. By the 1930s women equaled men in number of members.

Women in the Society certainly reinforced, if needed, its patriotic spirit. The 1920s were years when the *Mayflower* tradition was particularly honored and New England's contributions to the United States were celebrated with plaques, memberships, and named bequests. The Society's halls filled with memorials, perhaps none so celebrated as the tribute to Abraham Lincoln, whose family could be traced to Hingham. Nearly every room in the Ashburton building was named in honor of a deceased member. In 1944, the building itself was named for Greenlaw. Such names as Wilder, John Foster, Seymour Morris, and Robert Henry Eddy were mentioned each day as staff and members worked in the rooms. These names, admittedly, came from donors who wanted their fathers or grandfathers to be remembered. But most of the deceased had no written biographies, and historical memory did not long linger for any. Of all the founders of the Society only Charles Ewer deposited his papers in the Library. Nearly nothing from Wilder, Baxter, and Greenlaw, who brought so much renown to the Society, was collected by archivists. When its headquarters moved to 101 Newbury Street in 1964, much of this past memory was abandoned. Some of the old plaques were given to family members when the walls of the new building were judged not strong enough for such weight.[18] Eventually, both the Hancock and Knox papers were sold to other institutions when members showed little interest in them as genealogical sources.[19] For years, more-over, these papers were deposited at neighboring libraries where historians could more easily consult them. The Lincoln memorial was sold to an art dealer.

The Society never cultivated heraldry as it did genealogy. Since 1861, however, a committee met more or less regularly to review correspondence and requests for heraldic research, and won a limited popular response. Under the leadership of Robert Dickson Weston, who served on the committee for more than forty-five years (1911-1957), he and his colleagues encouraged the study of heraldry and developed liberal rules for authenticating arms.[20] Also on the committee was Harold Bowditch, who served from 1924. An artist and scholar, he published seven installments of the *Roll of Arms* between 1928 and 1958 and bequeathed to the Society in 1964 his rich library of heraldic books and charts.[21] Several of Bowditch's colleagues, including John Insley Coddington, Eugene Van Ness Goetchius, and Henry L.P. Beckwith, Jr. also served many years on the committee. Over these years they acted often independently of the Society. But the agenda for meetings has always been full, as members of the Society seek to trace arms and tie insignia to some personage or event of centuries past.[22]

Genealogists have always been interested in heraldry, but largely as another tool in tracing ancestors. Most genealogists begin as amateurs, or as historians and antiquarians, and their interests develop. In recent years some have become truly distinguished professionals who have perfected the craft by working as authors, editors, compilers, recorders, and librarians. Many experts in locating genealogical data work like sleuths of a police department, or bloodhounds in search of the bone. Clarence Almon Torrey (1869-1962) was a major example of a detective. His manuscript on New England marriages prior to 1700 indexed almost 2000 genealogical and historical works identifying these seventeenth-century New Englanders. Torrey's *magnum opus* was published in 1985, with a splendid introduction by Gary Boyd Roberts.[23] Also important were the works of John Eldridge Frost (1917-1992). His two volumes of *Maine Probate Abstracts* from colonial times to 1800 is a massive, invaluable collection of data. His *Maine Genealogy: A Bibliographical Guide,* and vital records of York and Berwick, Maine, are distinguished source books. Likewise invaluable are the works of Ruth (Wilder) Sherman (1928-1992). Her transcribing of vital records and editing of *The American Genealogist* put her at the forefront of genealogical publishing.[24] Perhaps the leading genealogical scholar of the past several decades was John Insley Coddington (1902-1991), who co-founded The American Society of Genealogists in order to define and recognize professional standards. Author of over 175 articles, he gave his collection of 110 boxes of papers, notes, and correspondence to the Society in 1987.[25]

These deceased leaders of the profession are the major recent authors, editors, and compilers of books that researchers consult in the library. Members are primarily interested in these leaders, however, not as persons or professionals, but as guides in their quest for information on their families. They are completely involved in this hunt for information—totally absorbed in a search on a single problem, family or cluster of families. Members may look up from their books while reading in the library to ask a person in front of them what he or she may be researching; an exchange takes place which might include lunch; but then both plunge back into their separate work.

Most genealogists are unusually generous people who contribute regularly to the Society. From the approximately 16,000 members has come most of the support for the Sesquicentennial Campaign of five million dollars. In leading the campaign, Executive Director Crandall has spoken with a much larger number of members than did Charles Ewer and Joseph Felt in the 1840s. He finds most members, at least those he meets, are older than he once thought, often in their 70s, 80s, and 90s, avid genealogists, long-time members of the Society, and frequent correspondents. Many are skilled users of the computer, travelers, and book collectors, and have attended meetings of the Society in their locality. Some move yearly in the fall from New England to Florida, Arizona, or California and also maintain memberships in local genealogical organizations. Most members, wherever they live, look upon the New England Historic Genealogical Society, its *Register* and NEXUS, as both friendly partners along the craggy paths of their research and a strong force in collecting and preserving genealogical books and records.

Notes

[1] An early announcement of instructional classes appeared in the *News-Letter,* 3 (1976). Gary B. Roberts was the teacher of six Saturday morning classes from February 21 to March 17, 1976. "The first lecture will begin with some definitions . . . . Later lectures will center on how to use libraries . . . ." The series cost $10.00 for members and $25.00 for non-members.

[2] A major feature of the NEXUS is the section: "Queries and Answers" where members ask for help. See NEXUS, 10 (1993): 189-197 for a good example of cooperative research and bewilderment.

[3] Since 1976 the Society has published an up-to-date catalogue of the Circulating Library. The catalog lists thousands of genealogies which may be borrowed by members. The current size of the library is 20,000 books and microforms, and fees are fourteen dollars for a three-book package.

[4] A report on the 1993 "Heart of Scotland" tour was given by Virginia B. Augerson in NEXUS, 10 (1993): 140. Twenty-three members took the tour. Her report begins: "We came to see the Scottish Highlands in full bloom. . . . The weather was perfect, and the heather at its peak (a bit behind schedule), covering the Highlands in purple."

[5] The conference at Salt Lake City was held in the fall of 1993, with the expected capacity enrollment. Other conferences (in early 1994) included two in Florida, and one each in Denver, Westchester County, New York, and Seattle. A British tour featured Northern England in early May. See NEXUS, 10 (1993): 95-96, 133.

[6] Marcia Wiswall Lindberg, *Genealogist's Handbook for New England Research,* 3rd ed. (Boston, 1993). It is published in both soft and hard covers and is 178 pages in length. Ms. Lindberg is editor of *The Essex Genealogist.*

[7] Gary Boyd Roberts, *The Royal Descents of 500 Immigrants to the American Colonies or the United States* (Genealogical Publishing Co., Baltimore, 1993) and *Ancestors of American Presidents* (Santa Clarita, California, 1989).

[8] Ruth-Ann M. Harris and Donald M. Jacobs, *The Search for Missing Friends: Irish Immigrant Advertisements Placed in the Boston Pilot* (NEHGS, 1989-).

[9] Laura M. Carpenter presented an unusually sensitive portrait of Natalie G. Marko in NEXUS, 10 (1993): 79.

[10] Other staff members with college degrees include managers or editors Virginia B. Augerson, B.A. Cornell University; Scott A. Bartley, M.L.S. Simmons College; Lynne Burke, B.A. Douglass College, M.L.S. Simmons College; Dennis P. Dahill, B.F.A. Massachusetts College of Art, M.A.E. Rhode Island School of

Design; Marie Daly, B.S. Northeastern University, M.A. Boston University; Allison D. Johnson, B.A. Swarthmore College, M.A. University of New Hampshire; Susan E. Moran, B.A. University of Montana; Janet Mullen, B.A. North Adams State College; Julie Helen Otto, B.A. Scripps College; Robert Shaw, B.A. Harvard University; Nathaniel Shipton, B.A., M.A. Clark University; D. Brenton Simons, B.S. Boston University, Ed. M. Boston Univeristy; and Neil Todd, B.A. University of Massachusetts at Amherst, Ph.D. Harvard University.

[11] Several incentive programs were announced at the Annual Meeting in April 1993, including this plan for sabbatical leaves. See Trustee Papers, 1993.

[12] The Trustee Committees and chairs in 1993-1994 were:

> Computer, Robert C. Stevens
> Development, William S. Olney
> Education, Oglesby Paul
> Facilities, John G.L. Cabot
> Finance, Dean C. Smith
> Great Migration Project, Dean C. Smith
> Library, Joan Ferris Curran
> Membership/Marketing, Dean C. Smith
> Personnel, Nicholas Benton
> Preservation, Judith Avery Newkirk / Megan Sniffin-Marinoff
> Publications, John A. Schutz
> CD ROM, Robert C. Anderson
> Executive, William M. Fowler, Jr.

[13] See "Memorial of John Farmer, M.A.," *Register*, 1 (1847): 9-20.

[14] In the first volume of the *Register*, there was an article on heraldry, pp. 225-231.

[15] See David L. Greene, "Samuel G. Drake and the Early Years of *The New England Historical and Genealogical Register*," *Register*, 145 (1991): 203-233.

[16] Quoted in "Do We Collect Old Books," *News-Letter*, 5 (1978). Of course Drake was not the first editor of the *Register*, but the quotation is essentially correct.

[17] See Albert Mathews, "John Tyler Hassam," *Register*, 58 (1904): 13.

[18] In NEXUS, 6 (1989): 142. Most of the memorial tablets were offered to interested members.

[19] The Hancock and Knox papers were sold in 1992. The Harvard School of Business bought the Hancock Papers which had been on deposit in its library for a half-century prior to their return to the Society in the late 1970s.

[20] See Gilbert Harry Doane, "Harold Bowditch, M.D.," *Register*, 119 (1965): 3-5.

[21] The editor of the *News-Letter* [4 (1977)] began a response to questions about heraldry in this way: "From time to time, many members ask us 'What in the world is the work of the Heraldry Committee all about? It seems mysterious and

secret.'" Henry L. P. Beckwith, Jr., probabaly the foremost heraldic authority in America, has chaired the committee in recent decades.

[22] Clarence Almon Torrey, *New England Marriages Prior to 1700* (Baltimore, 1985), with the introduction by Gary Boyd Roberts, pp. v-xvi. Torrey's extensive bibliography was omitted.

[23] Obituaries for Ruth (Wilder) Sherman and John Eldridge Frost appeared in NEXUS, 9 (1992): 156-157.

[24] See David Curtis Dearborn, "John Insley Coddington," *Register*, 145 (1991): 195-201.

[25] The Coddington collection is being catalogued and should be available for general use in 1995.

Portrait, at about age 5, of John Bonner, Jr. (1692-1762), son
of Boston mariner and mapmaker John Bonner and his
second wife, Mary Clark (artist unknown, 1698, 1884 gift of
Miss Mary Bonner Cazneau to NEHGS, in the Ruth C.
Bishop Reading Room at 101 Newbury St.). See the
Register 14(1860):240 and the Colonial Society of Massachusetts, *Boston Prints and Printmakers, 1670-1775* (Boston,
1973), pp. 3-14.

Portrait of Rev. Samuel Fayerweather (1724/5-1781),
graduate of Harvard, Yale, and Oxford, Episcopal minister
at Prince Frederick Wineyaw, South Carolina, and South
Kingstown, Rhode Island (attributed to Jeremiah Theus, ca.
1719-1774, Charleston, S.C., 1748, 1924 gift of Miss
Elizabeth Harris to NEHGS, in the Ruth C. Bishop Reading
Room at 101 Newbury St.). Full genealogical coverage of
Fayerweather appears in the *Register* 144(1990):227-32.

Portrait of Mrs. Esther McIntyre, wife of Neil McIntyre (ca. 1718-1776) of Boston (Joseph Badger, 1708-1765, undated, 1978 gift of Mrs. Brookings T. Andrews to NEHGS, in the third-floor Director's office at 101 Newbury St.).

Portrait of Mrs. Andrew Tyler (Mary Richards, 1730/1-
1785), wife of the Congregational minister of Westwood,
Massachusetts (John Singleton Copley, 1738-1815, dated ca.
1765, 1850 gift of Capt. George Jackson Tyler to NEHGS, in
the Ruth C. Bishop Reading Room at 101 Newbury St.).
Rev. Tyler, whose portrait is also owned by the Society,
was a Harvard graduate of 1738 and nephew of Sir
William Pepperrell, 1st Bt.

Appendix   Index

Appendix

CHARTER AND ENABLING ACTS

An Act to incorporate the New England Historic Genealogical Society.
Be it enacted by the Senate and House of Representatives, in General Court
assembled, and by the authority of the same, as follows:

Section 1. Charles Ewer, J. Wingate Thornton, Joseph Willard, their associates and successors, are hereby made a corporation, by the name of the New England Historic Genealogical Society, for the purpose of collecting, preserving, and occasionally publishing, genealogical and historical matter, relating to early New England families, and for the establishment and maintenance of a cabinet, and for these purposes, shall have all the powers and privileges, and, be subject to all the duties, requirements and liabilities, set forth in the forty-fourth chapter of the Revised Statutes.

Section 2. The said corporation may hold and possess real and personal estate, to an amount not exceeding twenty thousand dollars.

[Approved by the Governor, March 18, 1845.]

Acts and Resolves of the General Court of Massachusetts, 1845, chapter 152.

An Act to enable the New England Historic-Genealogical Society to hold an
additional amount of property.
Be it enacted, etc., as follows:

Section 1. The New England Historic-Genealogical Society may take, by purchase, gift, grant or otherwise, and hold, real and personal estate not exceeding one hundred thousand dollars, in addition to the amount authorized by the second section of chapter one hundred and fifty-two of the acts of the year one thousand eight hundred and forty-five.

239

Section 2. This act shall take effect upon its passage.
Approved April 1, 1868.
Acts and Resolves, 1868, chapter 100.

An Act to enable the New England Historic-Genealogical Society to hold
additional real and personal property.
Be it enacted, etc., as follows:

Section 1. The New England Historic-Genealogical Society may take by
bequest, gift, grant, or otherwise, and hold, real and personal estate not exceeding
two hundred thousand dollars in value in addition to the amount authorized by
section two of chapter one hundred and fifty-two of the acts of the year one
thousand eight hundred and forty-five, and by section one of chapter one
hundred of the acts of the year one thousand eight hundred and sixty-eight, and
exclusive of the value of all books, papers, pictures and statuary now owned, or
which may be hereafter acquired by said society
Section 2. This act shall take effect upon its passage.
Approved April 13, 1888.
Acts and Resolves, 1888, chapter 227.

An Act to enable women to become members of the New England Historic
Genealogical Society.
Be it enacted, etc., as follows:

The New England Historic Genealogical Society, a corporation organized
under the laws of this Commonwealth, may admit women to membership,
subject to such restrictions as the by-laws of said corporation may from time to
time impose.
Approved April 10, 1897.
Acts and Resolves, 1897, chapter 275.

The following is from the *Revised Laws of 1902, Corporation Acts, chapter 125,*
section 8:

Any corporation organized under general or special laws for any of the
purposes mentioned in section two [educational, charitable, antiquarian, historical, literary, scientific, etc.] . . . may hold real and personal estate to an amount
not exceeding one million five hundred thousand dollars.

APPENDIX

Laws of Massachusetts of 1954, Chapter 180, section 9:

Any corporation organized under general or specific laws for any purpose mentioned in this chapter (educational, charitable, antiquarian, historical, library, scientific, etc.) . . . may hold real and personal estate to an amount not exceeding five million dollars.

Laws of Massachusetts of 1986, Chapter 180, section 6:

Powers of charitable corporations: Any corporation may hold real or personal estate to an unlimited amount, which estate or income shall be devoted to the purposes set forth in its charter or articles of organization. . . . This provision shall be applicable notwithstanding the specification of a limited amount in any special law.

1845

CONSTITUTION

of the

NEW ENGLAND HISTORIC

GENEALOGICAL SOCIETY

Article 1. The Society shall be called The New England Historic Genealogical Society.

Article 2. The object of the Society shall be to collect and preserve the Genealogy and History of early New England Families.

Article 3. The Society shall be composed of Resident, Corresponding, and Honorary Members, who shall be elected by ballot, having been nominated by the Board of Directors at a previous meeting.

Article 4. Each Member shall pay into the Treasury, on his admission, the sum of three dollars, and two dollars annually.

Article 5. The officers of the Society shall be a President, Vice-President, Recording and Corresponding Secretaries, and a Treasurer, who, together, shall constitute the Board of Directors.

Article 6. The Society shall meet quarterly, in the city of Boston, on the first Tuesdays of January, April, July, and October, to transact business; and at such other times as the Board of Directors shall appoint. The officers of the Society shall be chosen at the January meeting, by ballot.

Article 7. By-Laws, for the more particular government of the Society, shall be made by the Board of Directors.

Article 8. No Alteration of this Constitution shall be made except at the Quarterly Meeting, on recommendation of the Board of Directors, and by a vote of three fourths of the Members present.

Object of the Society

The object of the institution is the good of the whole community. Nothing, therefore, like exclusiveness has governed its original founders. They have acted upon the principle, that, to make it extensively useful, its branches should be made to spread over all parts of New England, and over all lands, wherever the sons of New England are found. Hence, they have elected their corresponding members with especial reference to this consideration,—governed always by the interest manifested in the cause on the part of those invited to become members.—*From Circular Number Three.*

APPENDIX

FIRST CIRCULAR ISSUED BY THE SOCIETY

An institution has been formed in Boston, by the name of the New England Historic Genealogical Society, for the purpose of collecting and preserving the genealogy and history of the early New England families. The object of this Association has justly been regarded as one of great importance, as well as curiosity, both in a physical and social point of view. The minds of men are naturally moved to know something of their progenitors—those from whom they have derived their being; and there seems to be an increasing interest in this subject; many are trying to trace their genealogy back at least to the first settlers—the early pilgrims of this country. The Society propose to cultivate this taste, and give such a direction to these inquiries as well as facilitate their labors, and render them of practical importance to individuals and the public. We wish, by united action, and through the aid of our extensive collections of printed and manuscript works, to furnish the means to every person descended from an early inhabitant of New England, of tracing his genealogy and history. When our collection shall be sufficient, Society propose to publish a Genealogical and Biographical Dictionary or History of all New England Families. The present time is deemed a suitable one for instituting inquiries of this nature since the sources of information, by the death of elderly persons, and the destruction of records, are daily becoming lessened, and soon it will be impossible to obtain the desired information at all. In accomplishing their objects, the Society propose to obtain, by solicitation or otherwise, books, papers, original manuscripts, and written communications, relating to them. It is also their intention to suggest the best methods of making genealogical investigations, and the best forms for keeping family registers, and for the public records of births, marriages, and deaths. All donations, either in print or manuscript, will be deposited in the library of the Society, for the use of the members and others; and a description of them carefully entered on the records, in connection with the name of the donor. Should you feel disposed to forward to the Society any book, or original manuscript, or to compile a biographical or genealogical memoir of an individual or family, selected by yourself or proposed by the Society, and particularly your own family or connections, you will confer a public benefit, and particularly oblige its members. It is hoped you will so far favor our purpose as to make such contributions as your convenience may permit. The Society will be pleased to receive suggestions, and to correspond with individuals in relation to their objects.

With great respect, your obedient servant,

Boston   18   *Corresponding Secretary*

N.B. All communications may be addressed to the Corresponding Secretary. In forwarding documents to the Society, it is requested that a private conveyance may be adopted, instead of conveyance by mail.

A P P E N D I X

THE NEW ENGLAND HISTORIC GENEALOGICAL SOCIETY

BYLAWS-1991

Article I
The Corporate Seal

The seal of the corporation shall be the device herewith printed, namely:

Article II
Members and Dues

Section 1. The classes of membership shall be established from time to time by the Board of Trustees (hereinafter referred to as "the Board"). Any person who has paid the current dues for his/her class of membership shall be considered a member of the Society.

Section 2. The amount of the annual dues for the several categories of membership shall be determined by the Board from time to time.

Section 3. A member may be suspended or expelled by the Board for conduct which the Board finds has been or may be detrimental to the welfare of the Society. Before making such finding, the Board shall give such member fourteen days written notice and an opportunity to be heard at a stated time and place before at least three members of the Board. Such notice shall include a general statement of the grounds upon which the suspension or expulsion of such a member is to be considered. A member shall be dropped from membership by the Board for non-payment of dues after such dues have become six months overdue, or after two reminders are sent, whichever comes later.

Article III
Trustees

Section 1. Election: The governing body of the Society shall be the Board of Trustees. The Board shall be composed of the elective officers and fifteen individuals duly elected by the Society from its membership. Of these fifteen members, five shall be elected annually, each for a three-year term. On completion of an elected three-year term, one year must elapse before an individual member may be elected to another term as such Trustee. Trustees shall be chosen by ballot at the annual meeting by a majority of the votes of the members, either in person or by proxy.

Section 2. Resignation: Any Trustee may resign at any time by giving written notice of such resignation to the Board.

Section 3. Vacancies: Any vacancy on the Board (other than that of an elective officer) occurring during the year may be filled for the unexpired portion of the term by the Board or the Executive Committee. Any Trustee so chosen shall hold office until the next annual meeting, at which time the vacancy must be filled by the normal election process.

Section 4. Regular Meetings: There shall be no fewer than four regular meetings of the Board during the calendar year. The date, hour and place of each meeting will be determined by the Board by standing or special order.

Section 5. Special Meetings: A Special Meeting may be held at any time by order of the President or the Board, or by written request from three or more members of the Board filed with the Secretary.

Section 6. Notice of Meetings: Written notices of all Board Meetings shall be sent to Board members at least fourteen days prior to the scheduled meeting, unless waived in writing by all members of the Board.

Section 7. Quorum: At all meetings of the Board of Trustees, one third of all the then current Trustees shall be necessary and sufficient to constitute a quorum for the transaction of business, and the act of a majority of the Trustees present at any meeting at which there is a quorum shall be the act of the Board, except as may be otherwise specifically provided by statute or by these bylaws.

Section 8. Powers: The Board shall have general management and control of the property, business, and work of the Society. It shall have and may exercise all the corporate powers of the Society provided for in these bylaws and in the laws of the Commonwealth of Massachusetts. The Board may by general resolution delegate to committees of their own number, to officers of the corporation or to members, such powers as they may see fit.

Section 9. Director: The Board shall employ a Director who shall serve at such compensation and upon such other terms of employment as the Board may determine.

Section 10. Affirmative Action: The Board of Trustees shall establish and maintain an affirmative action plan for the employment of the Director and the staff.

Article IV
Officers

Section 1. Number: The officers of the Society shall be President, First Vice President, Second Vice President, Treasurer, Secretary, and other officers with such powers and duties not inconsistent with these bylaws as may be appointed and determined by the Board of Trustees.

Section 2. Election, Term of Office and Qualifications: The President, Vice Presidents, Treasurer and Secretary shall be elected annually for a one year term at the annual meeting of the members of the Society. No such person shall hold the same office for more than six consecutive years.

Section 3. Vacancies: Should the office of the President become vacant by death, resignation, retirement, disqualification, or by any other cause, the First Vice president shall become President and shall so serve until the next annual meeting of the members. If there is a further vacancy in this office, the succession of officers who shall assume the President's responsibilities until the election of his/her successor shall be in the following order: Second Vice President, Treasurer, and Secretary.

Section 4. President: The President shall be the principal officer of the Society, shall superintend and conduct its prudential affairs with the advice of the Board, and shall preside at all meetings of the Board and of the Society. The President shall be an ex officio member of all committees of the Board. In the absence of the President the succession of officers who shall assume his/her responsibilities shall be in the order set forth in Section 3 above.

Section 5. Vice Presidents: In the absence of the President the order prescribed in Section 3 above shall be followed for performance of his/her duties.

A P P E N D I X

Section 6. Treasurer: The Treasurer shall have charge of the management of all the invested property, funds, and financial affairs of the Society, and shall have full authority, in the name and behalf of the Society, to receive, collect, take charge of, and disburse all monies, and to give due acquaintances thereof, and shall arrange for the custody or the deposit of the Society's investments and funds with the approval of the Board, and such investments may be held in the name of any nominee approved by the Board. With the approval of the Board other officers of the Society may be given the authority to withdraw bank deposits, either jointly or singly.

The Treasurer shall:

a. keep, in books belonging to the Society, full and accurate accounts of all receipts and disbursements, bequests and devises by will, and of the various funds and the financial condition of the Society;

b. render a report at each annual meeting of the operations of the Treasurer's office for the year preceding and of the amount and condition of all property of the Society in his/her charge, with a detailed statement of all investments;

c. render periodic reports of receipts and expenditures to the Board, in such detail as the Board may direct;

d. furnish such bond, at the expense of the Society, for the faithful performance of the duties pertaining to the office as the Board may direct;

e. have charge of all real estate owned by the Society, and

f. have authority, with the consent of at least one other member of an investment committee appointed under Article VIII, Section 3C, to sell, transfer and deliver any securities, mortgages, or other intangible personal property of the Society; to invest and reinvest the funds of the Society; to accept unrestricted gifts and bequests paid otherwise than in cash; and to execute any contracts and instruments relating thereto.

The Treasurer shall have such assistance, including that of professional advisers, as the Board may authorize.

The Board may appoint an Assistant Treasurer to perform such of the Treasurer's duties as the Board may determine.

Section 7. Secretary: The Secretary shall be the clerk of the corporation, shall issue notices of the meetings, shall make and keep accurate records of the proceedings of the Board, of the annual meeting of the Society, and of such other Society meetings as from time to time may be designated, and shall have custody, except as otherwise provided, of the corporate seal, all papers and reports that are ordered to be placed on file, and all documents and letters relating to the official business of these bodies. All proceedings, documents, and records shall be kept on file at the Society's House.

Article V
Nominations and Elections

Section 1. All members of the Board shall be nominated and elected in the manner herein described.

Section 2. A Nominating Committee consisting of five members of the Society shall be appointed by the President with the approval of the Board no later than October 1.

Section 3. This committee shall report its nominations to the Executive Committee no later than January 1. Prior to March 1, a candidate for any office to be filled at the next annual meeting may be nominated by a petition signed by not fewer than twenty members and filed with the Secretary.

Section 4. A complete list of all candidates nominated, naming the offices for which they are candidates and the manner of their nomination, shall be made available to any member of the Society. A copy of such list shall be mailed to the members with the notice of the annual meeting.

Section 5. Only candidates nominated in the manner provided in this Article shall be eligible for election at the annual meeting.

Section 6. Election shall take place at the annual meeting according to these bylaws and the laws of the Commonwealth of Massachusetts.

Article VI
Duties of the Director

Section 1. The Director shall administer the policies of the Society as established by the Board, shall be an ex officio member of all committees of the board, and shall have the power to hire, supervise, and discharge all employees of the Society.

Article VII
Meetings of the Society

Section 1. The annual meeting of the Society shall be held at such time in April or May as the Board shall determine. It shall take place in the Society's House or such other place as may be designated by the Board.

Section 2. The President of the Society shall preside at all meetings of the Society. In the absence of the President, the meetings shall be chaired in the succession shown in Article IV, Section 1, above.

Section 3. A special meeting of the Society shall be held upon the written request, filed with the Secretary, of eight or more members of the Board.

Section 4. A notice of each meeting of the Society shall be mailed to all members at least ten days prior to the date of the meeting, or may be included in any publication of the Society so mailed. The notice shall give the place, date and hour of the meeting and any further information required by these bylaws.

Section 5. At any meeting of the Society two hundred members in person or by proxy shall constitute a quorum. Though less than a quorum be present, any meeting, annual or special, may, without further notice, be adjourned to a specified date.

Section 6. Members may vote at any meeting of the Society only when present in person or by proxy duly executed on a form provided for that purpose by the Society.

Section 7. At the request of the presiding officer any motion or resolution shall be submitted in writing.

Article VIII
Committees

Section 1. Executive Committee: The Executive Committee shall be comprised of the officers of the Society. The Executive Committee shall meet with the Director for the purpose of setting agenda for Board meetings prior to the regularly scheduled meetings of the Board and shall have the powers of the Board between meetings of the Board, with the obligation to report its actions to the Board at the Board's next regular meeting. The Executive Committee is not empowered to make policy changes, which require Board approval.

Section 2. Nominating Committee: The Nominating Committee shall be named as heretofore provided in Article V, Section 2.

Section 3. Finance Committee: The Finance Committee shall be appointed by the Board and shall be chaired by the treasurer. This committee shall:

a. review, with the Director, the annual budget prior to presentation to the Board for approval;

b. review and evaluate any financing needed for new programs or capital expense, for recommendation to the Board;

c. be responsible for the supervision of the Society's investments. This can be done by acting as a committee of the whole, or by naming a subcommittee as an "Investment Committee"; and

d. have such additional responsibilities as are determined by the Board.

Section 4. Personnel Committee: The Personnel Committee shall be appointed by the Board and shall develop, recommend, and maintain personnel policies for the Society. It shall:

a. develop and recommend methods of employee evaluation;

b. develop and maintain job descriptions, job classifications, and salary ranges, all of which shall be reviewed at least annually;

c. develop and oversee the affirmative action plan;

d. conduct an annual review of the Director, reporting the results to the Board in executive session;

e. review, with the Director, the annual reviews and evaluations of the staff, and report the results to the Board; and

f. have such additional responsibilities as are determined by the Board.

Section 5. Other Committees: The President, with the approval of the Board, may from time to time appoint such other committees for such purposes and for such terms of office as the Board may specify. The members of such other committees may include Trustees, members or non-members of the Society, and shall serve at the pleasure of the Board.

Article IX
Publications

Section 1. A quarterly publication, *The New England Historical and Genealogical Register*, shall be published under the direction of the Director, subject to policies and standards established by the Board.

Section 2. The Board may authorize other publications.

Article X
Indemnification

Section 1. The Society shall, to the extent legally permissible, indemnify each of its trustees, officers, employees and agents (hereinafter collectively referred to as "officer") while in office and thereafter (and the heirs, executors and administrators of such officer) against all expenses and liabilities which he/she has reasonably incurred in connection with or arising out of any action or threatened action, suit or proceeding in which he/she may be involved by reason of his/her being or having been an officer of the Society. Such expenses and liabilities shall include, but not be limited to, judgments, court costs and attorney's fees and the cost of reasonable settlements, provided as to which such officer shall be finally adjudged in any such action, suit or proceeding not to have acted in good faith in the reasonable belief that his/her action was in the best interests of the Society. In the event that a settlement or compromise of such had, but only if the Board shall have been furnished with an opinion of counsel for the Society to the effect that such settlement or compromise is in the best interests of the Society and that such officer appears to have acted in good faith in the reasonable belief that his/her action was in the best interests the Society, and if the Board shall have adopted a resolution approving such settlement or compromise. Indemnification hereunder may, in the discretion of the Trustees, include payment by the Society of costs and expenses incurred in defending a civil or criminal action or proceeding in advance of the final disposition of such action or proceeding, upon receipt of an undertaking by the person indemnified to repay such payment if he/she shall be adjudicated not to be entitled to indemnification hereunder.

The foregoing right of indemnification shall not be exclusive of other rights to which any such officer may be entitled as a matter of law.

Article XI
Amendments

Section 1. These bylaws may be amended at any lawful meeting of the Society by a two-thirds vote of all members of the Society present or voting by proxy. The text of the proposed amendment or amendments shall be included in the notice of the meeting or may be included in any publication of the Society mailed to members at least twenty-one days before the meeting at which the proposed amendment is to be considered.

Section 2. A proposal to amend these bylaws may be made by the Board; or by a petition signed by at least one hundred members or one percent of the members, whichever is the greater number, and received by the Secretary at least sixty days before the Society meeting at which it is to be considered. On receiving the petition, the Secretary shall submit it forthwith to the Board or to the Executive Committee, if the Board is not scheduled to meet within the next thirty days. The petition shall thereafter be presented at the next meeting of the members of the Society, with notice as provided in Section 1 of this Article.

PRESIDENTS OF THE SOCIETY

Charles Ewer	1845-1850
Joseph Barlow Felt	1850-1853
William Whiting	1853-1858
Samuel Gardner Drake	1858-1859
Almon Danforth Hodges	1859-1861
Winslow Lewis	1861-1866
John Albion Andrew	1866-1867
Marshall Pinckney Wilder	1868-1886
Abner Cheney Goodell	1887-1892
William Claflin	1892-1898
Edward Griffin Porter	1899-1900
James Phinney Baxter	1901-1921
John Carroll Chase	1922-1936
Frederick Silsbee Whitwell	1936-1941
Frederic Alonzo Turner	1942-1948
Walter Merriam Pratt	1948-1954
Thomas Temple Pond	1954-1961
Charles Moorfield Storey	1961-1963
Walter Muir Whitehill	1963-1971
Robert Churchill Vose, Jr.	1971-1974
Richard Brigham Johnson	1974-1977
Rodney Armstrong	1977-1982
Arthur A. Dunn	1982-1987
Theodore Chase	1987-1991
William M. Fowler, Jr.	1991-

APPENDIX

VICE PRESIDENTS OF THE SOCIETY
1901-1995

Caleb Benjamin Tillinghast	1901-1909
Henry Winchester Cunningham	1910-1912
Nathaniel Johnson Rust	1912-1917
Charles Sidney Ensign	1917
John Carroll Chase	1917-1921
Nathan Matthews	1922-1927
James Parker Parmenter	1928-1936
Frederic Alonzo Turner	1937-1942
Davenport Brown	1942-1947
Thomas Temple Pond	1948-1954
Robert Humphrey Montgomery	1954-1963
Robert Churchill Vose, Jr.[1]	1963-1971
Malloy Myron Miller	1971-1974
Mrs. Robert G. Fuller	1975-1980
Mrs. Shirley Goodwin Bennett	1980-1984
Mrs. Joan Ferris Curran	1984-1987
Theodore Chase	1986-1987
William M. Fowler, Jr.	1987-1989
Nicholas Benton	1988-1993
Dean C. Smith	1989-1990
W. Robert Mill	1990-1993
John G. L. Cabot	1993-
Mrs. Joan Ferris Curran	1993-

---

[1] Until 1971 the Society had vice presidents for each of the New England States, but always the vice president for Massachusetts was deemed senior. Since 1986 the Society again has more than one vice president.

TREASURERS OF THE SOCIETY

William Henry Montague	1845-1850
Frederic Kidder	1851-1854
John Ward Dean	1855-1856
Isaac Child	1857-1859
George Washington Messinger	1860
William Blanchard Towne	1861-1871
Benjamin Barstow Torrey	1871-1903
Nathaniel Cushing Nash	1904-1907
Francis Apthorp Foster	1907
Charles Knowles Bolton	1908-1912
Charles Edward Lord	1913-1915
Lew Cass Hill	1916-1917
George Lambert Gould	1918-1921
James Melville Hunnewell	1922-1943
Alexander Bigelow Ewing	1943-1944
Everett Jefts Beede	1944-1953
Ralph Sylvester Bartlett	1953-1957
Frederick Milton Kimball	1957-1974
Zane Albion Thompson	1974-1977
Ralph L. Pope	1977-1981
Arthur A. Dunn	1981-1982
Lowell A. Warren, Jr.	1982-1988
W. Robert Mill	1988-1990
Dean C. Smith	1990-

RECORDING SECRETARIES OF THE SOCIETY

John Wingate Thornton	1845-1846
Rev. Samuel Hopkins Riddel	1846-1851
Charles Mayo	1851-1856
Francis Brinley	1856
David Pulsifer	1857
William Mason Cornell	1858-1859
Rev. Caleb Davis Bradlee	1859-1862
Edward Franklin Everett	1862-1863
Edward Sprague Rand, Jr.	1863-1870
Samuel Hidden Wentworth	1870-1873
David Greene Haskins, Jr.	1873-1890
George Kuhn Clarke	1890
Gustavus Arthur Hilton	1891-1892
George Augustus Gordon	1893-1909
John Albree	1910-1915
Alfred Johnson	1916-1917
Henry Edwards Scott	1918-1937
Everett Jefts Beede	1938-1944
Mrs. Florence Conant Howes	1944-1946
William Carroll Hill	1946-1949
Mrs. Florence Conant Howes	1949-1951
John William Farquharson	1951-1964
Susan Parsons	1964-1967
Richard Brigham Johnson	1968-1974
Rodney Armstrong	1974-1977
Catherine Coolidge	1977-1978
Francis V. Lloyd, Jr.	1978-1981
Henry H. Thayer	1981-1986
Mrs. Shirley Goodwin Bennett	1986-1989
William M. Fowler, Jr.	1989-1991
Mrs. Joan Ferris Curran	1991-1993
Mrs. Sandra M. Hewlett	1993-
John A. Schutz[*]	1992-

---

[*]Assistant Secretary

LIBRARIANS OF THE SOCIETY

Directors Since 1973

John Wingate Thornton	1845
Edmund Batchelder Dearborn	1846-1848
David Pulsifer	1849-1850
Thomas Bellows Wyman	1851
William Blake Trask	1852-1854
Rev. Luther Farnham	1854-1856
Thomas Bellows Wyman	1856-1857
Edward Holden	1858-1859
William Blake Trask	1859-1860
John Hannibal Sheppard	1861-1869
William James Foley	1870-1871
James Frothingham Hunnewell	1872
John Ward Dean	1872-1889
Ezra Hoyt Byington	1891-1892
Henry Winchester Cunningham	1892-1893
John Ward Dean	1893-1902
William Prescott Greenlaw	1902-1929
Josephine Elizabeth Rayne	1929-1936
Howard Dakin French	1936-1940
Mrs. Franklin Earl Scotty	1940-1950
Pauline King (acting)	1950-1951
Arthur Adams[1]	1951-1959
Pauline King	1959-1971
Edgar Packard Dean[2]	1962-1971
Mildred E. Leavitt	1971
Robert Churchill Vose[3]	1972-1973
Richard Donald Pierce	1973
James Brugler Bell	1973-1982
Ralph J. Crandall	1982-1987
John W. Sears	1987
Ralph J. Crandall	1987-

---

[1] Adams was administrative head of the library and the library building until retirement. Pond (to 1961) and Storey (to 1962) were administrative heads until Dean's appointment.

[2] Dean became the first director of the Society and the positions of librarian and director were separated. (They were joined again in 1973.)

[3] Vose as President was administrative head in 1972 and part of 1973.

A P P E N D I X

EDITORS OF THE *REGISTER*

Rev. William Cogswell	1847
Samuel Gardner Drake	1848- Jan. 1849
William Thaddeus Harris	1849 Apr., July, Oct.
Samuel Gardner Drake	1850 Jan.
Nathaniel Bradstreet Shurtleff	1850 Apr., July, Oct.
Samuel Gardner Drake	1851
Rev. Joseph Barlow Felt	1852 Jan., Apr.
Timothy Farrar	1852 July
William Blake Trask	1852 Oct.
Samuel Gardner Drake	1853-1858
William Blake Trask	1859-1860
William Henry Whitmore	1859-1860
John Ward Dean	1859-1860
Samuel Gardner Drake	1861
William Blake Trask	1862 Jan., Apr.
Rev. Elias Nason	1862 Apr.
Charles Hudson	1862 July
John Ward Dean	1862 Oct.-1863
William Blake Trask	1864 Jan., Apr.
John Ward Dean	1864 July, Oct.
William Blake Trask	1865
Rev. Elias Nason	1866-1867
Albert Harrison Hoyt	1868-1875
John Ward Dean	1876-1901
Henry Ernest Woods	1902-1907
Francis Apthorp Foster	1908-1912
Henry Edwards Scott	1913-1937
Harold Clarke Durrell	1938-1943 July
William Carroll Hill	1943 Oct.-1949 Apr.
Arthur Adams	1949 Oct.-1959
Gilbert Harry Doane	1960-1971 July
Elsie McCormack[*]	1960-1969
Anne Borden Harding[*]	1969-1974
John D. Austin, Jr.	1971 Oct.-1974 Jan
Gilbert Harry Doane[†]	1974-1975

---

[*] Associate or Assistant Editors
[†] Consulting Editor

Ralph J. Crandall*	1975-1978
Susan L. Patterson*	1973-1977
Ralph J. Crandall	1978 July-1983
Anne O. Koopman*	1977-1979
Catherine L. Slichter*	1979-1981
Edward W. Hanson*	1982-1983
Donald M. Nielsen*	1983-1987
Edward W. Hanson	1983-1986
Jane Fletcher Fiske*	1987
Lili Van Zanten*	1987-1988
Jane Fletcher Fiske	1988-
Margaret F. Costello*	1988-1993
Allison Dyson Johnson*	1993-
Jerome E. Anderson†	1988-
Robert Charles Anderson†	1988-
Gary Boyd Roberts†	1988-

* Associate or Assistant editors
† Consulting editor

APPENDIX

OFFICERS 1994-1995

President: Prof. William M. Fowler, Jr.
1st Vice President: John G. L. Cabot
2nd Vice President: Mrs. Joan Ferris Curran
3rd Vice President: Robert C. Stevens
Treasurer: Dean C. Smith
Secretary: Mrs. Sandra M. Hewlett
Assistant Secretary: Prof. John A. Schutz

TRUSTEES 1994-1995

Term Expiring April 1995
Nicholas Benton
Harrison Black, M.D.
Elysabeth C. B. Higgins (Mrs. James H., II)
Oglesby Paul, M.D.
Margaret P. Speckman (Mrs. Carroll D.)

Term Expiring April 1996
Albert H. Gordon
Eleanor D. Grant (Mrs. W. Brewer)
Kenneth E. Haughton
William R. Marsh, M.D.
Robert H. Rodgers

Term Expiring April 1997
Dorothy B. Erikson (Mrs. Gordon I.)
Judith W. Freeman (Mrs. Louis M.)
Judith Avery Newkirk
William S. Olney
Meriwether C. Schmid

APPENDIX

DEPARTMENTAL STAFF LIST

September 1994

Administration

Executive Director Ralph J. Crandall
Executive Secretary Linda S. Skinner

Membership

Linda S. Skinner
W. Denis Hanley
Robert Shaw

Direct Mail/Marketing

Susan E. Moran

Business Office

Marie E. Daly
Shirley L. Bartlett

Reception

Ann L. Dzindolet
Eleanor Yee

Development

Virginia B. Augerson
Susan W. Gillespie

Education

D. Brenton Simons

Computers

Donald R.G. MacDonald
David A. Lambert
Susan W. Gillespie
W. Denis Hanley
Gomer U. Sanchez

Sales

Janet Mullen
Gomer U. Sanchez
Barbara J. Robinson

Publications

Books/NEXUS

Gary Boyd Roberts
B. Emer O'Keeffe
Julie Helen Otto
Robert Shaw

NEHG Register

Jane Fletcher Fiske
Allison Dyson Johnson

Great Migration Study Project

Robert Charles Anderson
Margaret F. Costello

APPENDIX

Library Services

Library

David Curtis Dearborn
Jerome E. Anderson
Marshall K. Kirk
Donald R.G. MacDonald
Gary Boyd Roberts

Technical Services

Lynne Burke
Jackie Kamlot
Kenneth S. Paulsen
George Freeman Sanborn, Jr.

Shipping/Receiving

Phlo (John) Phlay

Manuscripts

Scott A. Bartley

Archives

Nathaniel N. Shipton

Circulating Library/Preservation

Dennis P. Dahill
Mary S. Erlewine
David A. Lambert
Phlo (John) Phlay

Building Maintenance

Christopher P. O'Sullivan

A P P E N D I X

SOCIETY PUBLICATIONS SINCE 1974
Compiled by Gary Boyd Roberts

I. Books and Pamphlets Published by NEHGS

1975

1. Nancy S. Voye, ed., *Massachusetts Officers in the French and Indian Wars, 1748-1763* (co-published with the Society of Colonial Wars in the Commonwealth of Massachusetts, henceforth SCWCM, and the Office of the Secretary of the Commonwealth of Massachusetts, Archives Division, henceforth OSCMAD) (paper).

1976

2. Charles E. Hambrick-Stowe and Donna D. Smerlas, eds., *Massachusetts Militia Companies and Officers in the Lexington Alarm* (co-published with SCWCM and OSCMAD) (paper).

1977

3. Mary Ellen Baker, *Bibliography of Lists of New England Soldiers* (reprint of 1911 ed. published by NEHGS, with *Addenda* by Robert Mackay) (paper).

1978

4. Robert E. Mackay, ed., *Massachusetts Soldiers in the French and Indian Wars, 1744-1755* (co-published with SCWCM) (paper).

1979

5. Myron O. Stachiw, ed., *Massachusetts Officers and Soldiers, 1723-1743, Dummer's War to the War of Jenkins' Ear* (co-published with SCWCM) (paper).

6. Garrison Kent Hall, *The Pedigree of Fletcher Garrison Hall.*

7. Michael H. Gorn, ed., *An Index and Guide to the Microfilm Edition of the Massachusetts and Maine Direct Tax Census of 1798* (paper).

1980

8. Mary E. Donahue, ed., *Massachusetts Officers and Soldiers, 1702-1722, Queen Anne's War to Dummer's War* (co-published with SCWCM and OSCMAD) (paper).

9. David E. Maas, *Divided Hearts: Massachusetts Loyalists, 1765-1790: A Biographical Directory* (co-published with SCWCM) (paper).

10. Henry L.P. Beckwith, ed., *Ninth Part of a Roll of Arms Registered by the Committee on Heraldry of the New England Historic Genealogical Society* (published by the Committee) (paper).

1982
11. Carole Doreski, ed., *Massachusetts Officers and Soldiers in the Seventeenth-Century Conflicts* (co-published with SCWCM) (paper).

12. George Oakes Jaquith and Georgetta Jaquith Walker, *The Jaquith Family in America*.

13. Priscilla R. Ritter and Thelma Fleishman, *Newton, Massachusetts, 1679-1779, A Biographical Directory* (paper).

1983
14. P. William Filby, *American and British Genealogy and Heraldry: A Selected List of Books, Third Edition*.

15. F.G. Emmison, *Essex Wills (England), Volume 2, 1565-1571*.

1984
16. Harold Edward Woodward, *Some Descendants of Nathaniel Woodward who Came from England to Boston about 1630*.

17. Roger D. Joslyn, *Vital Records of Charlestown, Massachusetts to the Yar 1850, Volume I*.

18. Joseph Carvalho, *Black Families in Hampden County, Massachusetts, 1650-1855* (co-published with the Institute for Massachusetts Studies, Westfield State College).

1985
19. K. David Goss and David Zarowin, eds., *Massachusetts Officers and Soldiers in the French and Indian Wars, 1755-1756* (co-published with SCWCM) (paper).

20. Clare M. McCall, *Captain John McCall, 1726-1812: His Ancestors and Descendants*.

21. George A. Rice, *Vital Records of Pepperell, Massachusetts to the Year 1850*.

22. Willard Heiss and Thomas D. Hamm, *Quaker Genealogies: A Selected List of Books* (paper).

23. Thomas H. O'Connor, Marie E. Daly, and Edward L. Galvin (edited by Edward W. Hanson), *The Irish in New England* (a reprint, with preface and index, of three articles in the July 1985 *Register* [139:187-224]) (paper).

24. Marcia Wiswall Lindberg, *Genealogist's Handbook for New England Research*, 2nd ed. (paper) (for 3rd ed. see under 1993).

1986
25. Allen E. Marble, *The Descendants of James McCabe and Ann Pettigrew*.

26. F.G. Emmison, *Essex Wills (England), Volume 3, 1571-1577.*

27. Marion E. Allen and Nesta R. Evans, *Wills from the Archdeaconry of Suffolk: 1629-1636,* and *Wills from the Archdeaconry of Suffolk, 1637-1640.*

1987

28. P. William Filby, *American and British Genealogy and Heraldry, 1982-1985 Supplement.*

29. Elmer S. Small and Mary Ann Nicholson, *The Family of Daniel Shays* (paper).

30. Henry E. Scott, Jr., *The Adams Family of Martha's Vineyard* (published by Mercury Publishing, Rutland, Vt. in cooperation with NEHGS; copyrighted by NEHGS).

1988

31. Virginia Augerson, ed., *Ancestral Stirrings: A Cookbook Compiled from Family Recipes, Stories, Letters and Early Cookbooks Donated by Members and Friends* (paper).

1989

32. Ruth-Ann M. Harris and Donald M. Jacobs, eds., *The Search for Missing Friends: Irish Immigrant Advertisements Placed in the Boston* Pilot, *Volume I, 1831-1850.*

33. Perley M. Leighton, *A Leighton Genealogy: Descendants of Thomas Leighton of Dover, New Hampshire,* 2 vols.

34. Terrence M. Punch, *Genealogist's Handbook for Atlantic Canada Research.*

35. Ann Smith Lainhart, ed., *First Boston City Directory (1789) Including Extensive Annotations by John Haven Dexter* (a reprint, with a preface by John A. Schutz and an index, of articles published in the *Register* 140[1986]:23-62, 138-70, 230-63, 321-30).

36. Joan Ferris Curran, *Family History: A Legacy for Your Grandchildren* (paper) (for 2nd ed. see under 1993).

1990

37. Eugene Chalmers Fowle, *Descendants of George Fowle (1610/11?-1682) of Charlestown, Massachusetts* (edited by Gary Boyd Roberts and Neil D. Thompson).

38. Dean Crawford Smith, *The Ancestry of Samuel Blanchard Ordway, 1844-1916* (edited by Melinde Lutz Sanborn).

39. Theodore Chase and Laurel K. Gabel, *Gravestone Chronicles: Some Eighteenth-Century New England Carvers and Their Work* (with a preface by Ralph J. Crandall) (hardcover and paper).

40. Margaret F. Costello and Jane Fletcher Fiske, *Guidelines for Genealogical Writing: Style Guide for the New England Historical and Genealogical Register with Suggestions for Genealogical Books* (paper).

APPENDIX

1991

41. Ruth-Ann M. Harris and B. Emer O'Keeffe, eds., *The Search for Missing Friends: Irish Immigrant Advertisements Placed in the Boston* Pilot, *Volume II, 1851-1853.*

42. John Eldridge Frost, *Maine Probate Abstracts, Volume 1, 1687-1775* and *Maine Probate Abstracts, Volume 2, 1775-1800* (published by Picton Press of Camden, Maine, jointly with NEHGS).

1992

43. Henry C. Hallowell, Lee K. Kugler, and Caroline Lewis Kardell, *Vital Records of Townsend, Massachusetts: Town Records to 1850 with Marriage Intentions to 1873 and Cemetery Inscriptions.*

44. H.L. Peter Rounds, *Vital Records of Swansea, Massachusetts to 1850* (edited by Jane Fletcher Fiske and Margaret F. Costello).

45. George Freeman Sanborn, Jr. and Melinde Lutz Sanborn, *Vital Records of Hampton, New Hampshire to the End of the Year 1900, Volume One.*

46. Lester MacKenzie Bragdon and John Eldridge Frost, *Vital Records of York, Maine* (published by Picton Press jointly with NEHGS, copyrighted by Picton Press and NEHGS).

47. Dean Crawford Smith, *The Ancestry of Emily Jane Angell, 1844-1910* (edited by Melinde Lutz Sanborn).

1993

48. Ruth-Ann M. Harris and B. Emer O'Keeffe, eds., *The Search for Missing Friends: Irish Immigrant Advertisements Placed in the Boston* Pilot, *Volume III, 1854-1856.*

49. Marcia Wiswall Lindberg, *Genealogist's Handbook for New England Research*, 3rd ed. (hardcover and paper).

50. Joan Ferris Curran, *Family History: A Legacy for Your Grandchildren*, 2nd ed. (paper).

51. *Circulating Library Catalogue for the New England Historic Genealogical Society, Volume I - Genealogies* and *Volume II - Histories and Research Aids* (Jan. 1993 - 6th ed. of vol. 1, 5th ed. of vol. 2; earlier editions omitted from this list) (paper).

1994 - early 1995

52. *1994 Supplement to the 1993 Circulating Library Catalogues for the New England Historic Genealogical Society* (May 1994) (paper).

53. John A. Schutz, *A Noble Pursuit: The Sesquicentennial History of the New England Historic Genealogical Society, 1845 - 1995.*

54. Jane Fletcher Fiske, *The New England Historical and Genealogical Register: Index of Persons, Volumes 51 through 148*, 4 vols.

55. Ruth-Ann M. Harris and B. Emer O'Keeffe, eds., *The Search for Missing Friends: Irish Immigrant Advertisements Placed in the Boston* Pilot, *Volume IV, 1857-1860.*

II. Microfilm Publications by the Society

1. *The New England Historical and Genealogical Register,* vols. 1-146, 27 reels.

2. Walter E. and Lottie S. Corbin, *The Corbin Collection: [Genealogical and] Historical Material Relating to Central and Western Massachusetts,* 55 reels, 1982.

3. 1798 U.S. Direct Tax Census for Maine and Massachusetts, 18 reels, 1979 (for its *Index and Guide* see under Books and Pamphlets, 1979).

4. Clarence Almon Torrey, *New England Marriages Prior to 1700,* 7 reels, 1979 (for its later book format see below).

5. *Pepperrell Papers, 1689-1764* (of Col. William Pepperrell and his son, Sir William Pepperrell, 1st Bt.), 2 reels, 1974.

6. *Faneuil Papers* (of Andrew Oliver and his nephew, Peter Faneuil), 1 reel, 1979.

7. Fred E. Crowell, *New Englanders in Nova Scotia,* 1 reel, 1979.

8. Waldo Chamberlain Sprague, *Genealogies of the Families of Braintree, Massachusetts, 1640-1850, including the Modern Towns of Randolph and Holbrook and the City of Quincy,* 1 reel, 1984 (published in cooperation with the Quincy Historical Society).

III. Works of Other Publishers Authored, Co-authored, Compiled, Edited, Co-edited, or Introduced by Staff Members

1979

1. William Prescott Greenlaw, *The Greenlaw Index of the New England Historic Genealogical Society,* 2 vols. (Boston, G.K. Hall & Co.).

1983

2. Gary Boyd Roberts, ed. (selected and introduced by, as with 4,8,9,12 and 14 below), *Genealogies of Connecticut Families From The New England Historical and Genealogical Register,* 3 vols. (Baltimore, Genealogical Publishing Company, henceforth GPC).

1984

3. Ralph J. Crandall, ed., *Genealogical Research in New England* (GPC) (Six articles reprinted from the *Register,* 1976-82, with an introduction by R.J. Crandall, additions, and corrections.)

4. Gary Boyd Roberts, ed., *English Origins of New England Families From The New England Historical and Genealogical Register, First Series,* 3 vols. (GPC).

APPENDIX

5. Gary Boyd Roberts and William Addams Reitwiesner, *American Ancestors and Cousins of The Princess of Wales* (GPC) (chapter one of which was first published in the *Register* 136[1982]:85-103,307-36 and reprinted, with additions, in #2 above).

6. Edward W. Hanson, *The Hendersons of Cambridge: The Family of Robert and Marion (Johnston) Henderson of Cambridge, Massachusetts, with Appendixes on the Shattuck, Gage, Swan, Hurd and Hanson Families* (privately published, paper).

1985

7. Clarence Almon Torrey, *New England Marriages Prior to 1700* (GPC, book version, without references, 5 printings through 1994) (with an introduction, updated for recent reissues, by Gary Boyd Roberts).

8. Gary Boyd Roberts, ed., *English Origins of New England Famillies From The New England Historical and Genealogical Register, Second Series*, 3 vols. (GPC).

9. Gary Boyd Roberts, ed., *Genealogies of Mayflower Families From The New England Historical and Genealogical Register*, 3 vols. (GPC).

1986

10. Ralph J. Crandall, *Shaking Your Family Tree: A Basic Guide to Tracing Your Family's Genealogy* (Dublin, N.H., and Emmaus, Pa., Yankee Books, over a half-dozen printings through 1994) (hardcover and paper).

11. Robert M. Taylor, Jr. and Ralph J. Crandall, eds., *Generations and Change: Genealogical Perspectives in Social History* (Macon, Ga., Mercer University Press).

12. Gary Boyd Roberts, ed., *Mayflower Source Records: Primary Data Concerning Southeastern Massachusetts, Cape Cod, and the Islands of Nantucket and Martha's Vineyard From The New England Historical and Genealogical Register* (GPC).

1987

13. Jane Fletcher Fiske, *Thomas Cooke of Rhode Island: A Genealogy of Thomas Cooke alias Butcher of Netherbury, Dorsetshire, England, who came to Taunton, Massachusetts in 1637 and settled in Portsmouth, Rhode Island in 1643*, 2 vols. (privately published). Before joining the staff Jane Fletcher Fiske also edited Esther Littleford Woodworth-Barnes, *Huling Genealogy: Descendants of James and Margaret Huling of Newport, Rhode Island and Lewes, Delaware* (privately published, 1984).

1989

14. Gary Boyd Roberts, ed., *Genealogies of Rhode Island Families From The New England Historical and Genealogical Register*, 2 vols. (GPC).

15. Gary Boyd Roberts, *Ancestors of American Presidents*, preliminary ed. and preliminary ed. revised (Santa Clarita, Calif., Carl Boyer 3rd).

1992

16. Scott A. Bartley, ed., *Vermont Families in 1791, Volume 1* (Genealogical Society of Vermont, Special Publication Number 1, published by Picton Press of Camden, Maine) (with contributions by David Curtis Dearborn and Julie Helen Otto).

1993

17. Gary Boyd Roberts, *The Royal Descents of 500 Immigrants to the American Colonies or the United States* (GPC).

Note 1: Before joining the staff Marie E. Daly, who contributed a chapter to Jeffrey Willis, ed., *The Catholics of Harvard Square* (Petersham, Mass., Saint Bede's Publications, 1993, hardcover and paper), transcribed and edited *Gravestone Inscriptions from Mount Auburn Catholic Cemetery, Watertown, Massachusetts* (privately published, 1983). David Curtis Dearborn contributed a "Foreword" to the 1984 reprint, by New England History Press of Somersworth, N.H., of David W. Hoyt, *A Genealogical History of the Hoyt, Haight, and Hight Families* (1871). Preceding the *Register* reprint program in effect edited by G.B. Roberts, GPC published Michael Tepper, ed., *Passengers to America: A Consolidation of Ship Passenger Lists From The New England Historical and Genealogical Register* (1977); and, alongside the later reprint program, GPC also consolidated, without a named editor, *Suffolk County Wills: Abstracts of the Earliest Wills upon Record in the County of Suffolk, Massachusetts From The New England Historical and Genealogical Register* (1984).

Note 2: The Society has also photoduplicated, for its circulating and research libraries, and for sales, over 650 genealogies and over 350 local history or source record volumes published mostly before 1920. These latter include many volumes of Massachusetts town vital records to 1850, all 21 volumes of J.N. Arnold's *Vital Record of Rhode Island*, the six volumes of A.M. Hemenway's *Vermont Historical Gazetteer*, and 14 volumes (those covering Revolutionary War service and probate data, 1635-1771) of the *New Hampshire State Papers*. Since 1991 all of these photoduplicates have been listed in an annual *Sales Catalogue*.

Index of Names

INDEX

Index of Names

Harding, Anne Borden 159, 162, 168, 169, 173, 189, 190, 204, 257
Harding, Warren Gamaliel 102
Harris, Edward D. 41
Harris, Ruth-Ann M. 223, 234, 264, 265, 266
Harris, William Thaddeus 19, 20, 41, 257
Hart, Albert Bushnell 165
Hart, Wayne C. 218
Harvard, John 64, 65, 68, 230
Haskins, David Greene, Jr. 68, 255
Hassam, John Tyler 54, 56, 57, 58, 63, 64, 65, 66, 68, 69, 71, 77, 230, 235
Hathaway, Rufus 192, 217
Haughton, Kenneth E. 259
Hawes, Florence C. 69
Haywood, Carle Read 106
Hazelton, Edith Eliza (Hazel) 162, 163, 164, 188, 189
Healy, James J. 150
Heiss, Willard 263
Hemenway, A. M. 268
Henderson, Ernest Flagg, III 212
Henderson, Marion Johnston 267
Henderson, Robert 267
Henry, Patrick 31
Hewlett, Sandra M. (Mrs. Larry) 255, 259
Hicks, Lewis Wilder 93
Higgins, Elysabeth (Lys) C. B. (Mrs. James H., II) 205, 207, 213, 259
Hight family 268
Hill, Hamilton A. 67
Hill, Lew Cass 254
Hill, William Carroll 128, 130, 151, 255, 257
Hills, William Sanford 87, 94
Hilton, Gustavus Arthur 255
Hinckley, Gov. Thomas 18
Hitchcock, Thomas Barnes 94
Hoag, Ruth Wood 67
Hoar, Senator George F. 61
Hodges, Almon Danforth 27, 29, 42, 252
Holden, Edward 256
Holland, Rev. F. W. 38

Holman, Mary Campbell Lovering 128, 137, 151, 225
Holmes, Abiel 2, 13
Homer, James Kendall 69
Hoover, Herbert Clark 102, 108
Hopkins, Mrs. Roland Gage 105
Hornblower, Mrs. Ralph 124
Howes, Florence Conant (Mrs. Joseph Curtis Howes) 93, 100, 104, 110, 112, 118, 119, 120, 134, 141, 150, 255
Hoyt, Albert Harrison 38, 47, 66, 67, 257
Hoyt, David W. 268
Hudson, Charles 257
Huling, James 267
Huling, Margaret 267
Hunnewell, James Frothingham 256
Hunnewell, James Melville 100, 109, 111, 115, 122, 123, 127, 131, 150, 254
Hunt, John G. 70
Hurd family 267
Hutchins, Frank Miller 217
Hutchinson, Thomas 1, 18
Hyde, Myrtle Stevens 70
Ickes, Margaret 105
Jacobs, Donald M. 234, 264
Jacobus, Donald Lines 70, 98, 118, 151
Jaquith, George Oakes 263
Jenks, Rev. William 9, 10, 11, 21, 25
Johnson, Alfred 92, 94, 100, 255
Johnson, Allison Dyson 235, 258, 260
Johnson, Richard Brigham 170, 174, 177, 190, 191, 252, 255
Johnston, Marion 267
Jones, Eleanor H. 124
Joslyn, Roger D. 204, 225, 263
Kamlot, Jackie 261
Kardell, Caroline Lewis 265
Kaufholz, C. Frederick 217, 223, 225
Kellogg, Lucy Mary 159
Kidder, Frederic 21, 27, 37, 38, 48, 254
Kimball, Frederick Milton 132, 134, 146, 147, 151, 152, 155, 156, 161, 166, 171, 172, 187, 188, 190, 254

273

Index of Names

Index of Names

INDEX

Subject Index